*Legends of the Plumed Serpent*

also by NEIL BALDWIN

Edison: Inventing the Century

Man Ray: American Artist

To All Gentleness: William Carlos Williams, the Doctor Poet

The Writing Life (Co-Editor)

LEGENDS

OF THE

PLUMED SERPENT

Biography of a Mexican God

NEIL BALDWIN

PublicAffairs — New York

For information, address PublicAffairs, 250 West 57th Street,
Suite 1825, New York, NY 10107.

Book design by Smyth and Whiteside (BAD).

LIBRARY OF CONGRESS CATALOGING-IN-PUBLICATION DATA

Baldwin, Neil, 1947–

Legends of the plumed serpent : biography of a Mexican god / Neil Baldwin.

p.   cm.

Includes bibliographical references and index.

ISBN 1-891620-03-7 (hc)

1. Quetzalcoatl (Aztec diety) 2. Indian mythology — Mexico.

3. Kukulcan. 4. Aztec mythology. I. Title.
F1219.3.R38B36   1998
299'.73 — dc21
98-36524 CIP

First Edition

1 3 5 7 9 10 8 6 4 2

Contents

For Nicholas and Allegra

Glossary

agave: A type of cactus.

Aguila Sangrienta (bloody eagle): A goddess associated with Quetzalcóatl through her association with Tlaloc, god of storms.

alma nacional: National soul.

Alvarado, Pedro de: The conquistador in charge of the Spanish garrison at Tenochtitlán during the conquest.

Alvarado Tezozómoc, Hernando: Author of *Crónicas Mexicanas* and *Mexicayotl*, histories of the migration of the Aztecs drawn from Nahuatl accounts.

amoxcalli (houses of books): Libraries.

Anáhuac (near the water): The geographic area encompassing the Basin of Mexico, where Mexico City now stands.

Anales de Cuauhtitlán: An Aztec history written circa 1570.

Annals of the Cakchiquels: A Mayan text detailing the flight of Cakchiquel Maya ancestors from Tula in the wake of Plumed Serpent's departure.

Atetelco: One of the major outlying areas of Teotihuacán, distinguished by its surviving murals of Tlaloc, the Aztec storm god.

Atlantes: Four freestanding statues in the temple at Tula, depicting Plumed Serpent as an earthly prince.

Avenue of the Dead: The ceremonial center of Teotihuacán, bounded on the north end by the Pyramid of the Moon.

Axayácatl: Moctezuma II's father.

Aztec: Nahua-speaking culture originating in Aztlán that eventually migrated to the Basin of Mexico.

Aztec Mexica: One of the seven Aztec tribes that migrated to the Basin of Mexico to found the Aztec Empire.

Aztlán (place of herons): The Aztec mythical place of origin.

Cabrera Castro, Ruben: Director of the Mexican National Anthropological and Historical Institute's excavation of the Temple of Quetzalcóatl at Teotihuacán during the mid–1980s.

Brinton, Daniel G: One of the earliest American interpreters of Nahuatl poetry.

Calmécac: A training school for Aztec priests.

Campeche: A province of Mexico in the Western Yucatán.

Campesino: A peasant farmer.

Cancún: A resort town on the eastern coast of the Yucatán peninsula.

Cantares Mexicanos: Eighty-five folios of Nahuatl poems and history songs.

caracol: Snail.

Cardenal, Ernesto: Nicaraguan poet and Roman Catholic priest, author of the epic poem *Quetzalcóatl*.

casahuate: A type of tree found around the site of Monte Albán; the tree's white blossoms represent the current name of the site: White Mountain.

Caso, Alfonso: The archaeologist responsible for the discovery of the tombs and tunnels beneath Monte Albán.

Catherwood, Frederick: One of the original discoverers, with John L. Stephens, of the Mayapán archaeological site.

Ce Ácatl: The year One Reed in the Aztec calendar cycle; the year in which Plumed Serpent was born and in which he promised to return.

Ce Ácatl Topiltzin: "Our Dear Prince" Quetzalcóatl. This name is most often applied to Plumed Serpent in his legendary incarnation as an earthly prince.

Ce Cóatl: The year One-Serpent in the Aztec calendar cycle.

ceiba: The kapok tree, found in Central America, sacred to the Maya because a ceiba tree was one of the pillars that held up the four corners of heaven and earth.

Cempoala or Zempoala: A city of the Totonac people, who allied with Hernán Cortés against the Aztecs during the conquest.

cenote: A water hole in limestone, found at many Mayan archaeological sites, often used for sacrifices.

Cenote de los Sacrificios: The sacred Well of Sacrifices at Chichén Itzá.

Cerro de la Cantera: A mountain in the Mexican state of Morelos, site of the Olmec city of Chalcatzingo.

Cerro de la Malinche: A hillside at the archaeological site of Tula, bearing a carved relief of Plumed Serpent.

Cerro del Jaguar: Jaguar Mountain; the Aztec name for Monte Albán.

Cerro del Tesoro: The Hill of the Treasure; the site of the excavation of Tula.

Cerro Gordo: Big Mountain; a mountain at Teotihuacán.

Chac: The Mayan rain god.

Chalcatzingo: A major Olmec archaeological site in the Mexican state of Morelos.

chalchíuatl: Human blood.

Charlot, Jean: A French artist closely associated with the Mexican muralists of the 1920s.

Charnay, Désiré: A French expeditionary photographer who published landmark portfolios on Tula, Chichén Itzá, and other Mexican sites.

Chichén Itzá: Major city and religious center of the Yucatec Maya.

Chichimec: A tribe from the northern areas of Mexico that migrated to the Basin of Mexico toward the end of the Toltec era and was eventually assimilated by the Nahua-speaking population.

chicle: Sap from the *sapodilla* tree in Yucatán.

Chilam Balam: Spokesman of the Jaguar; a "prophetic history" of the Maya reaching back to the seventh century B.C.

chilam: A Mayan priest.

Chimalman: The Aztec cult personification of feminine divinity and the mother of Plumed Serpent.

Cholollán: "The Place of the Flight"; the Nahuatl name for Cholula.

Cholula: A city in Mexico; Plumed Serpent's resting place after his exile from Tula.

Chontal: A tribe of Maya from a region near the Gulf of Mexico; they may have invaded Chichén Itzá before the Toltec incursion.

Chontalpa: The eastern border of the Olmec "mother culture."

cielo estrellado: The starry sky; for the Olmec, it is reflected in the pattern of spots on the jaguar's flanks.

científicos: Advisors to President Porfirio Díaz.

Cihuatlampa: The Aztec Heavenly House of the Sun, the dwelling of the sun god; the western quadrant of the earth.

cipactli: Crocodile; Earth Monster.

Classic Maya: Mayan civilization from the late-third century to the mid-tenth century A.D., typified by the archaeological site of Tikal.

Coatepantli: A serpent wall of Toltec origin.

cóatl: Serpent; can also be another word for "road."

Cocijo: The Zapotec god of rain, closely allied with Plumed Serpent.

cociy: The Zapotec word meaning "lightning."

cociycobaa: The Zapotec word for "the dry season."

cociyquiye: The Zapotec word for "the rainy season."

Codex Bodley: A preconquest Mixtec codex detailing the migration of Plumed Serpent into the lands of Oaxaca.

Codex Borbonicus: A pictorial account, in part, of Plumed Serpent in his aspect as soul carrier and companion to the noble dead.

Codex Borgia: Pueblan or Tlaxcalan document showing Plumed Serpent in his allied identity as Éhecatl, the wind god.

Codex Chimalpopoca: Contains Anales de Cuauhtitlán; depicts Plumed Serpent in his aspect as a "teacher of all first things."

Codex Colombino: Mixtec account.

Codex Dresden: A preconquest Mayan document, "allegedly from Chichén Itzá" (Thomas).

Codex Florentino: Bernardino de Sahagún's *Historia General*.

Codex Telleriano-Remensis: Early postconquest Mexican manuscript with Spanish notations.

Codex Vienna: A postconquest text; "commissioned investigation" of Aztec culture.

Codex Vindobonensis: The "other" *Codex Vienna*; a preconquest document of Mixtec origin.

Codex Zouche-Nuttall: A Mixtec document showing Plumed Serpent in his allied identity as Éhecatl, the wind god.

Complex of the Thousand Columns (*Grupo de las Mil Columnas*): A colonnade at the site of Chichén Itzá that contains the Temple of the Warriors.

Conquest: The defeat of indigenous Mesoamericans (1519 to 1521) by a Spanish army of occupation led by Hernán Cortés.

conquistador, conquistadores: The Spanish troops brought to the New World by Hernán Cortés.

copilli: The ritual conical hat often worn by Plumed Serpent in Mesoamerican art.

Cortés, Hernán: The leader of the Spanish army of conquest.

Covarrubias, Miguel: A Mexican artist and ethnologist.

Coyolxauhqui: The Aztec moon goddess.

criollos (creoles): The first generation of Spaniards born in the New World.

Crónica Mexicana and *Crónica Mexicayotl*: Postconquest histories of Mexico written from Nahuatl accounts by Hernando Alvarado Tezozómoc.

Cruz Atrial: The sculptured crucifix Indian interpretation of the Passion of Christ at the monastery of San Augustín de Acolman.

Cuauhtémoc: The nephew of Moctezuma II and the last ruler of the Aztecs.

Cuauhtinchan: A Nahua settlement southeast of Cholula, where the *Historia Tolteca-Chichimeca* was written circa 1545.

Cuernavaca: The capital of the Mexican state of Morelos.

Cuicatl: Aztec songs, hymns, and poetry.

Danipa-an: The Zapotec name for Monte Albán.

Díaz del Castillo, Bernal: Hernán Cortés's lieutenant and the author of *The Conquest of New Spain*.

Díaz, Porfirio: The president of Mexico from 1876 to 1880 and 1884 to 1911.

Dios citbil: "God the remote" as he appears in the *Chilam Balam*.

Durán, Diego: A Dominican priest in Mexico in the mid-sixteenth century and the author of the *Historia de las Indias de la Nueva España* (History of the Indians of New Spain).

Dzibilchaltún: The earliest settlement in the northwest Yucatán.

Edmonson, Munro: The translator of the *Chilam Balam*.

Éhecatl: The Aztec wind god, often portrayed as an aspect of Plumed Serpent.

ejidos: Village lands.

El Caracol: The Snail; the observatory building at Chichén Itzá.

El Corral: A temple at Tula dedicated to Éhecatl.

El Mono: The Monkey; the Aztec personification of Éhecatl in his more destructive aspects.

El Quinto Sol: The Rising of the Fifth Sun; in Aztec mythology, the beginning of time.

El Rey: The King; an Olmec monument found at Chalcatzingo.

Felis onca: The species name for jaguar.

Gamio, Manuel: The first director of the Department of Anthropology at the *Museo Nacional* in Mexico and the primary excavator at Teotihuacán from 1917 to 1922.

García Bustos, Arturo: A contemporary Mexican mural artist, creator of the mural *Oaxaca en la Historia de Mexico*.

Grijalva River: One of the boundaries of Olmec-influenced territory.

guaje: Acacia tree.

Gucumatz: Quiché Mayan name for Plumed Serpent, also for all primordial beginnings.

Guzmán, Eulalia: The first archaeologist to describe the Olmec variants of the Plumed Serpent motif.

haab: The Maya "Vague Year."

hechicero: Sorcerer; Plumed Serpent's alter ego Tezcatlipoca.

henequen: The fiber of the agave plant, used for making rope.

Hildago y Costilla, Miguel: The leader of the New Spain independence movement.

Huitzilopochtli: The Aztec god of the sun and of war.

Hunab Ku: In the Mayan text *Chilam Balam*, "the unified god"; a parallel to Plumed Serpent.

icpalli: Throne.

inframundo: The underworld.

Instituto Nacional de Antropología e Historia (INAH): The Mexican National Anthropological and Historical Institute.

Insurgentes: A major avenue in Mexico City.

Isla Mujeres: An island off the eastern coast of the Yucatán peninsula.

Isthmus of Tehuantepec: In southeastern Mexico, between the Gulf of Tehuantepec and the Gulf of Campeche.

Itzamná: Son of the Mayan god Hunab Ku, he also shares many characteristics with Plumed Serpent.

Izapa: A preclassic site in southeastern Chiapas characterized by a baroque style of architecture.

Iztaccíhuatl: White Woman; the name of a volcano to the north of Cholula.

jefe: Hacienda boss; landholder.

katun: A period of twenty years in the Maya calendar.

kuk: The Mayan name for the "quetzal bird."

Kukul Can or Kukulkán: Yucatec Maya name for the Plumed Serpent.

La Ciudadela: The Citadel, a plaza at the site of Teotihuacán.

La Venta-Los Tuxtlas: An early Olmec archaeological site.

La Villa Rica de la Vera Cruz (The True Cross): The first town built by the conquistadores.

Laguna de los Cerros: An early Olmec archaeological site.

Lake Texcoco: The great lake that surrounded Tenochtitlán, present-day Mexico City.

Landa, Fray Diego de: A Franciscan priest in Mexico during the sixteenth century; author of the *Relación de las Cosas de Yucatán*.

Las Grutas: The subterranean caves at Loltun, in the Yucatán.

Lévi-Strauss, Claude: A French anthropologist.

Los Tres Grandes: The three great artists of the Mexican mural movement: Diego Rivera, José Clemente Orozco, and David Alfaro Siqueiros.

maguey: A Mexican cactus also called agave.

Malinalxóchitl (Maguey Flower): The shaman who led the Aztec tribes on their journey to Anáhuac, the area surrounding Mexico City; earthly sister to the god Huitzilopochtli.

Maya: One of the major pre-Columbian civilizations of Mesoamerica and the largest homogeneous group of Indians north of Peru.

Mayapán: A Maya site bearing a strong structural resemblance to Chichén Itzá.

Mérida: Capital of the state of Yucatán.

Mesoamerica: An area extending from central Mexico to Honduras and Nicaragua in which pre-Columbian civilizations flourished; defined in 1943 by Paul Kirchhoff.

mestizo: The child of a Spanish man and an Indian woman.

Miccaotli Phase: The Early Classic phase of Mesoamerican culture, dated from A.D. 150 to 250.

Michoacán: Province directly southwest of Mexico City.

Mictlán: The Mesoamerican underworld; Land of the Dead.

milpa: A tract of land cleared from the jungle, generally farmed for a few seasons and abandoned.

Mitla: Zapotec city near Monte Albán.

Mixcóatl: The husband of Chimalman and father of Plumed Serpent.

Mixtec: A Mesoamerican civilization centered in Oaxaca.

Moctezuma II: The king of the Aztecs at the beginning of the Conquest.

Monte Albán: The major ceremonial center of the Zapotec culture, near Oaxaca.

Monument 19: An Olmec monument dated to the tenth century B.C. bearing perhaps the oldest recorded image of the Plumed Serpent.

Motolinía (Fray Toribio de Benavente): One of the first priests in New Spain, author of the *History of the Indians of New Spain*.

nagual: Alter ego.

Nahachel: The Quiché Mayan name for Lake Atitlán, northwest of Guatemala City.

Nahua Aztec: The Nahua-speaking Aztec civilization centered in and around Tenochtitlán.

Nahua-Popoloca: The Nahua-speaking Popoloca Indians.

Nahuatl: The lingua franca of Mesoamerica.

Nahui Ollin: In Aztec legend, the Universe of the Fifth (current) Sun, containing the World of Man.

nepantla: A Nahuatl word meaning "in the middle."

nochtli: A Nahuatl word for "cactus."

Noh Ek: The Maya name for the planet Venus.

nopal: A kind of cactus.

Nuestra Señora de los Remedios: Our Lady of Consolation, a church built at Cholula during the Conquest.

Olmec: Mesoamerican "mother culture," dated between 1500 and 400 B.C.

Ometeotl: Lord of the Duality, heavenly mountain; the supreme (sometimes considered bisexual) Aztec deity.

Orozco, José Clemente: One of Los Tres Grandes, the three great artists of the Mexican mural movement.

Otomí: A Mesoamerican language-group near Tula.

País del Hule: The Country of Rubber, a name for the territory occupied by the Olmec.

Palacio de los Jaguares: A building at Teotihuacán incorporating Plumed Serpent imagery.

Palacio de Quetzal-Mariposa: A building at Teotihuacán incorporating Plumed Serpent imagery.

palapas: A thatched-roof building, usually open on the sides.

Palenque: A Mayan site in the state of Chiapas, Mexico.

Papaloapan River: A river in Central Mexico.

Patio de los Altares: The southern side of the pyramid at Cholula.

Paz, Octavio: The Mexican philosopher and poet.

peónes (peons): The labor class of colonial Mexico.

Petén region: A region of Northern Guatemala.

Pirámide Tepanapa: The pyramid at Cholula.

Plumed Serpent: The Mesoamerican god Quetzalcóatl.

Popocatépetl: A volcano to the southwest of Cholula.

Popol Vuh: The Mayan *Book of the Community*, the oldest written survivor of Mesoamerican "poems of origin."

pulque: An alcoholic drink made from the sap of the maguey plant.

Pyramid of the Magician: One of the pyramids at Uxmal.

Pyramid of the Moon: A pyramid at Teotihuacán.

Pyramid of the Sun: A pyramid at Teotihuacán.

quauhtecatl: The "companion of the sun"; the Aztec warrior heaven.

Quauhtitlán: One of the cities on the path of the Plumed Serpent's flight from Tula.

quequetzalcoa: The high priests in Tenochtitlán.

quetzal: An indigenous bird of Central and South America with golden-green and scarlet plumage.

Quetzalcóatl: The Mesoamerican god Plumed Serpent.

Quiché: The dominant Maya language of the Guatemalan highlands.

quinametzin: The "first men" of Teotihuacán, rumored to be giants.

Reyes, Alfonso: A Mexican historian and social philosopher, one of the founders of the *Ateneo de la Juventud*.

Rivera, Diego: One of Los Tres Grandes, the three premier artists of the Mexican mural movement.

sacbé: A holy path or causeway.

Sahagún, Fray Bernardino de: The first ethnologist of the New World; author of *The General History of the Things of New Spain*, also known as the *Florentine Codex*.

San Lorenzo Tenochtitlán: An Olmec archaeological site.

santos: Local spirits.

Sierra Madre Oriental: The mountain ranges of eastern Mexico.

Sigüenza y Góngora, Carlos de: A poet, historian, and former Jesuit in the seventeenth century; he originated the use of the name Mexico as an alternative to New Spain.

Siqueiros, José David Alfaro: One of Los Tres Grandes, the three leading artists of the Mexican mural movement.

Stephens, John Lloyd: American explorer of the mid-nineteenth century who visited Chichén Itzá and other major sites in Mexico and Central America.

Tamoanchán: Land of the Bird-Snake or The Place of Our Origin; a mythical paradise in Aztec legend.

Tedlock, Dennis: An American poet and anthropologist who translated the *Popol Vuh*.

Temple of Kukulkán: The temple of the Plumed Serpent at Chichén Itzá.

Temple of Quetzalcóatl: A temple dedicated to the Plumed Serpent at many major archaeological sites, including Tenochtitlán, Teotihuacán, and Cholula.

Temple of the Panels: A temple at Chichén Itzá.

Temple of the Warriors (Templo de los Guerreros): A temple at Chichén Itzá that shows striking structural parallels to the Toltec Atlantes Temple at Tula.

Templo de Xtoloc: A temple at Chichén Itzá.

Templo Mayor: The "Great Temple" recently excavated in Mexico City.

Tenan: Mother of waters; the ancient name for the mountain of Cerro Gordo, near Teotihuacán.

Tenochtitlán: Aztec capital city on the site of present-day Mexico City.

Teotihuacán: The earliest true urban complex in Mesoamerica; an archaeological site to the north of Mexico City that flourished from 100 B.C. to A.D. 600.

Tepanapa: The pyramid of Cholula.

Tepantitla: An outlying site of Teotihuacán.

Tepepolco: A town to the northeast of Mexico City.

Tepeyolotl: The Mesoamerican Earth Serpent, "god of the interior of the earth"; a mythic figure traced back to the Olmec.

teteuctin: Sons of Aztec nobility.

Tezcatlipoca: Smoking Mirror; Plumed Serpent's brother, adversary, and dark alter ego.

Tikal: The largest Mayan city in the northern lowlands of Guatemala.

Tlacaélel: The brother of the Aztec king Moctezuma I.

Tlacantzolli: Two-headed men said to have haunted the streets of Tenochtitlán as an omen of the Spanish Conquest.

Tlacaxipehualitztli: The "flaying festival," an Aztec ritual honoring Xipe Totec, performed in early spring to ensure a good harvest.

Tlahuizcalpantecuhtli: Plumed Serpent in his aspect as the planet Venus, Lord of the House of Dawn.

Tlaloc: The Mesoamerican rain god, closely allied with the Plumed Serpent.

Tlamachilliztlatozazanilli: *The Myth of the Suns and the Toltec-Chichimec Origins of the Mexica People.*

Tlapallán: The Land of the East or of the sunrise; Plumed Serpent's final destination after his flight from Tula.

Tlatoani: "Speaker"; an Aztec elder or hereditary ruler.

Tlaxcala: Allies of the Aztec empire, later allies of Cortés.

Tlili Tlapali, or variant, **Tlillan Tlapallán**: Land of the Red and Black; the Nahua name given to writing, glyphs, and mural paintings.

Tohil: The Quiché Maya's version of Plumed Serpent; associated with rain and fire, he led them into exile from Tula.

Tollán: The Nahuatl name for Tula.

Toltec: The people of postclassic Tula, legendary to the Aztecs for their abilities as craftsmen.

Toltecayotl: A Nahuatl term for successful craftsmanship in writing and the plastic arts.

Tonacacihuatl: The female dimension of Ometeotl, "Lady of our Flesh," in one version of the Aztec creation myth.

Tonacatecuhtli: The masculine dimension of Ometeotl, "Lord of our Flesh," in one version of the Aztec creation myth.

tonalamatl: A sacred ritual manuscript or Book of Days.

Tonantzin: Wife of the Serpent; earth goddess; mother of mankind.

Topiltzin: Our Dear Prince Quetzalcóatl; Plumed Serpent in his earthly aspect as a ruling prince.

Totonac: The first allies of Cortés against the Aztecs.

Tovar, Fray Juan de: A Franciscan priest in Cholula at the turn of the seventeenth century.

Tres Zapotes: An Olmec archaeological site.

Tula: The religious center of the Toltec culture, rising to prominence in about A.D. 800.

Tuxtla Mountains: A mountain range in coastal southern Veracruz, a border of the Olmec "nuclear area."

Tzabkán: The Mayan word for rattlesnake.

Tzompantli: A rack near a temple designed to hold the skulls of sacrificial victims.

Tzontémoc: The setting sun.

Tzotzil: A subgroup of lowland Maya in central Chiapas.

uinal: A Maya month of twenty days.

Usumacinta River: A river formed in Guatemala, emptying into the Gulf of Mexico.

Uuc-hab-nal: An older name for the site of Chichén Itzá.

Uxmal: A Mayan archaeological site fifty miles south of Mérida in the Puuc hills.

Velásquez, Diego: The Spanish governor of Cuba in 1520 and Cortés's immediate superior.

Veracruz: The first Spanish town built along the Gulf of Mexico, originally La Villa Rica de la Vera Cruz.

Villahermosa: A city on the Gulf Coast of Mexico.

Von Humboldt, Alexander: A traveler and writer, author of *Personal Narrative of a Journey to the Equinoctial Regions of the New Continent* and one of the first Westerners to evaluate Aztec art.

Xahil: A dynasty of the Maya; also, the name of one of the authors of the Sololá manuscript *Annals of the Cakchiquels*.

Xibalba: The underworld of the Highland Maya.

Xicalcoliuhqui: A stepped-fret design motif, used as a symbol of Plumed Serpent.

Xilotepec: An Otomí town near Tula, probably Xilotzingo.

Xipe Totec: Our Lord the Flayed One; the Aztec god of fertility.

Xiquipilli: A medicine pouch.

Xiuhcóatl: Plumed Serpent's aspect as "the soaring eagle," carrying the sun through the sky.

Xochicalco: A Mesoamerican city in the state of Morelos that rose to prominence after the fall of Tula.

Xocoyotzin: The Younger, usually applied to Moctezuma II.

Xólotl: A dog-headed god, one of Plumed Serpent's animal alter egos, as guide to the underworld.

Xul: November in the Mayan calendar; the sixth month.

Xux Ek: The Wasp Star or Venus God, possibly another Mayan version of Plumed Serpent.

Yahualli Éhecatl: The Wheel of the Winds; one of the earliest Nahua names for Plumed Serpent.

Yoo-paa: "Place of the dead"; the Zapotec name for the present-day site of Mitla.

Yucatán: A Mexican peninsula extending north into the Caribbean Sea.

Yucatec Maya: The Mayan civilizations of the Yucatán peninsula.

Yucu-cui: Green Mountain; the Mixtec name for Monte Albán.

Zapata, Emiliano: Farmer, revolutionary, reformer.

Zapotec: A Mesoamerican civilization centered in the valley of Oaxaca starting in approximately 300 B.C.

Zinacantec Maya: The contemporary Maya in the highlands of Chiapas.

zócalo: An open-air bazaar; the central square or plaza of a Mexican town.

zona arqueológica: An archaeological zone or area.

I gratefully acknowledge *Myths of Ancient Mexico* by Michel Graulich; *Facts and Artifacts of Ancient Middle America* by Curt Muser; and *Conquest: Cortés and the Fall of Old Mexico* by Hugh Thomas, all of which served as valuable resources for the amplification of many definitions in this glossary.

N.B.

The problems of research are so vast, the guidelines at our disposal so tenuous and uncertain, the past, over huge tracts of time, has been so irrevocably wiped out, and the basis of our speculations is so precarious, that even the most insignificant reconnoitering of the terrain puts the researcher into a state of uncertainty in which he oscillates between the most humble kind of resignation and the wildest ambition; he knows that the essential evidence has been lost and that all his efforts will amount to no more than a scratching of the surface; yet may he not stumble on some miraculously preserved clue that will shed light? Nothing is possible, so all is possible. The darkness through which we are groping is too thick for us to make any pronouncements about it; we cannot even say that it is doomed to last.

— CLAUDE LÉVI-STRAUSS, *Tristes Tropiques*

While a major concern of historians is to keep myth from replacing history and to purge the past of myth, they would have to admit that myths are an inevitable component of their regular subject matter. Myths are right there along with facts, working to determine and explain human behavior and the course of events. It would be stupid to ignore or underestimate them. Not all myths are associated with defeated or discredited causes and their defense. In fact the most hardy, secure, and numerous myths are the product of victories and vindicated causes, and embody live and cherished values.

— C. VANN WOODWARD, *The Future of the Past*

"My heart stirs just a little to the word Quetzalcóatl. Quetzalcóatl! Quetzalcóatl!" Cipriano repeated it several times to himself, smiling. "Curious!" he said. "But yet, Ramon, need we revive old gods? Isn't it an antiquarian thing to do? Do you know what Padre Ignacio once said to me about you? 'Ramon Carrasco's future is the past of humanity.' That always stuck in my mind. Can you find the future in the past?"

— D. H. LAWRENCE, *Quetzalcóatl: The Early Version of The Plumed Serpent*

The greatness of Mexico is that its past is always alive…. Mexico exists in the present, its dawn is occurring right now, because it carries with it the wealth of a living past, an unburied memory. Its horizon is also today, because today does not diminish the force of Mexico's living desire.

— CARLOS FUENTES, *A New Time for Mexico*

Geographies, too, are symbolic; physical spaces turn into geometric archetypes that are emissive forms of symbols. Plains, valleys, mountains: the accidents of terrain become meaningful as soon as they enter history.

— OCTAVIO PAZ, *The Other Mexico: Critique of the Pyramid*

DURANGO

Sierra Madre Occidental

ZACATECAS

NUEVO
LEÓN

Sierra Madre Oriental

TAMAULIPAS

SAN LUIS
POTOSÍ

NAYARIT

AGUASCALIENTES

Panuco

C. Rojo

MEXICO

Río Grande de Santiago

Guanajuato

QUERÉTARO
DE ARTEAGA

VERACRUZ-LLAVE

Guadalajara

GUANAJUATO

JALISCO

Chapala

HIDALGO

Ayutla

Lake
Chapala

MÉXICO

TULA

TEOTIHUACÁN

Acolman

Sa. Nevada Mts.

TLAXCALA

ZEMPOALA

Colima

MICHOACÁN
DE OCAMPO

MEXICO-CITY

CALIXTLAHUACA

D.F.

Tlaxcala

CHOLULA

Veracruz

COLIMA

MALINALCO

Cuernavaca

Puebla

XOCHICALCO

Anenecuilco

Tepeacá

*Presa del
Infiernillo*

Ayala

CHALCATZINGO

MORELOS

PUEBLA

Balsas

Papaloapa

GUERRERO

Sierra Madre del Sur

Oaxaca

MONTE ALBÁN

MITLA

OAXAC

GULF OF MEXICO

C. Catoche

Isla
Mujeres

DZIBILCHALTÚN
Mérida   YUCATÁN
Valladolid
MAYAPÁN   CHICHÉN ITZÁ
Mani
UXMAL   LOLTÚN
TULUM

Isla del
Cozumel

Campeche

Yucatan
Peninsula

QUINTANA
ROO

Bay of
Campeche

CAMPECHE

Laguna de
Términos

TABASCO   Grijalva
LA VENTA
Tuxtla Mts.   Uxpanapa   Villahermosa
SAN LORENZO-
TENOCHTITLAN   Chontalpa

CARIBBEAN
SEA

Isthmus of
Tehuantepec

PALENQUE

CHIAPAS   Usumacinta

TIKAL   Belmopan

BELIZE

Gulf of
Honduras

Grijalva
BONAMPAK   Río de la Pasión

Presa de
la Angostura   GUATEMALA

L. de
Izabal

Sierra Madre
de Chiapas   Quiché

HONDURAS

Gulf of
Tehuantepec

Sololá
Lake
Atitlán   KAMINALJUYU
Guatemala
City

Tegucigalpa

San Salvador

EL SALVADOR

© Copyright by HAMMOND INCORPORATED

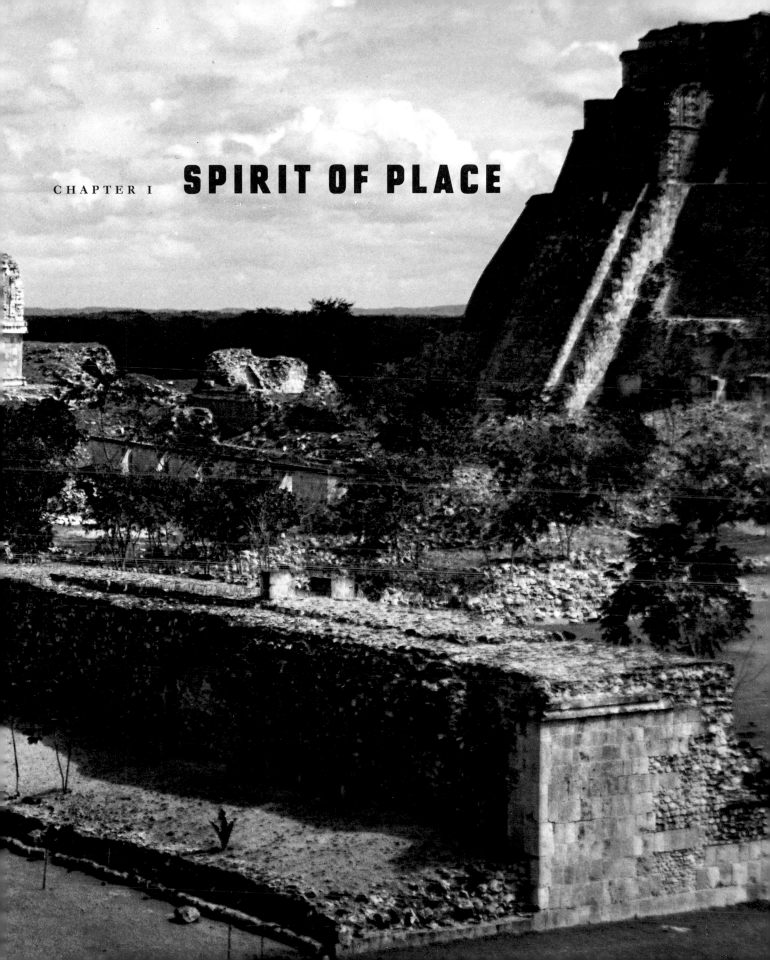

CHAPTER I **SPIRIT OF PLACE**

According to my handy guidebook, this was supposed to be The Temple of the Old Woman,
but as I scrambled to the top, grasping thick roots,
finding a toehold here and there in the dusty clay, it
seemed little more than a rocky, limestone-strewn
mound. Breathless, I crouched against the gnarled
stump of a long-dead *ceiba*, the sacred tree of the
Maya, and squinted out over the jungle into the
late-afternoon sun slant. Herds of tourist buses had
long since departed; the acrid tinge of diesel exhaust
hung in the still air. Now the Uxmal guards blew
mightily on their whistles, signaling that the ruins
would close in half an hour.

A constant, soughing breeze came at me across
the flat Yucatán lowlands, picking up hints of cool-
ness from the impenetrable green bush. Already it
was becoming difficult to conjure up a coherent
memory of the old colonial city of Mérida, only an
hour's drive north, where I had spent the past three
days in a gently seedy hotel with a fountain in its
well-swept stone courtyard. Directly across the street
was a twin-spired church; a hollow, tinny bell struck
every half hour starting at five-thirty in the morning,
awakening an insistent rooster. Mérida, capital of
the Yucatán—originally known as the "White
City"—had long since turned into a rather forlorn,
gray place, its moods heightened by brief, torrential
rain, swift black clouds, and intense sun.

I drove along narrow, eighteenth-century cobble-
stoned thoroughfares, built for horse-drawn car-
riages. Careening trams overloaded with workers
accompanied me, brakes screeching, past pavilioned
markets, tortilla shops, and cracked walls adorned
with huge posters advertising Cristal sparkling water.

But ten minutes out of the city, on the Avenida de
los Itzaes (Avenue of the Foreigners), I was overtaken
by a not entirely unpleasant fear that I was a stranger
in a strange land, striking off toward the middle of
nowhere, "toward the old prehistoric humanity, the
dark-eyed humanity" D. H. Lawrence had encountered and romanticized sixty years before.

The straight macadam road undulated over gentle hills past ranks of proud, spiky agave plants, and,
lo and behold, the cacophony dropped away. The
villages I passed blurred into vivid images: a dozen
thatched banana-leaf huts around a muddy yard
where dun-coated dogs sniffed and scampered after
children among discarded automobile tires; embroidered, stark-white *huipiles*, handmade peasant
blouses strung on clotheslines snapped like sails in
the wind; old *campesinos* on bicycles pedaled
methodically on and on in the brutal heat, expres-
sionless deep brown faces in even deeper shadows
beneath their straw hats; and women balancing baskets of fruit and bundled firewood on their heads.

Within an hour, even the villages receded, too,
and farmed-out *milpas*, patchwork charred fields still
smoking, alternating with waist-high verdant shrubbery, pressed up to the edge of the black tarmac.

Ubiquitous signs for the *Zona Arqueologica* try to
warn me, but even so, swerving out of a bend in the
road, gears grinding in the rented, vintage
Volkswagen sedan, suddenly—where before there
was nothing—the Mayan ruins appear. They simply
materialize: smooth, looming, tan facades erupt
from the green; they seem lit from within.

As I leave the car and approach, listening to the
crunch of my footsteps on gravel paths between
buildings, the seductive complexity of the structures
emerges and immediately becomes too much to
assimilate. But I hunger to look and keep looking:
corbeled archways; sneering, tongued, fanged, and
bug-eyed rain-god masks hewn from pitted rock;
peaked roof combs balancing upon frail latticework,

vines intertwining; recurrent, spiraling geometric motifs circumscribing hundred-yard-long walls in layered parades. There is the impassive way the buildings face off against one another: the manicured, I-shaped ritual ball court with its tiered spectator stands and stone hoop; the oblong palace, one story high, its sinister, pitch-dark doorways leading into labyrinthine, bare rooms.

And here is the all-too-familiar stepped temple, a benign image seen on countless travel posters and engraved comfortably into popular imagination. But up close the building is impossibly steep, vertiginous, hostile. Challenged, I grip a cold metal chain spiked into the rock and begin to climb, back rounded against the downward pull, not daring to look back over my shoulder at the receding ground below. I mount the narrow, worn steps ever higher into the palpable, humid quiet.

For no matter how dense with clamorous visitors the ruins become as the day wears on, once you begin this ascent, the space between edifices becomes filled with the pressing silence of past centuries, forcing you to forget everything except your ambivalent way up an incline that seems to say it is not meant to be pursued. A millennium ago, this same path was taken by four chanting, feather-robed priests flanking a joyful young girl, a virgin who would be beheaded and then flayed, obsidian knives penetrating her chest, her still-beating heart torn out as she lay spread-eagled upon the sacrificial altar at the pyramid's peak 120 feet above the ground.

Uxmal was a decade ago, when I first brushed up on my Spanish. My wife, Roberta, and I, very much the "accidental tourists," took two trips to the Yucatán on a whim (having been resolutely Eurocentric for my entire adult traveling life, never before venturing south of the border). We explored known and unknown historic sites and then lived near a fishing village with unpaved streets and beaches dotted with rustling *palapas*, thatched umbrellas, on the Isla Mujeres, off the coast near Cancún, a world away from that overbuilt place. Our island was reachable only via an interminable ride on a pitching and tossing blue ferryboat, accompanied by chicken farmers.

Lying on the sand one limpid afternoon, Margarita-drowsed, gazing out at the turquoise water through half-closed eyes, following the seaweed swaying back and forth just beneath the surface, I fancied (as any self-respecting writer must do) that it would be my turn to write a book about Mexico some day.

What kind of book would *mine* be?

The answer was already coalescing in my imagination, for in early travels through the country, I had become frustrated with the inadequate orientation materials—or, in many cases, no materials at all—at the remote ruins where the tourist trade had not yet reached critical mass. Even at Uxmal, one of the favored spots on *la ruta Maya*, the itinerary of most popular sites, the pamphlet I was handed, while visually helpful, was in poorly rendered English and lacked depth. There was no mythic background for the place, no sense conveyed of the intrinsic, underlying meaning, which predates the usual descriptions of what invading Spaniards saw and did when they arrived in the sixteenth century.

LEFT: *Agave plants, Yucatán*
PREVIOUS: *Uxmal ruins, Yucatán*

Beyond the rain-forested splendor of Palenque, beyond the austere, classic style of Uxmal, the warlike grandeur of Chichén Itzá, the peaks of Tikal—beyond these magnificent, parklike settings, there are hundreds of other sites, some only partially excavated, others little more than grassy mounds. At the end of a dirt road leading into the jungle, an Indian proprietor in a modest hut sits behind a wooden table. For a few pesos—less than a dollar—he will grant admission to roam among improvised clearings and view barely recognizable stelae clothed in vegetation.

One early morning, driving northwest from Mérida toward the Gulf Coast, I took an impromptu field trip to Dzibil-chaltún, the earliest-settled site on the entire Yucatán penin-sula. Thriving fifteen hun-dred years before the birth of Christ, it was a bustling metropolis of more than fifty thou-sand people. The place was now deserted except for a class of chattering parochial schoolchildren accompanied by two nuns. In the scrub grass, past the remains of a Spanish church con-structed out of limestone blocks from a destroyed Mayan palace, lay a depthless, dark *cenote*—a sacrificial well—where lost pottery, silver and gold jewelry, and human bones were discovered. At the remote end of a mile-long *sacbé*, a sacred path paved with white stones, was the domed "Temple of the Seven Dolls," thus named because of the miniature, homunculuslike clay and white chicle sap forms unearthed beneath its foundation. The temple was perched upon a low hill, and each of its

Aztec calendar stone

LEFT: *The author at the Temple of the Magician (El Adivino), Uxmal*

foot-thick walls was pierced precisely at the center with a small, porthole window, an observatory for viewing the heavens at certain ritual times of the calendar.

"But why did these buildings come to be situated here in the first place?" I asked myself, "What was the origin of the spiritual mind-set; the deep, reli-gious motivation; the rage for order of the driven people who constructed them? Where did these people come from and where did they go?"

As soon as these initial questions leaped to mind, my earliest notion for the book—simply to com-pose a thinking-person's guidebook to Mexico—seemed superficial. I was not going to write a conven-tional "travel" book, although my many subse-quent trips to Mexico over the coming years played an integral part in the structure of the book as I made it a point to *be* wherever I was writing about. Much as I might like to in some other fantasy life, I would never presume to live among the native peoples, learn a Mayan dialect, or hurtle in a bark canoe down the Usumacinta River. I would not presume to be an anthropologist or an archaeologist, although my readings took me into these and other related fields.

My essential curiosity about Mexico caught hold after the romantic veneer no longer satisfied me. The raw, surface beauty—and there is much of it throughout these pages—was always enthralling but only served as a portal. "I had staged in my head a *sham Mexico*," wrote the French artist and critic Jean Charlot in 1922, when he first arrived from Paris, "fanned with feathers of blue, green, and red, its trees feverish with tropical mimics."[1]

This was a literary tradition I was glad to find during my early, intuitive readings. What kind of Mexico did these outsiders expect, and what kind did they discover? At the very end of the eighteenth century, Alexander Von Humboldt came to Mexico from Germany (and went on to Washington to meet with a kindred spirit, Thomas Jefferson) and as a result of a five-year stay in Latin America wrote his trailblazing *Personal Narrative of a Journey to the Equinoctial Regions of the New Continent*. We now know that Humboldt was the first European to take Aztec art seriously. Visiting Mexico City, he was intrigued by the huge round calendar stone with its glyphic hints at an understanding of the cosmos. In preparing for his trip, Humboldt read accounts of earlier expeditions, "regret[ting] that travelers seldom possessed a wide enough knowledge to avail themselves of what they saw." Humboldt did not attempt to cover up his civilized background. He did not shy away from presenting himself as an erudite though inexperienced being in the midst of an alien environment. He liked to call himself a *"scientific traveler—* paying attention to the morphology of landscape, favoring panoramic description, valuing scientific accuracy, and avidly collecting all manner of detail and data." This mode of inquiry was meant expressly to disclose the "hidden, harmonic unity of nature" in Mexico. In the best romantic tradition, one traveled and observed closely, thereby "dissipating melancholy and restoring peace to the troubled mind."

Although I suffered my share of nightmares, alone and sweating as the only guest in a remote hotel during the off-season, with no telephone or television, awakening with a start at three o'clock in the morning in the pitch darkness, swearing I could hear the cattle in a field nearby murmuring to each other, in the best of my times in Mexico, Alexander Von Humboldt's was a soulful sensibility I looked to for solace: *"It is the man himself* we wish to see in contact with the objects around him," he

insisted. "His narration interests us far more if local coloring informs the descriptions of the country and its people."[2]

My room in the villa near Uxmal faced an open, central courtyard, and every morning at about six-thirty I would be gently awakened by two successive sounds: the swish (pause), swish (pause), swish of broom against concrete, as the porter made his solitary way from one end of the space to the other, unhurriedly gathering into a neat pile the dried palm leaves and husks detached by the prior evening's breezes; then came the *splash!* as he cast a bucketful of water across the ground just covered, as if to make this familiar terrain once more ready for the morning. While the sky brightened, his ritual was always the same. There was a certain seductive reassurance in that cyclic pattern. It was a bracing antidote to the "sham" image Jean Charlot had learned to resist, and to the "imaginary Mexico" that I, too, wanted to avoid.[3] The man's persistence in his daily round set me ruminating about a characteristic of Mexican life or even an archetype within the culture that I might be able to capture, that would have the staying power to become the center of my book.

Ingrained, habituated, unself-conscious movements of quotidian life were important to my understanding—from a great distance I was never able to bridge. But I had accepted my distance from the people. Whether I was looking out through the window of a cab speeding down the Insurgentes in Mexico City or confronting the bare, somber look of a peasant vendor crouched on the sidewalk outside the cathedral in the Oaxaca *zócalo*, the central square of the city, my gringo invisibility did not trouble me or make me feel guilty. As a matter of fact, it allowed me the intellectual latitude to seek the larger and deeper metaphor I required.

Quetzalcóatl, Telleriano-Remensis Codex

tierra.

ju   m   bue   ju

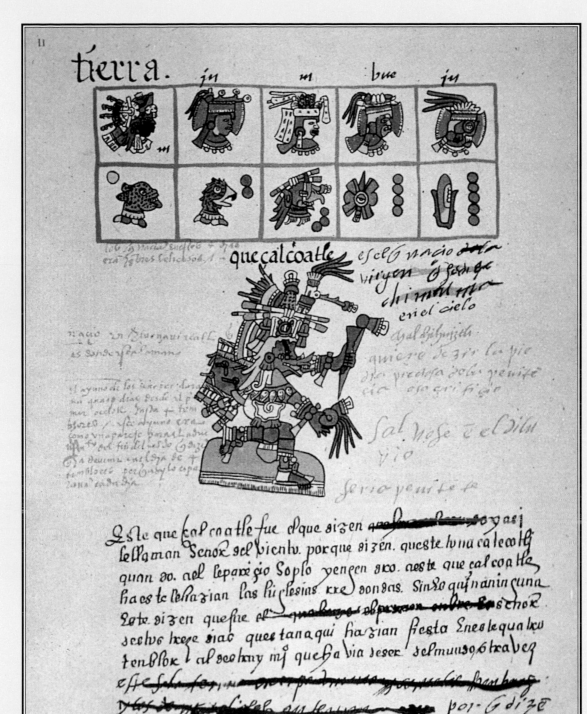

quecalcoatle

es el G nacio dela
virgen Ó Feade
chimalma
en el cielo

chalchihuitl
quiere dezir la pie
dra preciosa dela peniten
cia ó sacrifiçio

salyose el dilu
uio

seria penite...

nacio en Ouexquicatl
es sonde esta la mano

esta que calcoatle fue el que dizen
se llaman señor del viento. porque dizen. queste tuna catecotl
quando ael le parecio soplo yenen ...co. aeste que calcoatle
hacestelebrazian las lilesias rre sondas. Sinxo quinaninguna
Este dizen queste el
sestue treze dias questanaqui hazian fiesta En este qual ...
tenblor. al seoltuy mj que hauia deser delmuudosotra vez

por G dize
G seaperdido 4 bezes y seade perder o Ac

I spent my time watching, walking, taking photographs, eating meals alone, dozing fitfully in the midafternoon, jotting notes in my little journal, and, back home, omnivorously consuming history texts, browsing compulsively in the "Latin America" sections of bookstores, and combing through offerings under "Mesoamerica"[4] in rare book dealers' catalogues. At the time, my forays into Mexico seemed shapeless. Recounting them now, as I will do in the pages to come, I believe there was indeed a plan. And likewise with my endless, at times amorphous research, feeling my way through three hundred books I read in ten years: I know when the crystallizing moment occurred.

In the sultry summer of 1989, I reserved a spot in the Frederick Lewis Allen Room at the New York Public Library on Forty-second Street, and there, with the sympathetic assistance of the reference specialists Tim Troy and Wayne Furman, I set up shop in a study carrel, resolving to systematize my delving into Mesoamerican history, to find a single, underlying theme that would pull together all disparate threads, shards, intuitions, and good intentions. To get me going, Tim and Wayne brought out the twelve-volume *General History of the Things of New Spain*, also known as the *Florentine Codex*, by Fray Bernardino de Sahagún, a Franciscan friar and the first great ethnologist of the New World. Sahagún had come in the middle decades of the sixteenth century, after Hernán Cortés and the conquistadores resolved to destroy all "pagan" vestiges of the indigenous society. Aside from his mandate to proselytize and convert the native people to Christianity, Sahagún, who lived in the village of Tepepolco on the northeastern edge of the Basin of Mexico, set himself to learn the Nahuatl tongue, and then, with the aid of Indian informants, created an encyclopedic history of the Aztecs, their customs, and religious beliefs. The *Florentine Codex* appreciates in value when we realize that only sixteen books created in the entire span of Mesoamerican

culture before the Spanish Conquest remained intact after 1521.

I leafed through page upon page of parables, legends, and tales transcribed from the mouths of the "Old Ones" who described how life had been before the coming of the strange, bearded white men from across the waters to the east. "Another time it will be like this," Sahagún noted an ancient song, "another time things will be the same, some time, some place. What happened a long time ago, and which no longer happens, will be again, it will be done again as it was in far-off times: those who now live, will live again, they will live again."[5]

To the Aztecs and to the many other Mesoamerican civilizations preceding them by more than three thousand years, history was not a straight path, one event linked chainlike to the next, but rather a series of cycles, a spinning wheel spiraling forward through time, engendering repetitions as it goes.[6]

According to the tribal elders, the "First God" who set this wheel in motion was Plumed Serpent (Quetzalcóatl), the Lord of the Dawn and the Phoenix of the West. He was the great and benign namer of all things in the Universe: "mountains, forests, and sites." To my Westernized intellect, he appeared in the *Florentine Codex* like a figure out of *Paradise Lost*: "He was the wind, he was the guide, the roadsweeper of the rain gods, of the masters of water, of those who brought rain," Father Sahagún wrote of this transcendent being who gathered together the remains of the human race from *Mictlán*, the Underworld, the Realm of the Dead, after the primeval flood, and who then reestablished humanity in the "Time Before Time."

Plumed Serpent took this assemblage of bone ashes and clay, this thing that would become Man, infused him with his own sacred blood, and blessed him with maize, the arts of weaving and mosaic making, music and dance, the science of curing illness, commerce, crafts, time, the stars in the heavens, the calendar, prayers, and sacrifice. Plumed

Serpent was the performer of miracles, the supreme magician, the ruler of sorcerers, holding the secret of all enchantments.

The most potent mythologies present symbols of dualism and conflict. Plumed Serpent likewise confronted an alter ego, a dark side, his "Evil Twin": *Tezcatlipoca*, Smoking Mirror, the adversary who dogged Plumed Serpent through his peaceful mission and ultimately tempted him to fall from grace. According to Aztec lore, Tezcatlipoca posed as a servant and infiltrated Plumed Serpent's monastic household, concocting from the sap of the maguey plant a *pulque* brew with which he intoxicated the priestly god and his sister and deluded him into sleeping with her, thereby breaking his vows of chastity.

The legend tells us that the now fallible Plumed Serpent, cast out in anguish as a result of his transgressions, abandoned his earthly possessions and began an epic flight. A pilgrimage of purification resulted in the proliferation of his image and name throughout ancient Mexico, on and on toward the eastern horizon through Cholula, Quauhtitlán, Xochicalco, and as far as Chichén Itzá. There, when the angle of the sun is just right at the summer solstice, the shadow of an immense serpent ripples down the side of the many-tiered pyramid consecrated to Quetzalcóatl's Mayan name: *Kukulkán*.

When he finally reached *Tlillan Tlapallán*, the Land of Black and Red, his final place of spiritual enlightenment on the shores of the holy sea where the morning star announces daily the rebirth of the sun, Plumed Serpent declared with messianic flair to his weeping followers that he had been "called forth." He promised to return in the year named *Ce Ácatl*, One-Reed. He donned a turquoise mask and a robe of feathers and "ordered a raft to be made of snakes, and he entered it and sat down as in a canoe, and thus he left, navigating on the sea." Whereupon Plumed Serpent burst into flame, and the ashes of his heart rose upward, phoenixlike, and became the planet Venus.

Ironically, the fateful year 1519, when Spanish galleons were first sighted off the shore at Veracruz, coincided with *Ce Ácatl*, which cycled around every fifty-two years in the native calendar. Reports of giant, white-winged birds swooping over the seas bearing fair-skinned men reached Moctezuma, reigning king of the Aztecs. Surely this was the anticipated return of their beloved Prince Plumed Serpent, as it had been prophesied. Hernán Cortés and his musketed equestrian army—the Aztecs had never seen a horse or a gun before—were greeted with open embraces and offerings of gold. Within two years the Aztec world was destroyed.

"The myth of the Plumed Serpent is dazzling in its beauty. It is the complete fairy tale. All things change perpetually into something else. Everything is elusive, intangible, yet permanent and true. The great bird-serpent, priest-king Quetzalcóatl is the most powerful figure in all the mythology of Mexico and Central America."[7]

Indeed, I soon discovered that I was backing into a much vaster saga than the one unfurled by Fray Bernardino Sahagún. His was merely the very tip of the mountain, one act in a complex drama that had begun more than fifteen hundred years before Christ and is still enacted today in modern Mexico. This book is the mosaic mural depicting that vast myth. I use the term "mosaic" because it is composed of interlocking, contiguous bits and pieces fitted together, many brightly colored and varied iconographies, some foreboding and vicious, others noble and lofty, provided by a multitude of civilizations within the framework of Mesoamerica.

The great French anthropologist Claude Lévi-Strauss cautions that "*all* available variants of a myth must be taken into account. There is no single, true version."[8] I use the term "mural," though the story fabricated here is a narrative, necessarily presented in the conventional sense—from beginning to end, in a book, with chapters—because in fact (as we are striving to remain true to the ancient Mexican sense of time) the story of Plumed Serpent should authentically be seen as a simultaneous array, a swirl of impressions evolving over millennia.

Plumed Serpent is the only symbol with so much staying power that it can be found permeating nearly every formative culture of Mexico. As a biographer I set forth to understand and chronicle Plumed Serpent's persistent, indomitable "life," an undertaking that required me to go back to a time before he even possessed a proper name. Like the biography of a person, this story moves through stages—gestation, birth, infancy, childhood, adolescence, maturity, death—and into various transfigurations, including emotional crises along sacred and secular roads. I also try to recapture the spirit of place so vivid in widely varying geographic locations, encompassing the tropical Olmec world of Veracruz, Villahermosa, and the Gulf Coast; the magisterial ceremonial realm of Teotihuacán northeast of Mexico City and the societies engendered by its fall at Xochicalco and Cholula; the Toltec world of Tula so revered by the Aztecs; the Mayan empire at Uxmal, Chichén Itzá, and Mayapán; the literary culture of the Zapotec and Mixtec people in and around Oaxaca, Monte Albán, and Mitla, encompassed by the Sierra Madre mountains; and the final tragic efflorescence of the Nahua Aztec culture of Tenochtitlán, which was reborn in the search for a national identity during the long colonial centuries.

Revived and glorified, Quetzalcóatl, with all the hope inspired by his promise of return, was burned into the soul of the nation by the pioneering modernist philosophers, writers, and painters of the Mexican Revolution and the 1920s.

To begin this journey, we confront the elusive idea of an archetype and then visit an agricultural society where potent denizens of field and forest—animals such as the crocodile, the snake, and the jaguar—hold sway. We then move to the beginnings of organized religion, where the priestly class takes on a greater role, and examine Plumed Serpent's position in a pantheon, a community of gods, after which the god's mantle is assumed by actual men, the *hombre-dios*, kings who rose, flourished, and fell under Quetzalcóatl's banner. Next we view Plumed Serpent as the symbol for the diaspora of an entire people across ancient Mexico and follow him to his apotheosis and transformation as a warlike figure colliding with the conquering Europeans. We then see his problematic recasting in veiled Christian terms and examine the dilemmas this adaptation created in the psyche of the native peoples.

The wise words of the late Octavio Paz—philosopher, poet, diplomat, and voice of Mexico—are invoked and resonate often throughout this book because, more than any other teller of the Mexican tale in our time, he unerringly found the pulse of the nation. Paz says that to comprehend the whys and wherefores of Mexico, we must conduct "archaeological digs in the historical subsoil."[9]

The spade enters the earth.

CHAPTER II

TIME BEFORE TIME

OUT OF THE PRIMORDIAL REALM — PLUMED SERPENT
AS GOD OF MAIZE — SKY ABOVE, EARTH BELOW

Before "the science of men in time"—otherwise known as the discipline of history—was created,[1] and long before art began to depict imaginative beliefs, there came simply the tracks of men across landscapes. From northwest to southeast, twenty thousand years and more before Columbus, migrant peoples descended on foot through the plains of what we now name the North American continent.[2]

As they traversed the terrain, they encountered animals, plants, and hills, which became sacred neighbors and allies.[3] Before religion, before the advent (or invention) of gods and the "supernatural," rhythms and recurrences, the regular heartbeats within all manifestations of the cosmos and the natural world, formed the template for the spiritual feelings of early peoples in Mesoamerica: inevitabilities of

birth, maturity, and death; night succeeding day; seasons of the year; rain after lightning; and the movement of planets through the heavens.[4]

The human psyche was not, as it is today, alien or separated from the orderly processes of this world; rather, it aspired to be in harmony with them. The very land—even rocks that had to be cleared in order for fields to be cultivated—was as alive as those inhabiting it and responded to human contact as to a brother's touch.

Between seven and two millennia B.C., as the so-called hunter-gatherers became sedentary and settled into regions and what we would now call agriculture began in the basins of major river systems and on especially inviting fertile land, a sense of reverence prevailed.

At this juncture, the primal vision for what later was pronounced in the Nahua tongue as Quetzalcóatl found its birth in the synthesis, through the practice of agriculture, of two words—we could even say two worlds—sky (*quetzal*, bird) and earth (*cóatl*, serpent).[5]

Rain penetrated the ground and caused crops to grow. One of the first and most important domesticated fruits of this union was maize, the eternal staple of Mesoamerican life. The fresh green blades of young maize plants broke through the surface of the soil, and the new sprout divided into two leaves, like the quivering tongue of the rattlesnake. As the maize plant matured, its familiarly blunt, yellow-brown nutrient core of kernels arose, haloed by green, featherlike leaves. This flourishing image drew upon deep

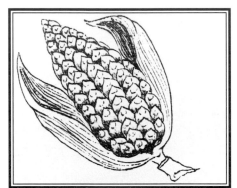

Mature maize plant, Florentine Codex
PREVIOUS: *Maize plant sprout*

roots from the epochs before mankind, when great reptiles ruled. From that common source both birds *and* serpents had evolved, two related and contrary forms of life, one aloft, the other earthbound.[6]

"The origin of myth must be looked for in imaginative tales dealing with the social life of the people," and this origin needs to be sought in "times when the world had not yet assumed its present form, and when mankind was not yet in possession of all the arts and customs that belong to our period."[7]

There is no reason to suspend disbelief. We can hold the plumed maize-serpent in our minds as a lived, everyday reality for the earliest Mesoamerican paleoplanters, remembering that "the primitive mentality did not *invent* myths" but rather "*experienced* them."[8]

When the practice of agriculture was still new to the Mesoamerican farmer, he had to reformulate his behavior from the routine of the predatory hunter, who ranged widely to seek food, to a structured manner of subsistence, controlling the growth of plants that required seeding, fertilization, and then harvesting. These changed patterns of life caused him to become more attuned to the soil and vegetation upon which he depended so intimately. He came to a new awareness of the world beneath his feet and its denizens, living and dead—for even departed family members, never-forgotten ancestors, were in a sense "planted," usually alongside the huts of those who remained behind.

Claude Lévi-Strauss elegantly terms *bons à penser* the native farmer's increased attention to the animals around him—meaning they became capable of stimulating new, more sophisticated *modes of thought* in man.[9]

In this dark, seductive realm, the serpent—more than any other beast in Mesoamerican lore before or since—achieved and maintained primacy as a doubled being, simultaneously inspiring fascination and veneration on the one hand and repulsion and fear on the other.

The serpent, the harbinger of rebirth after death, shed his skin and reappeared resurrected from his lair after long sleep, renewed with the shift from the dun colors of the dry season into the first fertile greens of spring. He was the bearer of wisdom, as his "watchful, lidless eye" shone forth with vigilant knowledge that man, who required sleep, could never attain.[10]

In his darker, dreaded persona, the serpent moved sinuously, slithering through the tall grasses without trepidation toward human habitats, and he struck unpredictably, with unerring accuracy, when angered. Even the sun's position and the waxing and waning of the moon seemed to affect the serpent's behavior. He embodied the threat of mortality. He was mysterious, enigmatic, at once quiet and wild.

Fixed indelibly in the imagination of Mesoamerica from formative times, the potent *cóatl* could be "hybridized, or plumed, twinned, grown gigantic and swift and all-seeing…a dream-mutant who both avenged and transmitted wisdom according to the vagaries of mood and circumstance." He flowered into "the primary archetype in Mesoamerican iconography…a channel of communication between the world of humans and the infernal world, both gods and ancestors appearing between his jaws."[11]

CHAPTER III

THE OLMEC

SIGNS OF SHARED KNOWLEDGE AMONG MESOAMERICAN CIVILIZATIONS —
FIRST PEOPLES ALONG THE GULF COAST — PLUMED SERPENTS CARVED
IN STONE — MAGICAL SHAMAN SPELLS — MEN BECOME BEASTS

Before embarking upon our journey through space and time across Mesoamerica, spanning from Nicaragua in the east to Michoacán in the west,[1] and from five millennia before Christ to two thousand years after, we need to pinpoint the correct place to start. In keeping with metaphors of the natural world, imagine a giant tree with diverse, autonomous "branches"—Teotihuacán, Toltec, Zapotec, Mixtec, Maya, Aztec—radiating outward from a "common bole."[2]

There is no other way to rationalize the coherent, recurring pattern of shared traits among the Mesoamerican cultures, the broad "constellation of achievements"[3] across national boundaries: ceremonial centers and cities designed by intelligent town planners, with pyramids, royal residences, meeting halls, and temples constructed around open plazas and marketplaces with hewn-stone irrigation ditches; a ritual, often sacrificial ball game played out in areas as big as a football field or as intimate in size as two tennis courts; painted books, called codices, crafted by learned sages into bark, paper, or deerskin pages folded accordionlike upon themselves, in which histories are divined, gods catalogued, the lives of rulers recorded, everyday customs and mores detailed. They also contain calendars; hieroglyphic writing; fables of love, war, and death; and seasonal rites born with fer-

Monumental Olmec head, Veracruz

tility cults observing sowing and reaping times, evolving into the worship of idols inside wood-thatched shrines at the pyramids' peaks, bearing testimony to the authority of the priestly class.[4]

The essential unity and crucial interdependence pervading the Mesoamerican community was set in motion by the Olmec, bearers of the "Mother Culture." Their name was derived from the Spanish, *País del Hule* (Country of Rubber). Their ancient domain, the so-called nuclear area or nexus of central Mexico, stretched between the basins of the Papaloapán and Grijalva Rivers, from the sultry, forested, and rainy lowlands of Chontalpa along the Gulf Coast in the east, over to the Tuxtla Mountains in the west.[5]

The earliest surviving evidence of "era dating" in Mexico has been deciphered from Olmec stelae inscriptions. The first Olmec hamlets of agriculturists and pottery makers in the region were established between 2500 and 1500 B.C.[6] Beyond these, the more developed settlements, or, more correctly, the four that have been excavated to date in the rather inhospitable tropical climate of "the Mesopotamia of the Americas"—San Lorenzo Tenochtitlán, Laguna de los Cerros, Tres Zapotes, and La Venta-Los Tuxtlas—are all noteworthy for presenting a single, large mound surrounded by smaller satellite sites. This pattern signifies a hierarchical society of elites and commoners.[7] La Venta, in the state of

Tabasco, is the prototypical Mesoamerican city.[8] Its Great Pyramid, more than one hundred feet high, was one of the most massive structures in the Americas when it was built—huddled and green like a volcanic serpent freed from his lair below the ground, coiled in ever-narrowing circles toward the sky.

The Olmec left no books. But they were the first Mesoamerican peoples (if, indeed, they *were* a defined race of people) to leave behind a corpus of permanent sculptured works. Perhaps the most dramatic metaphors for the top-heavy power structure of the culture are the imperious, carved stone heads believed to represent their ruling elite, "individual leaders of great force and charisma."[9] Weighing as much as fourteen tons and standing eight to fifteen feet high, the basalt boulders used to shape these colossal sculptures were shipped from the Tuxtla mountains by raft.

An important feature of Olmec style is its "classicism."[10] The austere, hieratic heads "stand free in space rather than being surrounded by the clutter of costumes and other details characteristic of the later, more 'baroque' [Mesoamerican] styles, like those of Izapa or the Maya." As a nation of sculptors, preceding the muralists of Teotihuacán, the Olmec spiritual thrust was aimed closer to man's integral aspects than his communal role. Beyond the giant heads for which they are best known, the overriding Olmec theme was a celebration of the human body.

No proven reasons have yet been put forth for the kind of religious need, emotional commitment, or intense "desire for form and meaning"[11] required to move masses of intractable raw material such long distances in order to make the monumental effigies. Only seventeen stone heads have been discovered. There must have been many more in their epoch of creation. On six of them, birdlike features supersede the more common personae, heavy-lidded, thick-lipped, supercilious, and somnolent of mien.

R ecent satellite surveys of Mexico indicate that despite the many *zonas arqueológicas* (archaeological districts) open to the general public and a recent, modest allocation of government funding to the *Instituto Nacional de Antropología e Historia* (INAH: the National Anthropological and Historical Institute) to continue digging in specially targeted sites, only a fraction of all Mesoamerican ruins have been revealed over the past century. Much of the accumulated pleasure gained in studying and visiting this enigmatic part of the world therefore comes with gradually developing the discipline to reserve judgment. We must observe, engage in what we hope will be intelligent speculation—but oftentimes all that will result is appreciation.

The "intrinsic meaning or content" of the icons, objects, carved and painted scenes selected for consideration as the Plumed Serpent biography unfolds can be apprehended only to the degree that we have

Monument 19, La Venta

knowledge of their context: the "other documents of civilization historically related to that work…bearing witness to the underlying principles…the political, poetical, religious, philosophical, and social tendencies of the individual, period, or country under investigation."[12]

For this kind of information, we are fortunate to be able to draw upon the wisdom of many intellectual and spiritual travellers. But we must always remember that in the case of the long-vanished Olmec, our range of "documents" is severely limited.

It is fitting that possibly the earliest image of Plumed Serpent arose from the Olmec nuclear culture. In 1955, during construction work on La Venta airstrip, a three-foot-high chunk of basalt boulder was unearthed. Unglamorously called Monument 19, and dated from the period between the tenth and sixth centuries B.C., it depicts a vivid, incised scene that has been the subject of much debate in the decades since its discovery.

What are the elements of the design? The dominant figure is a much-larger-than-life three-rattled snake, baring its fangs. Nestled into its curves and superimposed closer to the viewer is a seated man wearing a mask-headdress and extending a pouch forward from his right hand. Between man and beast are two connected panels containing paired quetzal birds.

The "crossed-bands motif" above the panel on the left is a geometric pattern that appears often in Olmec art, recurring in classic Maya with the meaning "sky" and "serpent." These two words are homonyms in the Mayan language, and the Olmec may have spoken an early form of Maya. The X-shaped design itself might have been based upon the markings on the back of a rattlesnake.[13]

The jaguar imagery in the man's headgear reflects the presence of another animal with tremendous power in the Olmec world. The serpent's body that embraces him provides a "sheltering, womblike enclosure," as if he were being nurtured while brought into the world.[14]

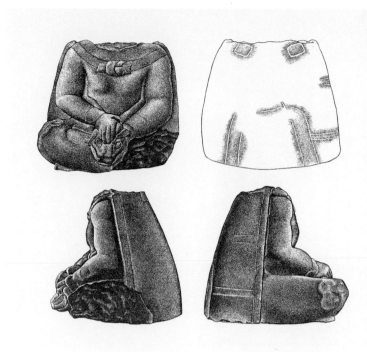

Monument 47

The "birthing" theme is important because the Olmec was the first culture to portray the blurring of men with animals: "The entire stela is strongly reminiscent of the man-bird-serpent of Tula [i.e., Quetzalcóatl], in spite of the differences of time, style, and perhaps even theme."[15]

The man's costume provides some tantalizing hints about his identity. The cape or mantle draped over his shoulders and chest shows that he is a "leader of men [possessing] authority and majestic elegance," as do the chest ornament, large earplugs, and helmet. The bag was a common accessory of priests in Mesoamerican theocratic cultures, and usually held *copal*, a ritualistic incense.[16]

Every feature of the giant serpent is shown realistically except the eyebrows and crest over the head, which "would never occur in the world of nature…. Some observers interpret the crest as feathers…"[17] and insist that we are looking at an "ancestral form" of Plumed Serpent.[18]

Olmec Man-Jaguar, Tabasco

The most ambitious verdict comes from Joseph Campbell, who approaches Mesoamerican religion from a broader, more universal overview, tying the feathered serpent of Monument 19 to an eternal tradition. He invokes the two opposing animal identities of the Hindu god Vishnu—the "sun bird" of the upper world and the serpent of the lower. Campbell further believes that the priest's jaguar mask resonates with Vishnu's other incarnation as "Man-Lion." Through this analysis Campbell identifies the tension that is an important ingredient of Plumed Serpent's story through the ages.

At San Lorenzo-Tenochtitlán, another important site in the land of the Olmec, archaeologists discovered the basalt statue now known as Monument 47: a seated, headless, caped figure who seemingly calms a feathered serpent, its body split around both sides of his captor. Elsewhere at San Lorenzo, a hieratic head was found with curved, shell-like ear pendants, strongly predictive of Quetzalcóatl's later recognized traits in the Mixtec and Aztec societies.

At Tres Zapotes, fragments of a box were found depicting what may be the profiled head of a feathered serpent.[19]

In Monument 19, as a sign of the obsessions of the Olmec world, the mystiques of bird and serpent were wedded to the jaguar, an animal central to understanding Mesoamerican culture from its earliest moments. And what a fearsome, fearless beast *Felis onca* was, reaching six feet in length, spending the day in caves and then prowling the jungle at night, undaunted by man and merciless against any animal who attacked. Ubiquitous yet insidiously stealthy, like the snake, he could become invisible even when letting loose his shattering nocturnal howl during mating time. His threatening jaws, like the snake's "great, gaping maw,"[20] could be fatal. Adding to these unnerving qualities, unlike other felines, the jaguar liked water and could navigate with ease and speed across rivers and small lagoons.[21]

In the pattern of spots on the jaguar's flanks, the Olmec saw reflected the *cielo estrellado*, the starry sky, home of wandering Venus, brightest of planets, appearing with nightfall and gradually fading with the dawn, later represented in Mayan iconography by a distinctively circular star glyph.[22]

In the jaguar as earthly predator, often represented with feathers along his back or flames over his eyes instead of eyebrows, the Olmec saw a soaring hunter, the harpy eagle, still named today by many Indians in South America "the jaguar of the sky."[23] And in the jaguar as a clawed swimmer, a spirit of the waters as well as the earth, the Olmec saw an aquatic serpent, a magical, avian dragon who could also fly, "journey[ing] from his watery underworld to the celestial realm."[24]

But above all these blendings of the spotted beast with other earthly and celestial forces, his most important mystical identity was that of the monstrous were-jaguar, its slanted eyes, forward-thrusting head, hunched shoulders, serpentlike fangs, and long, bifid tongue protruding from swollen, "inverted-U-shaped" lips, fists sometimes clenched—imagined as the offspring of a male jaguar and a human female.[25] The Mother Culture may have believed itself descended from this distant union; hence the proliferation of animal-human imagery in Olmec art.[26]

The were-jaguar represented the shamanic medicine man's ability, enhanced by hallucinogens, to transform himself ecstatically into "an animal spirit companion that transport[ed] him into the otherworld."[27] Many times, this anthropomorphic figure is depicted with slightly bent knees, as if preparing for a birdlike, flying leap beyond the human realm or shuttling back and forth in the mind in transitional states of being.

The combinations of men and animals we see in Olmec artifacts recur during the long chronology of Plumed Serpent and represent the interpenetrating relationship of the early Mesoamerican people with benign and forbidding dimensions of nature, and the spiritual feelings elicited by this relationship.

About two hundred miles west of the major Olmec sites discussed here, in the state of Morelos, fifteen miles southwest of the legendary volcano Popocatépetl, at the foot of the Cerro de la Cantera, lies the site of Chalcatzingo. Olmec-style rock carvings and bas-reliefs depicting important variants of the Plumed Serpent motif have been examined there by several scholars: first in 1934 by the archaeologist Eulalia Guzmán, twenty years later by Roman Pina Chan, and most recently and exhaustively by the American anthropologist David Grove and his team.

Monument 1, popularly known as *El Rey* (the King), shows a distinguished nobleman sitting in what has been described as an open cave or the jaws of a jaguar. In either case, the fact that he is in a niche brings immediate thoughts of the older Olmec Monument 19.

Monument 2, which dates from 500 to 700 B.C., is a relief depicting three standing caped figures wearing distinctive bird-serpent masks.

Monument 5, carved upon a low boulder, depicts "a large, serpent-like creature with a crocodilian head" that seems to be either disgorging or engulfing a human figure. There are three cloud-glyphs beneath the figure's jaw and body. It has a long, curving, bifid tongue, pointed scales, and three backward-slanting teeth. It seems to be closer in appearance to the *cipactli*, or crocodile (a beast sharing many attributes with the serpent), "an animal which dwelt in the primordial sea." Yet many other Chalcatzingo bird-serpent masks and designs of a serpent enfolding a man remind us of those found on Monument 19 in La Venta.[28]

Monument 1, Chalcatzingo

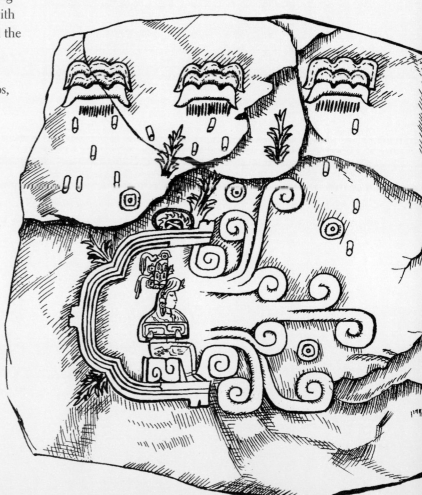

quando quiere picar yllenanta
se en alto, yarrojese sobre lo
que quiere picar: y quando pica
tambien ella muere. porque e
cha de vn golpe toda su poçon
ña y conella la vida.

¶ Parrapho septimo de
otras culebras mostruosas
ensi: ser y en sus propie da
des.

auh acan velittv, in canjn o
noc: auh nottem qujqua, ça
iquac neci intequa, injquac
tehoponja. Auh in aqujn quj
thoponja: çan njma mjctive
tzi, amo vel ce ora in njqrj,
çan vel athitonca: auh injc
tequa. achtopa patlanj, vel
tlacpac, vel aco miauh: auh
çan ipan oaltemo in aqujn
in noço tlein qujqua. Auh in
icpatlanj: in manoçe ic oal
temo, cenca ieheca: in quex
qujch icnemj, injc patlanti
nemj. Auh injquac tequa: nj
ma noiquac mjquj, qujl ipã
pa: çan njma mochi tlamj in
itenqualac, injztlac, canel
noço iehoatl inj tolca, inca
njn tehoponja, aocmo athi
contvca in thoponjlonj: auh
no vncan vetzi in in cooatvn
Hi: —

¶ Injc chicome parrapho: in
techpa tlatva cooame, veve
intin: auh cece tlamatli intv
Hi:

Two millennia after the Chalcatzingo carvings were made, the Aztec people created the books of the histories of their forebears. They looked back and told stories of the Olmec heartland in the Papaloapán Basin, the old places along the Gulf from the home of the Totonacs over to Campeche in Yucatán. Sahagún wrote down an illustrative tale of Quetzalcóatl stemming from the Gulf coastal terrain: "He was not only the god, or the King of Tollan [Tula], but also a particular, small, venomous snake from … the former region of the Olmec…. Its toxicity and mode of attack were similar to the arboreal palm viper. 'In order to bite you' [the Old Ones told Sahagún], 'first it flies, quite high up, well up it goes, and it just descends, upon whom or what it bites. And when it flies or descends, a great wind blows. Wherever it goes, it flies.'"[29]

With the winds came rain. The winds flew down from mountains by the sea and then broke open clouds collecting over hills. After the sweeping of the plazas and courtyards every morning in Mexico, there inevitably follows the cleansing, tossed water. As will become evident at the great pyramids of Teotihuacán—where he sat side by side with the rain god Tlaloc—and then at Uxmal, where the rain god Chac reigned, Plumed Serpent, first born as an agricultural deity, was always inextricably linked with the vital, nurturing flow of water.[30]

Flying Quetzalcóatl, Florentine Codex

CHAPTER IV

TEOTIHUACĀN

*Mexico's ruins are the vital ruins of the nation's origin,
the debris of projects promised and then abandoned or destroyed by other projects,
natural or human, but always proximate to something that an innocent look
can only identify as a perpetually original force.
That is the difference between the ruins of Mexico and those of classical antiquity.*
—CARLOS FUENTES, *A New Time for Mexico*

En el pensamiento mesoamericano nada es gratuito.
In the Mesoamerican mind, nothing is gratuitous.
—ENRIQUE FLORESCANO, *El mito de Quetzalcóatl*

Teotihuacán, the name of the magnificent and dramatic urban center thirty-three miles northeast of Mexico City, has been variously translated from the Nahua language of the Aztec people as "the dwelling place of the gods" and "the place where men become gods." According to the mythology of the Aztecs, it was here that time began, during *El Quinto Sol*, the rising of the fifth sun. The first gods of a nascent pantheon convened at Teotihuacán to create the sun and the moon, establish a race of men in the new world, and determine their fate. To this last and most important task was assigned Quetzalcóatl.[1]

First appearing between 200 and 150 B.C., the buildings of Teotihuacán grew out of an agricultural community that had lived at the site for thousands of years. It was originally thought that the ancient inhabitants of the Valley of Mexico were either Olmec-descended or Otomí peoples. But it seems more likely that they were proto-Nahua speakers, like the later Toltecs and Aztecs, who were proud to claim the Teotihuacános as their ancestors.[2] Teotihuacán reached the peak of its development in about the fifth century A.D.

Teotihuacán began as a theocracy, controlled and administrated by a priestly class. The priests had a sacred obligation to celebrate the creation story sanctifying the ground whereon they lived. It grew into a thriving metropolis with architects, artists, and artisans with workshops; a military class; and farmers who lived on the outskirts of the city and cultivated their fertile lands. By the time of its decline in the eighth century, more than two hundred thousand people lived there.[3]

When arriving at Teotihuacán today, take care to enter the site at 8:00 A.M., as soon as the wire-mesh

View of Pyramid of the Sun from the Pyramid of the Moon, Teotihuacán

gates swing open, and a good two hours before the day-trippers from Mexico City begin to appear. When the sun beats bright but not yet hot from an impeccably blue sky and the air at seven thousand feet above sea level is purely intoxicating, you become subsumed by the spare, silent dignity of this vast site.

The ceremonial center of the city is laid out along a broad, north-south axis, 1.2 miles long, named the Avenue of the Dead. At the northern end of this great avenue stands the Pyramid of the Moon, 138 feet high, but seemingly taller, because the avenue rises gradually by ninety-eight feet as you slowly walk its length. Breathing the crisp air deeply, you might pause every hundred yards to take an occasional sip from a bottle of mineral water or attend to plaintive bird cries and other small sounds: wind against stone and the low, brown grass or boots against gravel.

Religious man has always desired and attempted to live close to his gods: "In the higher regions … there dwell the gods; there, a few privileged mortals make their way by rite of ascent. He who ascends by mounting the steps of a sanctuary or the ritual ladder that leads to the sky ceases to be a man."[4] Ancient beliefs in the powers of the moon evolved out of the mystery of the three days of darkness necessary for its rebirth. It was likewise necessary for a man to die in order that he be reborn. All of humanity was caught up in this cycling rhythm, so important to the peoples of Mesoamerica.[5]

North of the summit of the Pyramid of the Moon there stands the dun-colored *Cerro Gordo*, the Big Mountain. Its ancient name was *Tenan*, Mother of Waters.[6] The symmetrical, geometric contours of the man-made, stepped hill upon which we stand gasping echo the sacred topography behind us, where the "Masters of the Storm Clouds" lie sheltered in the age-old earth.[7] The Teotihuacános believed that their rough-hewn limestone could harness and abet—or at least placate—the neighboring mountains' forces. More ambitiously, and more than in relation to any specific landscape, the architects of the Mesoamerican pyramids presented the design for a worldview. They strove to reiterate a "paradigmatic act," the creation of their world, and to capture the gods' everlasting time within man's built space through "the imitation of natural forms to fit themselves safely into nature's order."[8]

Southeast of the Pyramid of the Moon, across a tan field dotted with scrubby trees, rises the Pyramid of the Sun, the sheer magnitude of its facade facing west into the sunset. The pyramid has five sloping tiers interspersed with platforms, and it takes 242 narrow steps to reach the top, 213 feet above the ground. It was made from one million cubic feet of dirt and rock pulled together without use of the wheel or beast of burden. The workers who created its facing of painted stone used only carved and polished stone tools—no metal of any kind. Its gently rounded summit imitates the undulations of the molded hills bordering the south of Teotihuacán.[9]

A walk through the site reveals a spawning ground for a verdant melange of plumes, feathers, and wings affixed to depictions of all manner of real and imagined animals: serpents, of course, as well as coyotes, pumas, owls, quetzals, eagles, doves, deer, fish, shellfish—and, most especially, jaguars. Teotihuacán departs significantly from other major ceremonial locales in that no images of rulers are to be found.[10]

Descending from our vantage point atop the Pyramid of the Moon, adjacent to it we find the *Palacio de Quetzal-Mariposa*, the Palace of the Quetzal Bird-Butterfly, part of a complex where priests lived. The low reliefs reveal a beaked being with obsidian eyes, incised headdress, and a tail fashioned like a ruffled skirt.

To the west of the *Palacio de Quetzal-Mariposa* is the *Palacio de los Jaguares*. On its north side are three rooms. The middle chamber is decorated with a mural of enormous felines with feathered heads blowing into seashells held in their forepaws. The familiar signs are there: the jaguar's plumed headdress stretches back behind his ears; vacant-eyed star/Venus-glyphs with downturned mouths and two-pronged tongues keep watch above him. Elongated raindrops hang from the conch shell, itself a plumed sea symbol. The green-feathered jaguar frescoes and murals discovered at the foot of the Pyramid of the Sun and elsewhere on the site are "linked with the symbol of heaven, the quetzal or the eagle…representing the union of two opposites, heaven and earth."[11] Indeed, the red-and-orange-tinted Teotihuacán jaguars, agape jaws baring curved, tusklike teeth, spew forth with abandon puffy clouds, watery streams bordered with flowers, and wind-borne rain.[12]

In two outlying residential sites along the road circling around Teotihuacán, the god Tlaloc makes his appearance. At Tepantitla, there is a multicolored painting of a procession of chanting priests bordered by the body of a feathered serpent. The priests—*Tlaloques*, representatives of the rain god—wear jaguar headdresses and pour water or seeds to symbolize the sowing ceremony.[13]

At Atetelco, a sprawling apartment complex, three detailed murals are being painstakingly restored. In late afternoon light, the guard draws back thick protective curtains with a long, wooden rod, and the fine, chalk-white outlines glow against an ochre background set afire by the waning sun momentarily illuminating Tlaloc, bearing lightning, masked, and laden with all his finery. He will make a spectacular reappearance at our final stop, the third major building at Teotihuacán, the Temple of the Plumed Serpent or Quetzalcóatl.

The definitive excavation of the Teotihuacán site was carried out under the direction of Manuel Gamio between 1917 and 1922. The now dry San Juan River bed transverses the Avenue of the Dead from east to west. Just south and east of this inter-

24

section, at the center of the city, Gamio's team was removing earth and shrubs from a huge square named *La Ciudadela* (the Citadel) by the conquistadores and later changed more generically to the Great Compound, an enormous plaza, more than 1,300 feet on each side, enclosed around its periphery by four raised platforms resembling parapets. The diggers found to their astonishment that the apparently single pyramid just east of the center of the Citadel precinct actually had been built over a smaller, extraordinary one rising about seventy feet.

The Temple of Quetzalcóatl dates from A.D. 150 to 250, in Nahua language the *Miccaotli* Phase, "Early Classic," or "Classic Horizon" period of Mesoamerican culture.[14] It was the last temple to have been built at Teotihuacán by what is now believed to have been its last great ruler.[15] "One of the greatest tours de force of monumental stone sculpture in world history," its seven original tiers would have displayed exactly 365 heads, Quetzalcóatl alternating with Tlaloc, celebrating the passage of time, connected by reliefs of snake flanks in eternal motion. Only four echelons have been preserved.[16]

Directly below the parade of heads flow more scaled serpent bodies in relief, and at intervals ubiquitous bleached-white conch shells, some whole, others in transverse view. The conch shell is the spiraling sea image and swirling wind image, transported from the Olmec lands of the Gulf. It also represents the human heart, offered to the gods; the trumpet of priests summoning the faithful to worship; and, in cross-section, the serpent's coils.

Each Plumed Serpent head, tenoned into the facade of the building and weighing four tons,

Plumed Jaguar, Palacio de los Jaguares, *Teotihuacán*

protrudes from a roseate petaled collar. Are they maize leaves? Many still hold vestiges of ochre tint. The snout is square and open, and cavelike darkness reigns within. The jaw is fanged in a rictus grin, more proud than angry, and bears immediate resemblance to the jaguar snout, its lethal teeth curving backward, some still painted bone white. The nose, too, is feline, the eyes black circles surrounded by an outer rim, like targets.

The Quetzalcóatl temple facade is "a tribute to things that flow: the water in rivers, the course of a road, the sinuous winding of a serpent, blood through the veins, the ruffling of feathers on a banner in a breeze … presenting the visual statement of the sacred value of the nearby river."[17]

In an agricultural society what could be more important than water, the source of all life, venerated in the body of Plumed Serpent? Even in today's Mexico, in the Huastec region, a heavy shower is described as a *quetzalcóatl*.

Near the plumed serpents is Tlaloc's head, as if grafted from another world; it is square where Plumed Serpent's is round, except for the always open goggle eyes, paired discs superimposed against a checkered background. While Plumed Serpent's significance in the theology of Teotihuacán is forthright, Tlaloc's identity is problematic. In the earliest tales of his emergence, he was feared as lord over the *quinametzin*, the "first men" of Teotihuacán, reputed to be giants.[18] The proximity of the two contrasting heads might represent the succession of the dry season by the rainy season, in much the same way that the serpent has the magical ability to shed its skin and thereby "transform itself from an old into a young creature."[19]

Tlaloc's portrayal elsewhere in the city's frescoes as god of lightning is a precursor to his bearing as a god of fire,[20] thus making his presence next to Plumed Serpent an equally vivid metaphor for the later political transition in Teotihuacán from government by priest-sage to government by military.[21]

And in a far-less-aggressive guise as Plumed Serpent's *nagual*, or companion, Tlaloc is depicted in the ancient books of the Aztecs as striding forward before him waving an incensory. Tlaloc's robe is marked with the sign of the cross to show he is Lord of the Four Winds respectfully carrying his friend Plumed Serpent's *xiquipilli* (medicine pouch or copal bag).[22]

The 1980s excavations at Teotihuacán under the direction of Ruben Carrera Castro of INAH brought to light more than one hundred skeletons of sacrificed captive warriors accompanied by a profusion of tokens and tribute objects unearthed beneath the Temple of Quetzalcóatl. The ritual sacrifices took place when the construction of the temple began and again when it was concluded. The skeletons were in the fetal position: knees bent and arms in many instances tied behind their backs, heads bowed as if in prayer, ready to be born again in the way of the Plumed Serpent.[23]

Teotihuacán is vast, its architecture monumental, and its deities vivid. It feels like the center of an empire when we walk within. There was a city-state, a true civilization here, in the sense that "civilization may be thought of as the antithesis of the folk society."[24] It is an authentic manifestation of city life, a place with a formal layout where technical accomplishment was ubiquitous. Teotihuacán was built upon the remnants of a once-small folk society that had grown out of its self-sufficiency.

Teotihuacán exercised broad influence throughout the emerging Mesoamerican culture in the first centuries A.D. The natural flow into Teotihuacán from the Gulf Coast Olmec religions has been demonstrated. The far-flung flow of routes out of the city is evident in the other areas where Plumed Serpent reared his head: as far north as the Zuni of New Mexico, the Hopi in Arizona, and the Adena Mound Builders of

Temple of the Plumed Serpent, Teotihuacán

Temple of the Plumed Serpent, Teotihuacán

Ohio; and as far southeast as Costa Rica.[25]

Teotihuacán iconography has been detected as far east as the Usumacinta River drainage region of Guatemala.[26] By the third and fourth centuries A.D., "irradiations"[27] from Teotihuacán through the opening of trade routes and the spread of the Plumed Serpent cult reached Copán in Honduras, more than eight hundred miles away from the Valley of Mexico.

Homing in closer to nuclear Mesoamerica, Octavio Paz defines the Maya on the one hand and Teotihuacán civilization on the other as "two poles or extremes" threaded together by their common reverence for Plumed Serpent.[28]

Religious, commercial, and/or military "emissaries" from Teotihuacán did indeed appear in Mayan lowlands by the first century A.D. The Pacific coastal regions of Chiapas state and Kaminaljuyú in highland Guatemala have also been identified as sites with a wide variety of Teotihuacán characteristics.[29]

Likewise, the highland Mayan sacred book, *Popol Vuh,* which we will encounter later, tells that in the primordial darkness before the world began, only sovereign Plumed Serpent lived in the ocean.[30]

By the eighth century, Teotihuacán was abandoned, as were so many other magnificent cities in Mesoamerica. Why? Soil depletion, war, deterioration of the governing hierarchy—all have been offered as possibilities. The shock waves of the fall of this great city were a demarcation between one distinct cultural phase and another in the Valley of Mexico; its demise signaled the beginning of a sense of history in Mesoamerica—reverence for the sacred past that survived to be carried forward into the culture of the Aztec *Mexica.*

Reduced to rubble and overgrown with vegetation, Teotihuacán remained a renowned pilgrimage center for the Aztecs, a holy place to visit Plumed Serpent and Tlaloc.[31]

CHAPTER V

TULA

Claude Lévi-Strauss [in Structural Anthropology] compares the successive stages in man's ascent to a continuous card game, in which each culture is like a player who takes his place at the table and picks up cards that he has not invented. Every deal in the game is the result of a contingent distribution of the cards, unknown to the player at the time; he must accept the hand that he is given and employ it as best he can. Different players may vary their approach to a similar hand, even if the rules set limits on the game that can be played with a given set of cards.

— NIGEL DAVIES,
The Toltec Heritage

Long, long ago, according to the story in the sacred Aztec history, *Anales de Cuauhtitlán*, the Old Wise Men brought their books of paintings and their knowledge of the arts to the mythical city of Tamoanchán (the "Place of Our Origin"), surrounded by nine rivers, surmounted by nine heavens, and consecrated to the memory of the benevolent Quetzalcóatl. Here, it was written, he rested after his visit to the world of the dead and his tiring trip to "Sustenance Mountain" to seek maize for mankind before finally coming to Tula.[1]

Long ago, according to the Otomí peoples of Xilotepec, near Tula, there lived a god of the wind with two mouths like an alligator's, one on top of the other, who created the universe.[2]

And long ago, according to the neighboring Totonac peoples, *el hijo del sol*, the sun's son, disappeared into heaven, but promised one day to return, "bearing with him an era of delight and abundance."[3]

The mythic Tula, like storied Tamoanchán and Teotihuacán, was surrounded by a fairy-tale, halcyon haze, nostalgically imagined by the Aztec as the place where Plumed Serpent lived among men and "the air was filled with intoxicating perfumes, and the sweet melody of birds…. Wherever Plumed Serpent went, all manner of singing birds bore him company, emblems of the whistling breeze."[4] Here, for the pursuit of daily meditation and fasting, devoted to charity, Lord Quetzalcóatl built four palace sanctuaries in different colors filled with flower mats, feather hangings, and mosaics, each facing the cardinal points of the compass. According to the *Anales de Cuauhtitlán*, one house was encrusted with turquoise; one was made of pink shells; one of white shells; and the last and most important was of precious blue-green quetzal feathers.[5]

The Atlantes, Tula

Mythic Tula, as imagined by the Aztecs, was an "archetypal kingdom," an unreal city, phenomenally rich with houses of gold, where an ear of corn was as much as one man could carry, rainbow-tinted boles of cotton grew big as boulders, and the earth teemed with fruit and flowers. Tula was inhabited by a race who were the Aztecs' noblest dynastic ancestors, the chosen People of the Sun.[6]

The collapse of Teotihuacán in the eighth century A.D. signaled the beginning of the Postclassic Era, the "Second Epoch, the era of the great hegemonies" in Mesoamerica.[7] At that moment the actual historical Tula, in the state of Hidalgo, forty-five miles north and west of the present Mexico City, rose to prominence in conjunction with two other central highland centers, Cholula and Xochicalco. These we will visit in the next chapter, because they were also significant places where Plumed Serpent was centrally portrayed and worshiped.[8]

The name Tula is a variant of the Nahuatl *Tollán*, meaning "place of reeds." It was home to the original investiture ceremony of the royal lords who were the roots of Aztec nobility—although today, all I can see for endless miles across the surrounding dusty plains are maguey cactus and prickly pear. The peoples who settled here, a "nomadic warrior aristocracy" with still unclear roots, were called Toltec, a name that, in the reverential nuances of the Aztec Nahuatl tongue, came to mean "artist," so limitless were their sophisticated abilities to make beautiful objects, carved figurines, masks of jade, and knives of obsidian.[9]

The present site of Tula is west of the town, on the Cerro del Tesoro, the "Hill of the Treasure." What has currently been excavated represents only 10 to 25 percent of the original structures[10] and includes all the typical elements: a central plaza oriented to the four points of the compass, with traces of dwellings around it; a principal pyramid; and a ball court bearing a strong resemblance to the one at Xochicalco.

Across the river, about one mile from the central area, on a hillside called Cerro de la Malinche, an image of Quetzalcóatl was incised in a rock wall by Aztec artists as a walking male figure drawing blood with a sharpened bone from his left earlobe. Also carved into the wall is the glyph for Plumed Serpent's birth year, *Ce Ácatl,* "one reed." A giant, overarching vision serpent, reminiscent of images we have seen at Chalcatzingo and La Venta, rears up behind the man.

Cerro de la Malinche, Tula
RIGHT: *Quetzalcóatl,* Codex Telleriano-Remensis

At Tula Chico, "the small (Lesser) Tula," about 1.5 kilometers north of the central plaza, there is a two-tiered building, El Corral, with a distinctive shape—rounded in back and squared off in front; it is dedicated to *Éhecatl,* the wind-god identity of Quetzalcóatl.

"Deliberately harsh forms…aggressive asperities, gritty surfaces, and bellicose symbols" are evident in Tula's iconography, which abounds with warriors in quilted armor; wall reliefs of eagles, rattlesnakes, and jaguars devouring human hearts; and fleshless faces representing the souls of warriors killed in battle.[11]

Tula is a sparse, forsaken site, lacking the grandeur of Teotihuacán. It feels intimidating to me, walking here, knowing that at its height the city had a population of more than eighty-five thousand people. Its most striking—and, for my purposes, significant—feature is situated beyond the *Coatepantli,* the "serpent wall," which is crenellated with the ubiquitous conch shell fragments I have come to expect whenever Quetzalcóatl is near.

Here is the Temple of Tlahuizcalpantecuhtli, "Lord of the Dawn," Venus himself, who each day opens the path to the sun and is closely wedded to the transfiguration of Plumed Serpent. At the summit of this five-tiered structure, I find a flat platform populated by four immense columns in the shape of soldiers, the *Atlantes.* Shading my eyes against the powerful sun glare, I squint upward. Each statue is fifteen feet tall, weighs more than 8.5 tons, holds a copal bag, and features a geometrically decorated feathered headband, a quiver of darts, a butterfly-shaped breastplate, an ornately knotted apron held in place with a sun-shaped disc, and sandals. These prepossessing guardians, rebuilt from sections originally discovered at the base of the temple, are the first free-standing incarnations of Plumed Serpent anthropomorphized into an earthly prince.[12]

The codices *Telleriano-Remensis* and *Florentino* declare that Quetzalcóatl, as great artificer, "formed" and "molded" the first human beings in his image, and that only he—and no other god—"had a human body."[13]

Like the *Atlantes* before me at Tula—surrounded by space against a crystalline, overarching sky—the singular Plumed Serpent traveled alone in human guise. He was *el hombre-dios,* the god made flesh, man embodied with divine spirit.[14]

In the story of Plumed Serpent, like that of the city of Tula, fantastic and historical identities commingle. At this signal moment in the life cycle of our hero, standing so tall and proud at Tula, I will attempt to

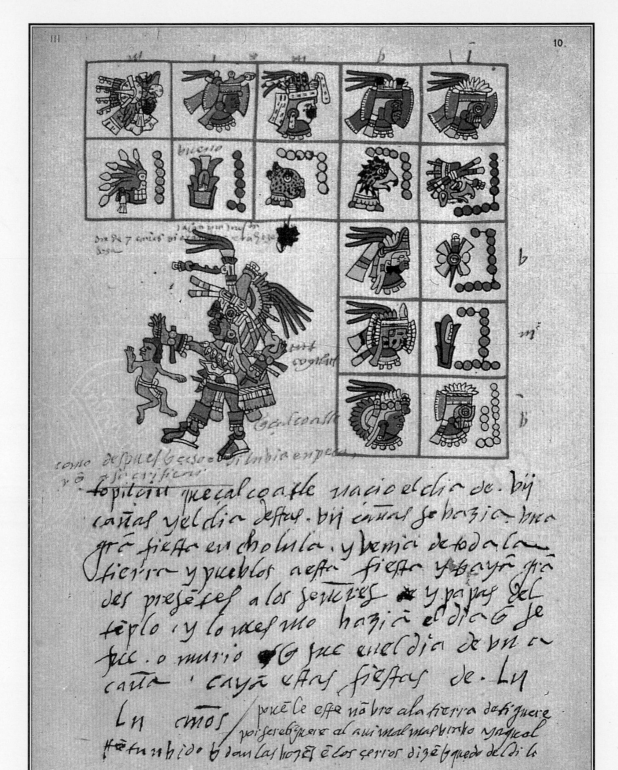

tease out the *dios* from the *hombre* and then try to ascertain the historical—as opposed to the mythical—moment when Plumed Serpent's identities melded.

According to Aztec legend, Quetzalcóatl came into the world at Tula/Tollán from the cloud-crowned peak of the highest mountain. He was born there of Chimalman, divine wife of Mixcóatl, "cloud serpent," ruler of the Chichimecs. From the time he was purely born, Quetzalcóatl stood for everything good and wise in the world. As "god of vital breath," blower of the conch shell, he was "the painter of words and sculptor of discourse," possessed with the encompassing power of speech.

When he descended to ground level through an opening in the sky, as if coming down the steps of a holy pyramid, he was able to instill this communicative ability within his sovereign creation— man— opening his eyes for the first time to "the delights and agonies of the world panorama."[15]

There are early hero-gods resembling Quetzalcóatl in every Indian culture of the Americas, "the great doers and teachers of all first things." The strong pedagogical strain in Plumed Serpent's identity recalls Iuskeha of the Iroquois and Manabozho of the Algonquins, benefactor gods of "dignified presence" worthy of love and reverence. The benign Quetzalcóatl instructed the first peoples on earth in domestic life, animal husbandry, curing and healing, copulation and child-bearing, agriculture, architecture (it was said that he built the cosmic pillars, the serpent columns and sacred *ceiba* tree holding up the four corners of heaven's vault), the art of divining, astronomy and science and the calendar, music and dance, writing and literature, and the arts of government. In the *Codex Chimalpopoca*, we read,

> *Truly with him it began*
> *Truly from him it flowed out*
> *From Quetzalcóatl*
> *All art and knowledge (sabiduría)*[16]

A complementary attribute of Quetzalcóatl led to his adoption centuries later as the patron saint of Aztec priesthood, the guiding spirit of the sacerdotal profession in the *calmécac* (training schools for the holy life).

This was his rigorous devotion to what Joseph Campbell calls "self-offering as the way to self-validation…[in which] *life lives on lives*" via symbolic sacrifice. In bold acts of extreme spirituality, Quetzalcóatl pierced his earlobes, calves, tongue, and penis with long, thin reeds; pulled knotted string through the wounds, drawing blood; and then dripped it onto leaves of lime-coated paper burned with copal in tribute to the life force. The priests imitated this practice in his name, often fasting for a week or more before the main feast days, drinking no wine and sleeping little.[17]

The same blood used to fabricate mankind took on penitential meaning when Quetzalcóatl in his priestly actions sought bliss through pain. He is often represented in masks as the "weeping god."[18]

Every hero must have his downfall. There was a reason for Plumed Serpent's blood penance. In the ever-turning wheel—the cycle of the Mesoamerican mind—every illuminating state of grace requires a dark and cloudy consequence,[19] every benign force engenders an evil one. In Plumed Serpent's story, the evil force assumed the shape of his own brother, Tezcatlipoca, "Smoking Mirror." He was the *hechicero*, the "somber sorcerer," the adversary "capable of inconceivable deeds" and possessed of "the secret knowledge of the seer," allowing him to cast a spell on his victims. What more threatening name could there be for this doppelgänger, this foe of goodness, than the "evil twin," the demonic alter ego of Plumed Serpent?[20]

Some of the codices say that the resentful Smoking Mirror defeated the good Quetzalcóatl in a "magical duel".[21] Others say that Plumed Serpent was duped into sleeping with his own sister after drinking *pulque* prepared by Smoking Mirror and his cohorts.[22] After a fierce struggle, the beloved ruler of the spirit realm—man of classic Toltec knowledge—was lured into drunkenness and carnality, brought down by the polluting, corrupt, and worldly wiles of the trickster.

In a hope-filled reversal of the tragedy representing yet another spin of the wheel,[23] Quetzalcóatl came back seeking revenge after thirteen times fifty-two years, in the anniversary of his birth year One-Reed, to re-establish the golden age he had spawned. He chased after Tezcatlipoca with "a big stick and knocked him out of the sky." Smoking Mirror tumbled into the ocean and came out on land in the shape of a jaguar.

Like the planet Venus, the sign of his transfiguration in the cosmic cycle—like the very earth itself, passing in and out of rainy and dry seasons—Plumed Serpent was fated to die and be reborn over and over again, through eternity.[24]

For now, however, the only path for the victim of temptation was expulsion and exile. Such a dire fate caused deep anxiety among the people Plumed Serpent had so devotedly taught.

"Why do you leave your capital?"

"I go to *Tlapallán*," replied Quetzalcóatl, "from whence I came."

"For what reason?" persisted the enchanters.

"My partner the sun has called me thence," replied Quetzalcóatl.

"Go then, happily," they said, "but leave us the secret of your art, the secret of founding in silver, of working in precious stones and woods, of painting, and of feather-working, and other matters."[25]

Tlapallán is a variant of *Tlili Tlapali*, Nahua for "land of the red and black," the name given to writing, glyphs, and mural paintings. Learning through these means at the feet of Quetzalcóatl, who possessed sovereignty over intellectual matters, mankind first gained wisdom.[26]

Quetzalcóatl as "The Weeping God"

Then Quetzalcóatl fixes his eyes on Tula and in that moment begins to weep; as he weeps, sobbing, it is like two torrents of hail trickling down; his tears slip down his face, his tears drop by drop perforate the stones. [27]

It was a sad and dangerous time for the Toltecs. They were losing their mainstay, their moral center. The society was fractured, as some of the devout inner circle of Plumed Serpent's priestly cult decided to venture forth with their chastened leader in his flight (and return) south and east to the realm of *Tlapallán* rather than risk never seeing him again.

They set forth to places real and imaginary, names echoing over millennia, some surviving in the Mexico of today—Cuauhtitlán, Temacpalco, Tepanohuahan, Coahapan, Cochtocan, Cholula, Mitla, Tlatlayan. And wherever Plumed Serpent alighted, it was said he left an indelible sign in the landscape: the imprint of a hand in the rock, or the sign of a cross upon two trees.[28]

Leaving the godly Plumed Serpent at the end of his long trek and rite of passage toward the eastern land; standing on the shore with his weeping followers shrouded in black; watching him drift slowly out to sea on a raft of snakelike reeds, burst into flame, and assume his apotheosis as Phoenix of the West—what can we say with historical certainty about the other side of the equation, the *hombre*, the man?

"The two worlds, the *divine and the human*, can be pictured only as distinct from each other—different as life and death, as day and night. The hero ventures out of the land we know into darkness … his return is described as a coming back out of that yonder zone. Nevertheless…the two kingdoms are actually one. The realm of the gods is a forgotten dimension of the world we know."[29]

"A poorly understood interregnum separates the early and late phases of the final period in the culture history of pre-Contact central Mexico."[30] This is another way of saying that the end—or gradual degeneration—of Tula society, estimated as having occurred between A.D. 1000 and 1200, was symptomatic of a massive transformation of Mesoamerica that resulted in the decline of all the high cultures and sparked a continual war among the Mesoamerican city-states that lasted until the Spanish Conquest.[31]

One of the destructive factors building within Tula was a simmering division between theocratic powers in the culture and more militaristic groups that eventually erupted into open conflict.[32] Out of this unstable setting in Tula's waning years, there emerged, according to traditional accounts, one of the great city's last kings, a man born in A.D. 935 or 947, who added the symbolic birth year and name of earthly respect to the mythic name: *Ce Ácatl Topiltzin* ("our dear prince") Quetzalcóatl. He would have been one of the final representatives of a royal dynasty of "Quetzalcóatls" at Tula that had decided to don the mantle of the figure revered for hundreds of years in Teotihuacán—and perhaps even before.[33]

This "actual" Plumed Serpent, or a succeeding chieftain assuming his name, fought to stave off an invasion by the "brutish, rude, and grub-eating" *Chichimec* peoples, a wild and savage tribe about whom not much else is known except that they are always portrayed as scapegoats for the misfortunes of the Toltecs. The Chichimecs swept down into sedentary Tula from depleted farming lands to the northwest, driving the civilized Toltecs away.[34]

What is true of myths in the collective sense is also true in the individual sense. A single person may step out of his culture pattern at any time, producing dreams or acts which bring again to life myths which might have been thought to be dead or outgrown.[35]

The exile of the legendary Plumed Serpent may be a dramatic metaphor, passed down through the ages, for the movement of an entire culture.

Whether or not it was attributable to a Chichimec invasion, there definitely was a Toltec diaspora. Led by kings posing as chosen ones blessed with Plumed Serpent's attributes, it extended in a broad swath from northwest to southeast across the heart of Mesoamerica, more than seven hundred miles into the land of the Maya. Evidence of this major migration movement, which rippled onward for four centuries, is found in the Mixtec territories around Oaxaca.

Penetrating across the jungles of the Isthmus of Tehuantepec, the Toltec culture culminated in the Yucatán at Chichén Itzá, which underwent an architectural and iconographic metamorphosis into a shrine to Quetzalcóatl, a sprawling haven for stone serpents.[36]

CHAPTER VI

CHOLULA AND XOCHICALCO

And so greatly did the Toltecs believe
in their priest Quetzalcóatl,
and so greatly obedient
and given to the things of their god were they,
and so fearful of god,
that all obeyed him,
all believed in Quetzalcóatl
when he left Tula…

Suddenly he went towards the center of the sea,
toward the land of black and red, [tlili tlapali]
and there he disappeared,
he, our prince Quetzalcóatl.

— MIGUEL LEON-PORTILLA,
Los Antiguos Mexicanos a través de sus Crónicas y Cantares
[The Ancient Mexicans Through Their Stories and Songs]

Imagine Plumed Serpent's mythic-historic journeys superimposed like a palimpsest upon one another, the sacred roads he traveled etched upon parallel sheets of glass. The French explorer and photographer Désiré Charnay declared that he had no doubt that Plumed Serpent's exodus began at Tula/Tollán with the breakup and diffusion of the "doomed" Toltec nation. After an exhaustive study of Aztec manuscripts such as the dirge cited above, and his documentary trip to the Valley of Mexico in August 1880, Charnay published a portfolio illustrating the irresistible visual parallels between monuments at Tula and at Chichén Itzá, "tempered slightly," he observed, "by the tastes of the conquered tribes and the nature of the locally available materials."[2]

Just as every "road" can represent the "road of life," by extension every "walk" can become a "pilgrimage."[3] In the Aztec painted books (at least to my incurably Western eyes) Plumed Serpent's trip from west to east, following the transit of Venus, takes on a heroic quality, like the poetry of Milton. I see our hero striding to meet his destiny, engaged in the penultimate act in his life's drama, meeting "a new world naked."[4]

His face was ritually painted red and black, prefiguring his destined goal. Plumed Serpent periodically set down his black and red thrones decorated with eagle feathers (*icpalli*) and paused to name the sites where he stopped to pray: "Beneath the Old Age [*pochotl*] Tree," "The Place Where the Handprints Are," "The Serpent Spring," "The Stone Crossing," and "The Sleeping Place."[5]

"Where the water of the sky met the water of the sea" Plumed Serpent's body was consumed by fire, and his heart departed to reappear as Venus in the heavens. But he himself did not die. In one of the statues consecrated to Plumed Serpent, he was represented as lying down and covered with blankets, as if asleep; "when he should wake from that dream of absence, he will rise to rule the land [of Tula/Tollán] again."[6]

Over a succession of world ages, Plumed Serpent would overcome the threatening powers of darkness and be reborn "from the shining East" with the brilliant springtime sun that year after year without fail brings forth the staple crop of maize, which evokes Quetzalcóatl's earliest embodiment.[7]

Désiré Charnay, Temple of Kukulkán, Chichén Itzá, 1860
PREVIOUS PAGE: *Désiré Charnay, Excavations on the Second Palace at Tula, 1880*

Tracing an arc south-southeast from Tula (around what is now Mexico City), across the corrugated Sierra Nevada range rimming the Basin of Mexico, Plumed Serpent's first stop was Cholula, named from the Nahuatl *Cholollán*, "the place of the flight." The earliest construction at this city in Puebla state has been traced to 200 B.C. Today pastel-colored, modest, low-lying houses are scattered like fallen dominoes around the edges of a scrub-adorned plain that runs up to the base of a hill covered with thick vegetation—in fact, this is not a hill, but the huge *Pirámide Tepanapa*— more than 1,300 feet long on each side and 200 feet high, the largest ancient pyramid in the Americas.

Consecrated to Quetzalcóatl, it is actually five successive pyramids that were layered atop one another in the course of six hundred years. They can be explored through a labyrinth of four miles of tunnels built by archaeologists over the past hundred years—low stone archways lit with bare electric bulbs, hollowed-out catacombs, and dark, dank passageways where it is sometimes impossible to stand erect; these tunnels lead up into barred, unreachable places and down into claustrophobic, dungeonlike depths that intersect the stone accretions of the centuries. Emerging cramped and blinking into the sunlight at the end of a particularly twisted subterranean tunnel at the eastern edge of the pyramid, I walk around to the "back" or southern side, the approach to the structure when it was first built. In the *Patio de los Altares*, the multileveled nature of the pyramid is dramatically evident in the fantastic varieties of stonework, including a low, flat platform incised around its boundaries with fanged serpents permanently pursuing each other.

When Alexander Von Humboldt visited the village of Cholula during his year in Mexico, 1803–1804, the townspeople referred to this monumental conglomeration of structures in Nahua as *Tlachihualtepetl*, which Humboldt interpreted as *"el monte hecho a mano"*—"the hand-made hill" that joins the tradition of the many Mesoamerican temples pieced together stone by stone without the use of beasts of burden.[8]

From up here, on the walled, grassy peak of Tepanapa, the precise location of Cholula becomes instantly apparent, centered dramatically like the apex of a triangle between the celebrated volcano across the valley, Popocatépetl (*Señor de la Tea Encendida*—Smoky Mountain), to the southwest and his mate to the north, *Iztaccíhuatl* (*Mujer Blanca*—White Woman). On this crisp, clear morning in late April, within days of the start of the rainy season, Popocatépetl lives up to his name, a thick white plume drifting slowly, almost imperceptibly from his jagged mouth.

On just such a day as this one, in early November of 1519, Hernán Cortés stopped at this very spot with his conquistadores and their Tlaxcalan Indian allies after a bloody massacre in Cholula, before making the final push through the pass between the mountain mates and down into Tenochtitlán, the golden kingdom of Moctezuma. Like many ritual pyramids throughout Mexico, the *Pirámide Tepanapa* is crowned with a church built during the Spanish Conquest, the ironically named *Nuestra Señora de los Remedios*, Our Lady of Consolation.

Literature coming out of the Conquest epoch is filled with references to Quetzalcóatl's importance at Cholula. One of the first priests to arrive in New Spain (as Mexico was called by the Spanish conquerors) was Fray Toribio de Benavente, affectionately named *Motolinía* ("the poor little one") by the Indians among whom he lived and proselytized beginning in 1524.

Motolinía's *History of the Indians of New Spain* is based in large part upon interviews with the residents of Cholula: "They say that Quetzalcóatl began the practice of fasting and scourging himself… drawing blood from his tongue and ears [using

cactus spines]," Motolinía wrote, "not as an offering to the devil, but as a penance for the vices of the tongue and ears." According to the people of Cholula in the early decades of the sixteenth century (in Father Motolinía's account), Quetzal-cóatl was recalled as

an honest and temperate man…who preached the natural law…of whom it is said that he had his principle seat in their village. Throughout this province there were many of [his] temples…. After they had built the square foundation and made the altar, they surrounded the latter with a high circular wall peaked by a spire. This was the temple of the god of air [Éhecatl, or wind, another attribute of Plumed Serpent] whom they said was a native of Tollan, whence he had gone out to build up certain provinces and had disappeared. "And they were always expecting him to come back."[9]

Seventy-five years later, at the turn of the seventeenth century, Father Juan de Tovar, a Franciscan priest in Cholula, witnessed a performance "at the outer steps of the great temple" during the festival dedicated to Plumed Serpent. He wrote,

a lively series of comic episodes was presented against the background of an elaborately decorated stage…. Certain actors played the parts of buffoons, others masqueraded as animals. A ballet, in which all performers took part, ended the spectacle.[10]

Native peoples living in Cuauhtinchan, a Nahua-Popoloca settlement southeast of Cholula, composed their own account, the *Historia Tolteca-Chichimeca*, circa 1545, a book based upon memories of a much older, preconquest codex which had been—like countless native texts—destroyed by the Spanish. This "anonymous native document"

40

View of Popocatépetl and Iztaccíhuatl from the Piramide Tepanapa, Cholula

confirms the deeper significance of Quetzalcóatl's role as a "patron god" for the Puebla province. It states that even before the first documented arrival of the Toltec diffusion from Tollán, there stood a statue or shrine built in Cholula ("beyond the [two] volcanoes") representing Plumed Serpent's *hombre* image; other accounts describe the statue as having wavy long hair and a beard.[11]

Xochicalco is Nahua for the lyrical name *En el lugar de la casa de las flores*, "in the place of the house of flowers." Surrounded by the lore of mystery, this remote, terraced hilltop city is more than three thousand feet above sea level, twenty-four miles by twisting road southwest of Cuernavaca in the state of Morelos; it lies halfway between the south and the center of Mexico.[12] It may very well be the original site of mythic *Tamoanchán*, where the wise astronomer-priests convened at the beginning of the first fifty-two year cycle in the history of the world and at the beginning and end of every One-Reed cycle thereafter.[13]

As a boy and after his mother died, *Ce Ácatl Topiltzin* was sent to Plumed Serpent's great sanctuary at Xochicalco to complete the spiritual education that prepared him to become a high priest, leader of his people, and devotee of the god Quetzalcóatl, and earned him the right to assume this holy name upon his return to Tula.[14]

Xochicalco flourished between the seventh and tenth centuries A.D., during the "late Classic era" — after the abandonment of Teotihuacán and roughly contemporaneous with Tula and Cholula. It covers about six square miles in an intricate network of

Temple of the Plumed Serpent, Xochicalco

platforms and courtyards rigorously laid out along the cardinal points of the compass. The Temple of the Plumed Serpent stands at the center of the public square, at the highest point of the hill, the virtual *axis mundi* of Xochicalco—oriented east-west to mimic his journey.[15]

At Teotihuacán Quetzalcóatl thrusts his serpent head aggressively outward toward the observer, whereas here he flows in a low-relief frieze, "a river of stone ... a long, all-powerful symbology of death" around the four sides of the building, almost square at sixty-four by sixty-nine feet.

His *hombre* personae nestle in the upward and downward crooks of each curve in the serpent body. These noble gentlemen are seated with legs crossed and wear plumed headdresses. With their gracefully cupped hands, strong profiles, and adornments they present a distinctively Mayan aspect. This sophisticated iconography might have arrived with visitors

along a trade route from the Yucatán, through the Gulf Coast, and then up into the adjoining area now called Guerrero province.[16]

Leaning in closer, I remember that vestiges of red, green, yellow, blue, black, and white paint have been detected on the walls of the temple, subsequently painted entirely in red, to underscore the increasingly warlike inclinations of the society out of which it sprung. The Quetzalcóatls on the walls of Xochicalco "breathe" their plumes from flared nostrils, while immense bifid tongues droop and curl downward from open mouths. Their headdresses are swept back like meticulously combed manes; their segmented bodies are punctuated every few feet by vertebra-sculpted joints that shade and then cradle conch shapes and fire glyphs. The total effect is reminiscent of Plumed Serpent's origins in murky waters and of his fate as a burning star in heaven.[17]

CHAPTER VII

MONTE ALBĀN AND MITLA

PLUMED SERPENT'S BROTHER-GOD, COCIJO — PEOPLE OF THE BOOK — HIDDEN
RICHES IN MIXTEC TOMBS — THROUGH CAVES INTO THE OTHERWORLD

It is dawn, fifteen hundred feet above the Oaxaca Valley and five miles west of the city. I understand why the Zapotecs called themselves *"los pueblos de las nubes"* — the people of the clouds.[1] I watch the gossamer morning mist, floating above meadows and forest remnants, ever so slowly dissipate. The sun rises with a breath of breeze. First light touches the *flor blanca*, delicate white dogwoodlike blossoms of the diminutive *Casahuate* trees. Grasping the hillside, they inspired the Spanish to give this place its colonial name: *Monte Albán*, White Mountain, the fourth name over two millennia.

When the Zapotec people first emerged here five hundred years before Christ, they called it *Danipa-an* — their Sacred Mountain.[2] To the Mixtec successors this was the Green Mountain — *Yucu-cui*. To the Aztecs, it was the *Cerro del Jaguar*.

There have been so many different identities for Monte Albán, the largest urban center in all of Oaxaca, the province at the absolute heart of Mesoamerica. To the northwest — whence we have just come — are the Tehuacan Valley, the Puebla-Tlaxcala kingdoms, and the Basin of Mexico. Directly to the north is Veracruz and the Gulf Coast, birthplace of the ancient Olmec. And to the east — where we will head next, following Plumed Serpent's path — lies Mayaland: Chiapas, the Yucatán, and Guatemala.[3]

A center within a center, Monte Albán covers two and one-half square miles on a leveled hilltop at the convergence of three sprawling valley systems: Tlacolula, Etla, and Zimatlan. To walk through Monte Albán is to be encircled by the territory of several Indian cultures and sense the quietude and insularity created by the massive *Sierra Madre Orientale* range, which over many centuries has given this place and people their distinctive character.[4]

Perhaps because I know that it rose to prominence, fell into disuse, and was subsequently venerated by a later culture in tandem with Teotihuacán, its great sister city to the west, Monte Albán evokes in me the same intrinsic spiritual mood as that distant City of the Gods. Perhaps it is the rarefied atmosphere, the isolation from city sounds, or the weathered, multihued stones. Perhaps it is the unimpeded vista across the rectangular central Plaza, dominated at each end by huge platforms and bordered by stepped temples, all of which face inward, enhancing the cloistered atmosphere of this sanctuary that seems to have emerged from nature.

Yet upon closer examination, Monte Albán is much less decorated than its contemporary, Teotihuacán. It is refreshingly free of the overt, oftentimes baroque adornment of other large sites. Its ball court is modest and deep, almost claustrophobic.

The spirit of the place comes from its human scale and dignity rather than from any intent to overwhelm the respectfully intruding tourist (or the humble worshiper of ages past) with martial imagery.

Because of its geographical isolation, Aztec conquerors did not manage to reach the Oaxaca area until the middle of the fifteenth century, establishing a garrison on a hill at the meeting of the Rio Atoyac and Rio Salado and imposing their "tribute control" upon the valley Zapotecs, giving Oaxaca the name by which we now know it. Diminutive, edible pod-producing *guaje* (acacia) trees dot the piedmont slopes in the valley, and some can even be found among the Monte Albán ruins. In the Aztec Nahuatl tongue, *Huaxyacác* means "at the point [nose] of the acacia"—and thus we have the Hispanicized "Oaxaca" of today.[5]

The evolution of Monte Albán, and its relationship to the iconography of Plumed Serpent, was manifested in the life of Cocijo, the most venerable god in the Zapotec pantheon. Just as Teotihuacán and Monte Albán evolved at about the same time, Tlaloc and Cocijo were siblings who represented parallel cultures. "Every temple [at Monte Albán] stood over half a dozen temples of centuries before.... Buried in the great temples were high priests of legendary powers, now semi-deified; centuries of accumulated wealth in offerings, centuries of mana in ceremonies, centuries of power and success, lay deep inside that masonry."[6]

Monte Albán's vast network of more than one hundred and seventy tombs laced together by underground passageways was slowly uncovered by the Mexican archaeologist Alfonso Caso from 1931 to 1949. Caso was the first to examine the earliest clay funerary urns from the fourth century B.C.

LEFT: *Dawn, Monte Albán*
BELOW: *Casahuate trees, Monte Albán*

45

He established that they repeatedly showed the visage of a rain god whose name meant "lightning." Cocijo was also the important root demarcation (*cociy*) for the two-season division of the yearly calendar into rainy (*cociyquiye*) and dry (*cociycobaa*). A life-size, bronze, stela-shaped monument in tribute to the bespectacled Dr. Caso, who dedicated all of his professional life to studying the Zapotec-Mixtec cultures, greets today's visitors to Monte Albán at the northeast corner of the site. Archaeologists have excavated only a fraction of the sprawling city, which at its peak was home to more than twenty-five thousand people.[7]

In addition to his power to bring down rain, which allied him with Tlaloc, Cocijo possessed physical attributes that tied him to Quetzalcóatl, the rain god's shoulder-to-shoulder neighbor on the facade of Teotihuacán's Temple of the Plumed Serpent. Caso described a Zapotec glyph similar to Cocijo's mouth as the "jaws of the sky"; its centered set of feline teeth are framed by two symmetrical "lips" turned downward, as if snarling. Once again, jaguar and serpent blur into each other. "In profile, the jaguar's teeth become bird's eyes; perhaps the deity derives from a mythical bird-jaguar combination."[8]

Many-faceted and powerful, Cocijo moved through the stages of Monte Albán's history for more than one thousand years with his familiarly curled serpent's tongue, the very same one we have seen emanating from the jaguar's mouth in the ochre-tinged Teotihuacán murals; his "squared-off frames around the eyes" are reminiscent of Tlaloc. In later theocratic manifestations, Cocijo's visage metamorphosed into a mask covering the face of a holy man. His serpent's mouth metamorphosed into a crocodile's, "with up-turned snout or nose," tellingly adorned with conch ornaments. Later still, the Cocijo mask became so detailed and grotesque that it migrated to its own realm above the head of a seated figure, his extended hands cupped downward as if in blessing (or to send the rain), resulting in a true *hombre-dios*—the supernal god dominating the earth-bound man.[9]

Alfonso Caso's excavations were launched on a disappointing note. The first six tombs he found had been severely vandalized. But down the hill, past the northernmost temple, away from the main ceremonial center, Tomb No.7 was a much different story. Beneath two floors of stucco, a roof, and a stone slab lay "the treasure that was to make history as the richest archaeological find of the New World."[10] It took more than a week for Caso and his men to bring more than five hundred splendid items to the surface: solid gold masks, "strings of pearls as big as pigeon's eggs," jade, turquoise mosaics, obsidian implements, gold beads, bells—and nine skeletons: eight priests and one woman.

The god Cocijo, Monte Albán

After extensive study of the contents, Caso determined that the tomb was within the general parameters of Monte Albán and had been originally dug by the Zapotecs. But the rich contents dated from the later postclassic period, after A.D. 1250 and before the Spanish Conquest. Caso announced that Tomb No.7 was a Mixtec burial site, established by the people who had pushed the Zapotecs out of Monte Albán yet still worshiped the sacred ground; they brought their highest nobility and priesthood here to be interred, just as their contemporaries, the Aztecs, continued to visit hallowed Teotihuacán and use it as a burial site.[11]

Among the splendid items yielded by Tomb No.7 were more than thirty strips of carved jaguar bone inlaid with turquoise. One of the most noteworthy depicted Quetzalcóatl being born out of a tree. The Mixtec people in the fourteenth century (by which time they occupied most of western Oaxaca and the adjoining regions of Puebla and Guerrero) claimed that they were direct descendants of Plumed Serpent, "rooted" proprietarily through him into their land since "the time before time."

Plumed Serpent continued to reveal himself around Oaxaca as the centuries unfurled. "An elaborate, multicolored feathered-serpent pictograph" was incised into a cliff face in the deep and rugged region called the *Cañada*, north of the Zapotec Sierra mountains.[12] Near Tontepec ("the mountain of the sun"), fifty miles east of Oaxaca, sixteenth-century Indian informants spoke of Quetzalcóatl "in the form of a serpent with green feathers passing from one sierra to another, making loud hissing sounds and cries that spread terror."[13]

When the Zapotec-Tehuantepec tribes rose up against the Spanish oppressors in 1550, they were led by a native priest "who claimed to be an incarnation of the god Quetzalcóatl," who had evolved into a symbol of insurrection and an advocate of a return to preconquest traditions. As we shall soon see, the special revolutionary appeal of Plumed Serpent continued to flower for another four hundred years.[14]

On my last day in Oaxaca, I decided to make one final visit to the *zócalo*, the central square of the city. I was drawn back there time and again during my stay by the benign atmosphere of the outdoor cafés, the seamless flow of music drifting in the balmy evening air, the cooing pigeons nestled in the deep shade of ageless laurel trees, the twinkling

Birth of Quetzalcóatl from a tree, Tomb 7, Monte Albán

lights strung from branch to branch, and the Indian merchants, who displayed their wares on multi-colored blankets as serious-faced children did their homework.

This bright morning, I walked down the broad Andador Macedonio Alcalá, paved with green stone. I passed in front of the cathedral. An elderly peasant lady, her hand outstretched toward me, was sitting on the ground below a sculpture of the Ascension of the Virgin. Because it was the first day of December, following the local custom, I gave her three coins for luck.

On impulse, I headed down to the far end of the square, to the nineteenth-century *Palacio de Gobierno del Estado*, which I had not yet visited. I stepped into the cool courtyard. It reminded me of the painted interiors of the *Palacio Nacional* and the *Museo de San Ildefonso* on the immense *zócalo* in

Mexico City. Here, too, the walls of a two-sided, curved staircase with a wrought-iron banister leading up to a balcony were decorated with a three-paneled mural crammed with images of a nation's history—this time, the people of Oaxaca from ancient times, through Independence and the Revolution, and into the present.

The artist, Arturo García Bustos, was unfamiliar to me, even in my studies of *Los Tres Grandes*—Diego Rivera, José Clemente Orozco, and David Alfaro Siqueiros—and all their contemporaries. García Bustos lives today in a house once occupied by Hernán Cortés and his Indian translator and mistress, "La Malinche," in the colonial neighborhood of Coyoacán, Mexico City. García Bustos studied in his youth at the Academy of San Carlos, where he met Rivera, Orozco, and Frida Kahlo, who guided and encouraged his work during the early 1940s.[15]

The vast mural, more than two hundred square meters, took two years to execute and was completed in November 1980. It is done in the classic encaustic method invented in ancient Greece: dry pigments are mixed with melted beeswax and resin and applied to the wall while still warm. In the final stage of composition, a heat element, such as a light bulb inside a reflector, is passed above the surface, essentially "burning" the color and the wax together, fusing them to the wall.[16]

The most vivid theme running through García Bustos's mural, *Oaxaca en la Historia de Mexico*—slashed at its topmost heavenly corner with Cocijo's lightning bolt—emphasizes the studious literary tradition of the Mixtec. In one section, two tribal elders sit cross-legged on a reed mat. One man, with grave expression, eyes downcast, dressed in a ceremonial cloak adorned with jaguar heads, presents a bleached-white codex page to his comrade, while

the second man, wearing a green-feathered quetzal headdress, points to the painted pictures, as if offering his interpretation. A wide-eyed auditor sits to the right, transfixed. Nearby, a younger scribe, adorned with gold tiara, necklace, armbands, and earplugs, cradles a deerskin screenfold book in his lap and delicately wields a paintbrush above the page coated with white lime. The aura of respectful concentration is palpable.

The term "codex" applies broadly to painted manuscripts that are the written legacy of the Mesoamerican peoples. But these historical records actually took other forms besides what we would perceive as a conventional "book." There were accordion-pleated or screenfold manuscripts, often hung for display in the homes of their proud owners; *tira* scrolls wound from one staff to another; and

LEFT AND RIGHT: *Arturo García Bustos*, Oaxaca en la Historia de Mexico (*details*)

49

one-page *mapa* broadsides. A few were to be read vertically, in columns; others from right to left ("*boustrophedon*"-style). For the most part the codices narrate from left to right. Some Mixtec books, however, proceed *en meandro*, seeming to have no specific linear narrative line, but rather slithering snakelike over and among the pages.[17]

Mesoamerican literature was systematically obliterated in the Spanish Conquest. The painted manuscripts contained the cultural history of the people. "Reading" these surviving books is like leafing through a collection of photographs—the image depicts the occasion or subject. This was the earliest narrative method employed; it was followed gradually over the centuries by symbolic pictures and then, more recently, by phonetic ones, which are closer to writing as we conceive it today.[18]

The codices enumerated divinatory rituals, assigned values to each day of the year, prescribed herbal remedies for illnesses, and advised prayers for all occasions. This information, which comes directly from the written record of the pre-Hispanic epoch, is gleaned from the meagre *sixteen* (or it may only be fourteen) surviving books remaining from the Mayan and Mexican period before the Conquest. And of these sixteen (or according to some scholars fourteen) books, no less than eight (or six) come from the Oaxaca region.

Man-serpent, Codex Zouche-Nuttall

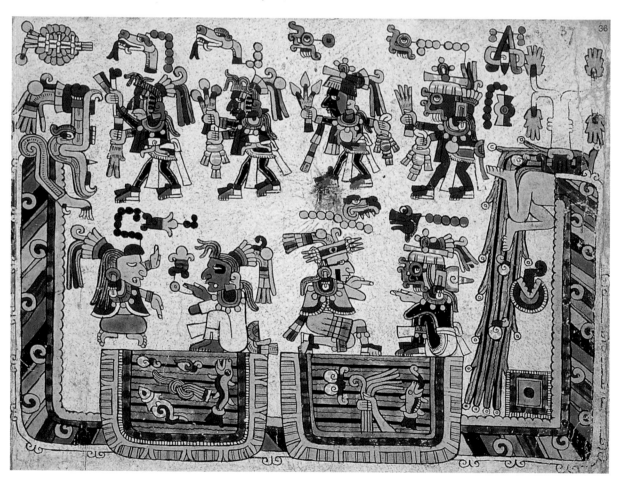

Equally impressive is the fact that according to a census of all known surviving Mesoamerican manuscripts—preconquest and postconquest—more than 20 percent are of Oaxacan origin; and they are considered the most colorfully realized. These were truly "people of the book" as well as "people of the clouds"; they copied and updated earlier histories, as if passing a baton from one generation to the next, to ensure that the chain would not be broken.

One thousand years of history is contained in the Mixtec Codices,[19] and Plumed Serpent is the most pervasive character. In the deerhide, fifty-two paneled *Codex Vindobonensis* (Vienna), which probably originated in western Oaxaca, he is familiarly cited as the founder of all royal dynasties. He appears under the local name 9-*Viento*, which not only represents the day he was born but also incorporates his persona as he who brought the wind with him, "sweeping" the path of life for men to follow and representing "speech, the *breath* of life."[20]

His stepped temple, shown in the *Codex Zouche-Nuttall* (like *Vindobonensis-Vienna*, also from western Oaxaca and dated before 1350), is adorned with the combination beak-monkey face resembling Éhecatl, another Plumed Serpent identity associated with wind. Meanwhile, approaching the temple is the formidable goddess *Aguila Sangrienta* ("bloody eagle"). Also named for her birth date 4 *Lagarto* ("four lizard"), she wears a Tlaloc mask, an elaborately layered visual analogue with Plumed Serpent.[21]

Elsewhere in this codex are pages bracketed down one side, along the bottom, and up the other with a ferocious serpent, noteworthy for its human feet and animal head. In these sequences, Plumed Serpent embraces the entire knowable world.

There is concrete evidence of Plumed Serpent's migration to the lands of Oaxaca in two other preconquest Mixtec codices, *Bodley* and *Colombino*, where it is written that in the eleventh century, at the same time as the attenuated Toltec exodus from the west, "four ambassadors from the king of Tula visited

Patio interior, Mitla

[Mixtec] King 8-*Venado* ('deer'), known as Tiger-Claw" and that this courtesy was reciprocated. Elsewhere in the *Codex Bodley*, 9-Wind's wife is tellingly nicknamed *Blusa de Tlaloc* ("Tlaloc's blouse"). These kinds of overlapping names, with the knowledge that Plumed Serpent dwells in close proximity to Tlaloc, show how proud the Mixtecs were of their link with the Toltecs, devotedly sharing that culture's veneration of Plumed Serpent and other gods.[22]

The open, windy, mountainous dignity of Monte Albán is counterbalanced by the introverted valley protectiveness of Mitla, twenty-four miles to the southeast along Highway 190. The name of this sanctuary in Zapotec was *Lyobaa* (also written *Yoo-paa*), translated by later Aztec-Nahuatl speakers as *Mictlán*, "the place of the dead," or "where the soul comes to rest."

Past the village enlivened by oleander, pomegranate, orange, and lemon trees and hedge-cacti fences between houses, Mitla's bleached buildings stand huddled in groups within declivities down the hill to my right near the dry *Rio Grande* river bed. The site abuts a colonial church with six-foot-thick walls on a higher rise of land to my left.

These are not noble pyramids but rather low-slung and layered-forward structures with ornamental moldings; higher levels often jut farther out than lower ones in a manner reminiscent of Uxmal's "palaces." Although caves in the hilly surrounding area were inhabited several thousand years before Christ, the main buildings at Mitla date from A.D. 800 onward. The facade walls are broken up with perfectly spaced, capacious doorways that open into silent patios within, decorated with varieties of a "stepped-fret" design in a mind-boggling display of mosaic art. Tiny pieces of volcanic stone, shaped with stone tools, were fitted together without mortar and then set obsessively into red stucco.

The Mexican artist and ethnologist Miguel Covarrubias, after visiting the site in the 1940s, marveled that "there are over twenty varieties of patterns in these panels, all based upon a *single motif*, the stepped spiral called *xicalcoliuhqui*, perhaps the most characteristic of Middle-American aboriginal art motifs, derived from the stylized head of the 'Sky-Serpent,' and thus a symbol of Quetzalcóatl."[23]

The human scale of Mitla's walls permits sunlight to pour in and play upon the incised and protruding (almost Greek) geometric swirls and arabesques, pure forms encompassing me with a dizzying chiaroscuro homage to Plumed Serpent. I reluctantly leave this unbearable brightness for the shadowy realm of *subterráneos* that earned Mitla its name. At the *Patio de las Cruceros* ("the crosses"), I stoop down, easily escaping the attention of the somnolent guard, and I almost double over into a square hole cut in the rough cement floor. I descend a short flight of stairs, pass through a fortunately unlocked iron gate, and then step over a wooden barrier into the midst of a clammy, cruciform tomb, its walls patterned with ubiquitous stepped-fret designs. Whatever physical contents and artifacts there were have long since been rifled. But the Zapotec spiritual legends remain—this resting place

and others like it, networking beneath Mitla's surface, "led to a dark tunnel that ran for thirty leagues … approaching the spirit world at the interior of the earth … the universal womb."[24]

As it was written in the *Tlamachilliztlatozazanilli* (*The Myth of the Suns and the Toltec-Chichimec Origins of the Mexica People*),[25] "Quetzalcóatl went off to Mictlán to take away the jade bones" of his forbears and deliver them to the surface of the earth.

> *He made a bundle and carried them at once to Tamoanchán. And as soon as he brought them, the goddess named Cihuacóatl ("the mother of mankind") ground them in her jade bowl, and then Quetzalcóatl bled his penis over it…. And then [all the gods] said, "The gods have given birth to men, the common people."*[26]

With his perilous and daring feats—"passing through the tenuous curtain which separates the living from the dead," invading the dreaded *inframundo* (underworld), and triumphantly "return[ing] with his life-transmuting trophy"—Plumed Serpent in the time-before-time demonstrated his heroism for all times to come, establishing a standard for the succession of shamans, priests, and princes who followed him and assumed his name.[27]

His intrepid down-going allied Plumed Serpent with Venus, herald of the sun and a hero among planets. Venus passed through its *own* inferior conjunction to survive day after day into eternity, "looming up in the dawn sky big as a snowball, shining with inexpressible brilliance."

This cosmic connection, indelible within Mesoamerican mind and literature, will help us understand the Aztecs' absolute conviction when Hernán Cortés arrived. Surely, Plumed Serpent was fulfilling his predestined, promised revisitation.[28]

Stepped-fret design, Group of the Columns, Mitla

CHAPTER VIII

THE MAYA LEGEND

*The culture of a people
is an ensemble of texts,
themselves ensembles,
which the anthropologist
strains to read over the shoulders
of those to whom
they properly belong.*
—CLIFFORD GEERTZ,
The Interpretation of Cultures

Wood carving, Caves of Loltun, Yucatán

*Whatever might be is simply not there:
only murmurs, ripples, in the dark, in the night.
Only the Maker, Modeler alone,
Sovereign Plumed Serpent, the Bearers,
Begetters are in the water, a glittering light.
They are there, they are enclosed
in quetzal feathers, in blue-green.
Thus the name, "Plumed Serpent."
They are great knowers,
great thinkers in their very being.*

Popol Vuh: The Mayan Book of the Dawn of Life,
translated by DENNIS TEDLOCK

"Our people have endured a bitter history
of 500 years of marginalization,"
said Macario Zabala Can, a Maya priest
who is president of the Council of Elders
advising the Guatemalan Fund
for Indigenous Development.
"But we have a prophecy that talks
of the return of the Wise Men,
and that is exactly what is happening now:
we are entering a period of gestation."

"*Maya Renaissance in Guatemala Turns Political,*"
by LARRY ROHTER, *The New York Times*, August 12, 1996

From the Uxmal ruins, I took highway 261 north to Muna and then highway 184 seven miles southeast to the town of Oxkutzcab. The impenetrable scrub grass bordering fertile corn fields edged up to the side of the two-lane black macadam road that cut straight through the undulating landscape. Through town and then two blocks from the central plaza, dominated by a Franciscan church, there was a hand-lettered sign with an arrow that read LAS GRUTAS (Maya for "the rock of flowers"), the largest known caves in the Yucatán, at Loltun.

Descending the slippery steps into the darkness, it was easy to understand how the place got its name: there were carvings of flowers everywhere on the high, gloomy walls, and here and there a solitary palm-print in black or red. The guide aimed his flashlight at some of the glyphs on the walls dating as far back as two millennia before Christ.

The final chamber opened up more than two stories high, and sunlight filtered down, lighting dust motes swimming aimlessly around a huge tree bursting upward from the cave floor. Drops of water spangled its leaves as tiny birds darted among vine-draped branches, their sharp calls reverberating against rocks.

Near the top of the ladder that we climbed to reach the surface, there was a solitary Maya Indian crouched in concentration, grasping a smoothed wooden panel in his left hand and carving away with his right. He had arranged wares around him on a ledge: grotesque feathered beings, shaman snakes, and imagined gods. The work in progress was intriguing. From the gaping beak of a bird with a peering, oval eye, a man's face emerged, his hands seemingly becoming claws. The artist's eyes met mine. He grinned and nodded, raising his eyebrows a millimeter, while slightly tilting the piece toward me so the brown contours caught

the sun. "I'll buy it, if you'll sign it," I said without a thought. The plumed man passed from Vicente Chable Canul to me.

There was a strong underlying unity to the worldviews of all Mesoamerican peoples. But it is not a contradiction to hold in mind the simultaneous fact that each culture also possessed its unique character. To understand the centrality of Plumed Serpent among the Maya, we will roll back the years to the era before the disturbance of the Toltec incursion and—despite the paucity of information available—survey the character of the "Classic Horizon" in Guatemala and the Yucatán.[1]

Maya texts inscribed on plaster-coated fig-bark paper within jaguar-skin covers fared even less well at the hands of the Spaniards than Mixtec deerskin books. There are *absolutely no known Maya codices extant* from the Classic period (ca. A.D. 400–900), and only three, perhaps four, authentic preconquest manuscripts survive from the thousands known to have been in existence in the 1520s: the Dresden, Madrid, and Paris (and perhaps Grolier), each named after the library archive in which it is housed.

Nevertheless, the Maya left testimonies of their inner lives in other narrative forms: meticulously painted stories around the circumference of glazed clay pots; glyphic carved surfaces of tilting but unbowed stone stelae sheltered in makeshift, thatched lean-tos in the jungle, bearing complex linguistic codes that have gradually yielded to interpretation during the past two decades; engraved friezes; and chipped, fading murals along temple facades.[2]

From these shards, what can be gleaned of the early Maya ethos? We know that the Mayan culture was above all else "a theocratic society whose economic base permitted a tremendous channeling of energy to the service of the gods and the dead."

The important idea here is channeling. The small group of priest-sages—the spiritual leaders of Mayan society in cities and towns large and small—had to have been men of tremendous persuasive power. They defined and declared or chanted beliefs which, in turn, were reinforced every day by the people's willing acceptance.[3]

Mayan gods were mercurial. They could be helpful to man at one moment, destructive at another.[4] To maintain equilibrium in an uncertain universe and to make day follow night and rain follow the planting of seeds, the gods had to be appeased. The traditional portrait of Mayan civilization as benevolent and tranquil in contrast to its vicious Aztec successors does not bear scrutiny. Rather, "blood was the mortar of ancient Maya life.... Through ceremonial bloodletting, Maya lords renewed the world and paid back the 'blood debt' they owed powerful gods."[5]

Blood cascaded from the flayed bodies of white-robed sacrificial victims subjected to a variety of tortures: they lent their hearts to be ripped from their breasts; or they were tied to stakes and walls and slowly, methodically killed by one arrow after another piercing their chests; or they gave up newborn babies and virgin daughters to be bound hand and foot and then cast into the sixty-foot-deep Well of Sacrifice at Chichén Itzá in service to the common weal.

The Maya would not have understood our separation of religious and secular life. The focal point of their society, providing its magnetic coherence, was the king. He was a religious man who incarnated godliness in human form. When he approached heaven and stood within the wooden sanctuary at the top of the steps of the pyramid in the center of the city, he did not "represent" or "symbolize" the pivotal, intermediary point between men and gods. He *was* that point. He *was* a vessel, and an elite one, into which the gods were poured before their authority could be transmitted to the people below.[6]

When the Maya king's earthly life concluded, it was well understood that he should be equipped in his tomb with provisions to help him make a journey "down the road to *Xibalba*," the Otherworld, there to vanquish the Lords of Death, after which he would be reborn as a heavenly body.[7]

Even as an unbroken chain of dynastic kings sustained by blood offerings managed to keep body and spirit in unity, every aspect of the Mayan environment possessed divine life. All things in the world, animate or inanimate, had a living essence indistinguishable from human beings: "He who makes an enemy of the Earth makes an enemy of his own body," said the Wise Men. This conviction provided an unvarying moral order in the daily existence of the Maya.[8]

The farmer in his *milpa* (cleared field), the tradesman in his marketplace stall, and the obsidian carver peddling his craft would not have understood (or perhaps, might have been bemused by) the nineteenth-century Romantic poets' intellectually urgent attempt to seek solace by "interpreting" in verse the meaning of a nature divorced from themselves.[9]

The Classic Mayan compulsion for moral order in everyday life was consistent with other Mesoamerican cultures' predication on a cyclic calendar depicting cosmic order. The thirteenth-century *Dresden Codex*, showing precise knowledge of the comings and goings of Venus—called *Noh Ek*, "the great star"—is the finest example of this moral imperative, bearing witness to the auguries and allure of this most luminous of heavenly spheres.[10]

The ebb and flow of planets in the sky was a metaphor for the Mayan sense of man's earthly history, in which every event in the present was a reflection of everything that had happened in the past and a projection of what would inevitably come.

Munro Edmonson, translator of the great Yucatec Mayan text *Chilam Balam*—which we will consider shortly—interpreted this worldview as "tragic fatalism ... the essence of the literature of the Mexican and Guatemalan Indians ... an ethic so distinctive that its flavor has survived four centuries of impingement from outside influences."[11]

The conquest of the Maya dragged on for more than two decades into the mid–1540s, long after the Aztecs had fallen to Cortés. Resistance to the invading culture was strong and quiet, evincing the stubborn reluctance to relinquish the precious stories of their ancestors. European script came into Guatemala and the Yucatán through the Spaniards, giving rise to alphabetic books in the native community. But until then the texts had been passed on through a centuries-old oral tradition. The earliest painted books were meant to supplement or cue the oral passing down of tales from the Wise Men to their students.[12]

In just such a transitional situation, the *Popol Vuh* (literally, "the book of the community," or "council book") was born. It is the oldest written survivor of the "poems-of-origin," representing a sacred practice common to all tribes living in North America before the European conquests. These monumental works told of the creation and emergence of animals and gods and of the first movements of man across the new landscape of earth.[13]

In the years between 1554 and 1558, in the town of Quiché, northwest of what is now Guatemala City, near the great sacred Lake Atitlán (*Nahachel* in Quiché), more than three thousand feet up in the mountains, members of the once mighty ruling families of the Quiché Maya resolved to preserve in writing the story of their forefathers and the origin of the gods they venerated.

Of the creator gods, the one with the most powerful spirit and the most awesome powers of change—the "lord of genius"—was *Gucumatz* (*guk*, "quetzal bird"; *cumatz*, "serpent"). His was the ancient Quiché name for all primordial beginnings, "in a world that [had] nothing but an empty sky above and a calm sea below"; here was Plumed Serpent's identity even before he took on a shape. And that shape could be protean:

Every seven days he ascended to the sky
and every seven days he followed the path
to the abode of the dead
and every seven days he put on the nature
of a serpent
and then he truly became a serpent
and every seven days he assumed the nature
of an eagle
and then he truly became an eagle
then of a jaguar
and he truly became a jaguar
then of coagulated blood
and he was nothing else
than coagulated blood.[14]

True to the responsibilities he bore here (as in other Mesoamerican cultures), the "Maker, Modeler, Bearer, Begetter, Sovereign Plumed Serpent" created man and woman, "the first mother-fathers"—but not, in the Quiché rendition, out of crushed bones or ashes. He used yellow and white corn for flesh and water for blood. His creations thanked Plumed Serpent profusely for their newborn lives:

Truly now,
double thanks, triple thanks,
that we've been formed, we've been given
our mouths, our faces,
we speak, we listen,
we wonder, we move,
our knowledge is good, we've understood
what is far and near,
and we've seen what is great and small
under the sky, on the earth.[15]

In his modern translation of the *Popol Vuh*, the American poet and anthropologist Dennis Tedlock notes the *hombre-dios* theme in the Quiché representation of Gucumatz/Plumed Serpent. He is a being who entered life as an all-encompassing, generative god, setting the wheels of creation in motion, subsumed, in Book Four—the penultimate section of the epic story—into a "mythohistoric" leader "whose face was not forgotten by his grandson and sons."[16]

This charismatic leader had convinced his people, the ancient ancestors of the Quiché, to leave their magical city of Tula/Tollán and had set the wheels in motion for their migration eastward from this "diffusion center." He was called *Tohil*, and, as it was written in the *Popol Vuh*,

> *But really storm [thunder, totoh, or tohil]*
> *was the name*
> *of the god of the Mexican people.*
> *Rattlesnake,*
> *Quetzal Serpent was his name....*
> *Even though Tohil is his name*
> *he is the same as the god of the Yaqui people*
> *who is named Yolcuat and Quitzalcuat.*

This Tohil, a questioning and restless leader, believed his people belonged elsewhere, even as they had previously come into Tulan from an unnamed place, "on the other side of the sea." With sorrow but with faith in his wisdom, they acquiesced, "[crying] in their hearts when they came away, when they made their departure from Tulan."

> *Alas! We won't be here when we see the dawn,*
> *when the sun is born, when the face of the earth*
> *is lit....*
> *We are going to the east, where our fathers*
> *came from....*
> *We're not dying. We're coming back, they said....* [17]

Another Guatemalan book, begun by members of the *Xahil* dynasty—neighbors of the Quiché—and preserved in the village of Sololá, overlooking Lake Atitlán, provides an important historical sequel to the *Popol Vuh*. It was called *Annals of the Cakchiquels* and was initially composed in the Spanish alphabet toward the end of the sixteenth century. It is thought to be a copy, in part, of a much older manuscript. It briefly corroborates the general narrative of the *Popol Vuh* relating to the origins of the universe and man. But the deeper and more sustained interest of the *Annals* resides in

the detailed migration story of the Cakchiquel Maya people, "from the great city of Tulan at the place which lies between Santiago de los Valles and Xilatepeq, fifty leagues from Mexico, from whence [sic] went forth a great number of noble men and women, directed by their Oracle [Plumed Serpent] to emigrate and found their monarchy elsewhere." [18]

The account describes a two-pronged route from Tulan, "The Golden City of the Sun," that passed through the Oaxaca region and across Tehuantepec into the provinces now known as Tabasco and Campeche. There, the wanderers rested by a lake that is now thought to be the *Laguna de Terminos* ("the meeting place for emigrant peoples"), which indents the southwestern shore of Campeche province, before heading south into the interior of Guatemala, "seeking mountains and valleys where they might prosper and settle under the sun of civilization." In addition to the Cakchiquels, these new arrivals included ancestors of the Gumarcaah, Iximche, and at least eleven other "dynasties who became linguistically Mayanized." [19]

Parallel to the *Popol Vuh* and the *Annals of the Cakchiquels* in the Guatemalan highlands, beginning in the mid-sixteenth century, the fourteen *Books of Chilam Balam* ("the spokesmen of the jaguar") emerged from the northern Yucatán lowlands. Over the next three hundred years, in gradual and fragmentary composition throughout the Yucatán, these eclectic documents of "prophetic history" chronicled the story of the Maya up to the seventh century A.D. [20] They describe the accepted succession of dynasties and include a pantheon of more than twenty fundamental gods and their moody temperaments.

But in their melange of languages, the *Chilam Balam* stories also serve as a patchwork reminder of the incessant struggle by the Maya to maintain the integrity of their beliefs despite "indisputable contamination" by Biblical literature, Nahuatl tales,

Spanish phraseology, church and lay Latin, and lunar tables from modern Europe.

In the *Chilam* creation story, "God" shows two faces: Hispanically, as *Dios citbil* ("God the remote") and, paralleling the Sovereign Plumed Serpent of the *Popol Vuh*, as *Hunab Ku* ("the unified god").[21]

The *Chilam Balam* is filled with "confrontational" references to recurring tensions beginning with the Maya of the Classic era, when their world was sullied by wave upon wave of western incursions: Toltec, Mexica, and Spanish colonizers, followed by the burdens of full-fledged republicanism in the modern era.

"They did not wish to join with the foreigners," reflected a melancholy *Chilam Balam of Chumayel* scribe during the late 1500s. "They did not desire Christianity.... At that time [before the Spanish came] the course of humanity was orderly. The foreigners made it otherwise when they arrived here."[22]

"This is history in the Mayan manner, dominated by a profound faith that correct calendrical calculation will enable the priests to predict the fate of the next cycle." The cycles came in twenty-year periods called *katuns*, set in motion 3,115 years before Christ to roll forward as implacably as a snake with its tail in its mouth. The priests understood this world wheel had long since been determined for them: "They knew the measure of their days," said the *Chilam Balam*. "Complete was the month; complete the year; complete the day; complete the night; complete the breath of life as it passed also."[23] This fatalism is evoked in this excerpt from the *Chilam Balam of Tizimin*, from about A.D. 1500:

> At Chichén Itzá
> Was the seat of the katun.
> Come is the quetzal;
> Come is the blue bird;
> Come are the yellow deaths;
> Come is blood vomit.
> For the fourth time
> Come is Kukul Can *after the Itzas.*
> For the fourth time
> Is the word of the katun's return.[24]

Kuk is the quetzal bird. *Kukul Can* is the Yucatec Maya version of the first Quiché god, *Gucumatz*—Plumed Serpent in another of his multiple guises, reaching full flower in Chichén Itzá. Illustrating this passage is a drawing of the "Lord of the Katun," adorned not only with feathers but also with stars that unite Plumed Serpent with Venus, his familiar heavenly counterpart.[25]

True to the solemn dictates of Mayan prophecy, *Kukul Can* reappeared later in the *Chilam Balam*. He returned, in the company of his priests, "Masters of the Earth," wearing white loin cloths and white robes.[26] His precious name would live on for millennia after his presence at the giving-birth of the world—until the final day, when it was written that Sky Serpent, together with the god of death, would bring an apocalyptic deluge upon his creation.[27]

Kukul Kan, Lord of Chichén Itzá, from Chilam Balam of Chumayel

CHAPTER IX

CHICHĒN ITZĀ

Deep in the troubled highlands of Chiapas, Mexico, which border Guatemala, the Zinacantec Maya still speak the ancient Tzotzil language. They have no words to represent the directions north or south, but the east-west axis is expressed as *lokeb-kakal* (rising sun) and *meleb-kakal* (disappearing sun). This eternal arc is known among the native people as the "Route of Our Divine Father." The authors of the *Chilam Balam* had written, "You see your guests upon the road, O Itza! It is the fathers of the land who will arrive!"[1]

The path of the sun; the transit of Venus; the transit of peoples, which began in the millennia before Christ; the movement of the Olmec from the Gulf Coast through the Isthmus of Tehuantepec—the west-east passage, which is an underlying theme in our legend of Plumed Serpent, comes to an end in the Petén region of northern Guatemala, forty miles south of the Campeche border, at the monumental jungle city of Tikal. This was the third sibling of Teotihuacán and Monte Albán, reaching full flower in concert with them. Among the closely spaced stepped skyscraper temples, archaeologists discovered inscriptions on stelae marking the inauguration of the Classic Mayan era, which began a thousand years before the scribes of the *Chilam Balam* launched their work of history acknowledging the Toltecs. These stone markers, dotted throughout the Yucatán, Guatemala, Belize, Honduras, and El Salvador, bear witness to the deeds of Mayan kings whose dominion spanned from the late third century to the mid-tenth century A.D.

Viewed in sequence, Mayan stelae tell the story of the systematic spread of governmental rule out of the Petén region and the establishment of rival Mayan city-states that eventually went to war with one another. They also tell the simultaneous story of "the long period of gradual infiltration of foreign elements" over the same seven hundred years, culminating in the domination of Chichén Itzá.[2]

How much of the cult of Kukulkán (Mayan Plumed Serpent) was imported from central Mexico, how much came from the coastal area, and how much was indigenous to the Maya? As with so many issues pertaining to the origins of the sophisticated Mayan culture, the question still hangs tantalizingly in the air.

ABOVE AND LEFT: *Temple of Kukulkán, Chichén Itzá*

The much vaunted (and much prophesied) Toltec arrival was more in the nature of a building sea swell than a sudden shock wave. By the time of the Toltec aggression (if indeed it *was* an aggression), an indigenous Mayan civilization had already expanded geographically from its Petén heart. An essentially naive agricultural society had long since given way to a state-managed society, which had begun in turn to weaken and collapse upon itself for reasons still incompletely known.[3]

Itza is Mayan for "those of twisted speech." The Chontal Maya (a "foreign" people by virtue of speaking a different dialect and inhabiting a region bordering the Gulf of Mexico) were already under Nahua influence and might have invaded the Yucatán early in the tenth century A.D., fifty years before the Toltec Plumed Serpent cult arrived. The *Chilam Balam* makes explicit reference to "Kukulcan [coming] for a second time," a third time, and, as we have seen, even a fourth time: "It is the word of god. The *Itza* shall come."[4]

As in their ancient myths, "the Maya sacred hymns also show similarities in comparison with the texts of the [Aztec region] Nahuas," because "there had been many contacts between the two cultures ever since the Teotihuacán period." The Maya believed, as did the Nahua peoples, that man was created by the gods in order that someone would exist to "invoke and praise" them. Previous ages of men did not know how to pray and therefore were destroyed. The *Popol Vuh* recounted a wishful hymn sung by more recent, wiser mortals, mindful of their obligations, "in large part prudence, in large degree piety":

> *O Gods…*
> *May the Sun move along and give light.*
> *May it dawn, may the light come!*
> *Give us good roads,*
> *level roads.*
> *May the people be at peace,*
> *enjoy a long peace.*[5]

The ground may also have been prepared for the flowering of Plumed Serpent in Mayaland by a predisposition among Mayan gods to assimilate their comrade. The supreme Mayan deity known as *Hunab Ku* (the "God Behind the Gods" or the

"Great Hand") corresponded to the Nahua *Ometeotl* ("Twice God," or "Two Gods in One").

Quetzalcóatl in the Nahua language was translated into the Yucatec Mayan name Kukulkán, *K'uk* meaning "sprouts" or "shoots," as in vegetal growth (or quetzal plumes, or even the split tongue of the serpent). This Kukulkán bore a telling resemblance to Hunab Ku's son, *Itzamná*, another early god legendary for having established culture, the arts, and writing — and for introducing maize as the staple food of the Maya.[6]

Were the tenth-century Toltecs who arrived in the Yucatán a raw, predatory lot, overwhelming the people of Chichén Itzá with the sole intent of dominating the remaining vestiges of the Mayan empire at the northern tip of the peninsula, levying harsh tributes upon the residents of the surrounding provinces?[7] Or was theirs primarily an ideological victory, setting new calendrical feast days in place, and moving Toltec wise men into prominent positions of authority?[8] Or did the pious Mayan laborers and artisans of Chichén Itzá "lend their talents and labors *willingly*" to help the Toltecs revive the religious stature of their Classic-era buildings, many of which had fallen into disrepair? Was the Toltec incursion an evangelical more than a military victory, during which the teachings of Quetzalcóatl as Kukulkán were readily adapted because reverence for his character and principles had already preceded him?[9]

The ambiguity of Chichén Itzá, the best known of all Mesoamerican ruins, starts with the name, which is Mayan for "at the mouth of the *well* of the Itza" and refers to the two sacred *cenote* ("wells," Hispanicized from the Yucatec Mayan *ts'onot*) within the known boundaries of the place. But, like temples built upon earlier versions, even Chichén Itzá's name has an ancestor: *Uuc-hab-nal*, variously translated as "the seven bushy places," the "seven great properties," or "the seven years of corn."[10]

Its ambiguity continues with Chichén Itzá's identity as perceived by most visitors, who know little or nothing of Mayan civilization but already feel familiar with the Pyramid of Kukulkán, which stands at the center of the site. This four-staircased temple is a deceptive symbol for Chichén Itzá, dominating the northern Yucatán plains and appearing at first glimpse to be so well preserved and clear. In fact, according to the most recent survey by the National Museum of Anthropology in Mexico City (1994), the site's excavation and restoration remain woefully incomplete. There is far more of Chichén Itzá still hidden below the lime-crust soil surface than is revealed above.[11]

Even as the tip of an archaeological iceberg, Chichén Itzá is frightening. It feels as if every visible stone has been forcibly invaded by an image, usually bold or malevolent, in the "unsympathetic" Toltec style.[12]

Chichén Itzá possesses the customary hushed atmosphere, comforting in early morning and late afternoon—yet within the shadowed silence resides a never-ending scream that pounds through my brain long after a full day's hot trek across its uneven terrain.

In contrast to the respect succeeding generations showed for the spiritual powers of Teotihuacán and Monte Albán, local tradition has it that the Maya who lived in surrounding towns in the centuries preceding the Conquest were afraid to go near the abandoned, weed-strewn Chichén Itzá ruins at night, when, they believed, "the souls of their forefathers"[13] roamed the grounds, their likenesses upon the painted sculptures, panels, Atlantean columns, balustrades, and friezes leaping forward when moonlight lanced through rapidly moving clouds.

"Chichén Itzá fairly crawls with feathered serpents, a motif which haunts the Toltec art of this site like an obsession."[14] At Chichén Itzá, the jaguar also

Maya Vision Serpent, Yaxchilan

lurks, never too distant from his serpent ally. There is a "close association" of the snake and the jaguar throughout the site, instances where the "clawed forefeet" of the latter support the body of the former. The trail of two hybridized beasts had its origins in the Olmec world and continues in full flower at Chichén Itzá at the Temple of the Jaguars, the rear of which faces the ball court. At the front of the temple, there begins a parade of thirty-two jaguars marching in pairs, flanked by "monstrous reptiles." The rear is decorated with feathered serpents.[15]

The looming Pyramid of Kukulkán is a compendium of calendrical signs. Its basic form and construction are Classic Mayan; the decorative details are Toltec.[16] There are ninety-one steps to the top on each of its four sides, which slope at a strict forty-five-degree angle—364 steps altogether,

with the uppermost platform, one hundred feet above the ground, making it 365. There are nine gently rounded terrace corners bracketing each of the four faces of the temple—rubble contained with stone and then finished with lime cement on both flanks of the central stair, making twice eighteen—the months (*uinal*) of the Mayan "vague year" (*haab*).

Each month had twenty days (*kin*), followed by the Ill-Fated month of five days. Each of the fifty-two inset panels on the pyramid represents a year in the Mayan "calendar round." After this interval, "New Year's Days of the same name would repeat themselves." Among the Mexica in Central Mexico, this fifty-two-year cycle was called a "year bundle," often represented as a knot in a rope showing that the period had been "tied up."[17]

At sunset on the spring and fall equinoctial days of March and September, shadows are cast downward from the top of the Temple of Kukulkán by the northwest corners of the nine platforms along the edge of the principle facade stairway; they create what appears to be the body of a huge serpent descending the pyramid. Its last wave concludes at the neck of a massive stone serpent head that rests on the ground at the staircase base, "the sacred serpent of light entering into the physical world of matter."[18]

The "fear and terror" of the mighty Earth Serpent whose origin was at the center of the volcano caused the Olmec at La Venta to elevate their temples in ever-narrowing concentric coils in tribute to the snake and the spirals of passing time. Similarly, the Pyramid of Kukulkán began as a man-made mountain modeled after the serpent. His forbidding head, hewn with stone tools from a single stone, still guards the foot of the restored staircase leading up to the sanctuary where he was worshiped.[19]

At the summit of the temple mountain of Kukulkán, breathing laboriously, lightheaded to the degree where sight becomes strained through tears, the climber beholds a dramatic panorama. The vistas of the site—even more than what the guidebooks' mantras promise—are thrilling. Among Plumed Serpent's spirit guardians at the peak threshold to his realm, in the pivotal zone pierced by sunlight, I am protected by dark arches, caught between the jaws of the shrine's mouth.[20]

The shrine entrance columns are serpentine: head at the base, body as the shaft, rattles as the capitals. For the Mayan high priest (*chilam*) who here wielded perhaps the same sacrificial quartz knife that archaeologists dredged from the mucky bottom of the Sacred *Cenote* (well), its wooden handle carved in the shape of two intertwined scaled

Priest's head emerging from serpent jaws, Temple of the Magician, Uxmal

serpents with eyes that sprout feathers, this was the promised gateway to the spirit world.[21]

Down a gently sloping hill and into woods to the southwest of the Pyramid of Kukulkán, I come to the Tomb of the High Priest, or Ossuary, so-called because seven superimposed burial vaults were found within. Its facade is decorated with images of a man-bird-serpent. It could be a miniature replica of the Pyramid of Kukulkán. There are unconfirmed rumors that a secret underground tunnel connected the two buildings. Directly across the small plaza in front of the tomb, past a circular altar, a Venus Platform—consecrated to Kukulkán in his familiar persona as Son of the Morning Star and decorated with incised panels representing the god in human form—bears a striking resemblance to a structure with the same name on higher ground to the north of the great pyramid. This persistent duality in Mesoamerican culture in general and Mayan thought in particular adds to the mystique of Chichén Itzá.[22]

The buildings of the Central Group, standing farther to the south, exemplify delicately formed vestiges of the Classic Mayan style at Chichén Itzá, a mode of expression that dates back to the early sixth century A.D. When the Toltecs first arrived, they joined the Maya in this sector of the city.[23]

The Snail (*El Caracol*), a building named by the American explorer John Lloyd Stephens in 1841, contains two circular passageways, and within them a spiral staircase leading up eighty feet to a round observatory oriented to the four cardinal points of the compass.[24]

The Snail building is an important signpost on our Plumed Serpent trail for several reasons. The round shape of the building links it to the chain of structures throughout Mesoamerica consecrated to *Éhecatl*, the Wind God, one of Plumed Serpent's personalities. Whirling winds—which rose up in the evening when the yellow, fading light of sunset merged into the dark sky of nightfall—threaded between the ruined buildings of Chichén Itzá and were considered evil by thirteenth-century Maya.[25]

The borders of stairs leading to platforms on the first and second levels of the *Caracol* are decorated with intertwined, scaled rattlesnakes (*tzabkán*) that are reversed so that the head of one lies next to the rattles of another.[26] The Classic Mayan period rattlesnake imagery on this building is further evidence that *Crotalus durissus* was a "deeply venerated cult animal" at Chichén Itzá before the Toltec incursion.[27]

The Temple of the Panels (*Templo de los Tableros*) southeast of the Observatory catches my eye on this dew-laden morning. Its human scale and absence of bellicose imagery create a decidedly contemplative air. I write the "Temple of the Animals" in my field notebook because of the veritable menagerie carved into the north and south exterior walls: all manner of birds, jaguars, monkeys, fish, and Plumed Serpents, once portrayed gaily in multicolored stucco, now long since faded.

The Spanish conquerors named the sprawling, many-chambered Nunnery (*Edificio de las Monjas*). An undulating stone rattlesnake runs around the building cornice, and below it, spaced between the eyebrows of *Chac*, the rain god, are human faces. A similar motif, combining ring-tailed snake,

Serpent design gold facial ornaments, Cenote of Sacrifice, Chichén Itzá

66

pendulous-snouted rain god, and man, also appears on the exterior walls of the western wing of another Hispanicized Nunnery at Uxmal, the quintessential Late Classic site fifty miles south of Mérida in the Puuc region ("land of low hills").

Chac's long nose and eye-scroll—interpreted as resembling flickering tongue and feathered brow—place him in direct association with the Olmec were-jaguar.[28]

I hear a soft, low call—"hu…hu…hu…hu"—and then, suddenly, something flits out of thick vegetation as I approach. Could it be the fabulous quetzal bird, blessing me with its presence, a good omen for my travails—a long, pendulumlike, spatula tail, a rustle of leaves, a flash of iridescence! Sadly no. Paging through my handy *Guide to Birds of the Mayas*, I see that I have encountered the Blue-Crowned Motmot, a denizen of "lowland, humid, dim jungle growth" nicknamed *bobo* ("fool") by the locals.[29]

Before leaving the Central Group and moving back north, I stop for a quiet pause at the *Templo de Xtoloc* (named for the lizards common to the area) next to the smaller of the two sacred wells at Chichén Itzá, overshadowed by drooping trees and vines. Upon stones numbered in black paint, arranged in the purple-flowered grass, and prepared for reassembling, I see the Venus star glyph.

Diving god stela, Ballcourt, Chichén Itzá

Set within the bleached-white Complex of the Thousand Columns (*Grupo de las Mil Columnas*), dramatically posed against the deep green jungle backdrop, receding to an infinite distance, the four-tiered Temple of the Warriors (*Templo de los Guerreros*) requires consideration in the Plumed Serpent story because of its explicit "plastic and structural" parallels with the Toltec Atlantes temple at Tula. The wooden entrance lintel (now gone) was supported by the rattlesnake tails of a formidable pair of feathered-serpent columns. The roof (also now gone) was held up by square columns incised with low-relief warriors.[30]

The "taloned Kukulkán" image in the Temple of the Warriors portrays a kingly head emerging between open, beaklike jaws. This *hombre-dios* brings to mind the manner in which the Olmec serpent in Monument 19 served as a curving backdrop to the copal-bearing man. At Uxmal, an elaborately tattooed, sculptured limestone head of a priest issuing forth from grotesquely gaping serpent jaws was found at the highest reaches of the Pyramid of the Magician. It can be viewed in the National Museum of Anthropology in Mexico City.

The vision of a serpent-bird was created during emotional extremes of fasting, sexual abstinence, and ritual bloodletting, temporarily uniting the hallucinating penitent with his departed ancestors. The feathered aspect of Plumed Serpent was tied to the clouds and to rain, the veils of the upper heavens, which represent the airy, spiritual aspect of the religious experience. The snake, "earthly and palpable," like the Olmec Earth Serpent, curls up from below in the shape of a holy pyramid.

When the winds came and disturbed the surface of the Well of Sacrifices (*Cenote de los Sacrificios*) at Chichén Itzá, the learned priests saw the ruffled feathers of Kukulkán in another guise, that of the "Water Serpent."[31]

If their crops failed in arid months, the Maya cast people into the *cenote* in hopes of pleasing *Chac*, whose dwelling place lay at the bottom: heavily drugged men, women, and children, some adorned with jewels, their hearts already cut out, bodies weighted with stones. The fortunate ones, still living, were rescued if they survived the plunge into the *cenote*, which they called the "Well of God" (*Chen-ku*). "The elliptical well of silent, jade-green water sixty feet deep and seventy feet below the brink of the almost vertical stratified limestone walls which encircle it" has not changed all that much since the American writer T. Philip Terry described it in 1909 as a serene place at the end of a holy path (*sacbé*) through the woods. The silence is interrupted only by "the muted trilling of tropical birds, the moaning of the wind through the tall cork trees, and the slithering rustle of harmless crested lizards and armored iguanas moving through the thorny underbrush." During almost a century of intermittent dredging and suction pumping, more than thirty thousand gold, copper, jade, pottery, wooden, and stone artifacts—even fragments of carbonized fabric and human bones of "the betrothed of Chac"—have been retrieved from the well.[32]

Frederick Catherwood engraving, Caracol, Mayapán
RIGHT: *Frederick Catherwood engraving, Temple of Kukulkán, Mayapán*

The cavernous ball court at Chichén Itzá is the largest in Mesoamerica, 230 feet wide and, at 551 feet, almost the length of two football fields. The serpent heads peer down from the slanting side walls three stories high, presiding over a game last played centuries ago. At the north end is a raised platform resembling a reviewing stand. Its murals hold some remaining touches of red ochre pigment. A series of Atlantes-type squared pillars on the southern platform catch my attention. The lowest quadrant stone of the pillars depicts a winged being with an ever-so-slightly (to my eye, at least) sad expression and drooping, bifid tongue, crouching low almost as if he had just accomplished a sudden, vertical landing, the palms of his hands flat on the ground.

Contemplating my melancholy friend, I am reminded of two sights: the eerie upside-down torsos incised into the limestone surface of the arrowhead-shaped Building J (thought to be an observatory) at Monte Albán and the figure popularly known as the "Descending (or Diving) God" at Tulum, the site on the eastern Yucatán coastal lowlands overlooking the translucent Caribbean. This character was also known as *Xux Ek*, the "Wasp Star" or Venus God.[33]

It was the fate of all Mesoamerican cultures that after the rise would come the fall. The descent of Chichén Itzá occurred in the early decades of the thirteenth century. In its wake, sixty miles to the west, the city of Mayapán emerged. Here, the Carnegie Institution of Washington conducted extensive excavations in the 1950s. Among the discoveries were shards of pottery and clay figures presenting an anthropomorphic Plumed Serpent, completely decked out as in the *Codices* with "peaked cap, loincloth with rounded ends, red and black face painting, pentitential bone dagger, hook-shaped ear pendants, and spiral wind jewel [a section of conch shell]."[34]

Careful study of the Mayapán site confirmed what the American trailblazers John Lloyd Stephens and Frederick Catherwood had first stumbled upon more than a century before: centrally located, virtual replicas on a smaller scale of the Temple of Kukulkán and the round Caracol at Chichén Itzá.

"For ages they had been unnoticed," Stephens wrote of the Mayapán structures, "almost unknown, and left to struggle with the rank tropical vegetation.... Like the mounds at Uxmal and Palenque, [the Temple] is an artificial structure, built up solid from the plain.... Four grand staircases, each twenty-five feet wide, ascended to an esplanade within six feet of the top.... The summit ...was probably the great mound of sacrifice on which the priests, in the sight of the assembled people, cut out the hearts of human victims."[35]

Yucatec Maya today say that "the King of the Maya is hiding, perhaps underground at Chichén Itzá. Someday he will return with *our brothers in work*," the ancient forefathers who built the ceremonial cities of their land.

CHAPTER X

THE AZTEC ARRIVAL

In 1978, workers digging a trench for electrical cable just northeast of the cathedral at the heart of Mexico City unearthed a stone disc carving of the Aztec goddess Coyolxauhqui—moon goddess, daughter of Coatlicue, and sister of Huitzilopochtli. The discovery triggered a decision to excavate the entire site, leading to the unearthing of remnants of the Aztec *Templo Mayor* (Great Temple). Walking along the *Calle Seminario*, I find myself on a railed path around an open pit, within which lie the foundations and fragments of this focal point of the Aztec capital city, Tenochtitlán. I look down upon the S-shaped curling serpent, frozen in his tracks, and then across to a silent, solemn parade of stone figures staring into the past from a place the Aztecs believed was the center of the world.

When most of us think of ancient Mexican civilizations, naturally the Aztecs come to mind. But long before the Aztec nation came to power, the beating heart of Tula controlled the ebb and flow of peoples throughout ancient Mesoamerica. The eventual decline of Tula led many of its inhabitants to head eastward toward Mayaland. Attracted to the lake-studded, verdant Basin of Mexico, where the gargantuan metropolis of Mexico City now sprawls, the Chichimec and other tribes from barren northern regions penetrated the promising territory of *Anáhuac*, "Near the Water." At first threatening the remaining Toltecs, the Chichimec seem to have gradually and inevitably adapted their more sedentary way of life and *Nahuatl* tongue.

Anáhuac evolved into a vast, densely populated region of militant, competing city-states, including Tenayuca, Culhuacán, Atzcopotzalco, Xochimilco, and Texcoco. Joining this unstable, factionalized network—perhaps emigrating originally from an island in the Pacific Ocean off what is now the northwestern state of Nayarit—came a group of nomads, "unwelcome squatters." These were the precursors of the people who have become known today as the mighty Aztecs.[1]

How ironic that the most flagrantly imperialistic Mesoamerican nation of all, the quintessential "tribute empire" most familiar to our modern popular imagination, was an "uncouth…upstart latecomer on the scene."[2] "Why must the Mexican archetype be only Aztec, and not Mayan or Zapotec or

Templo Mayor, Mexico City
LEFT: *Serpent, Aztec Templo Mayor, Mexico City*

Tarascan or Otomí?" asks Octavio Paz, echoing the sentiments of advocates for a corrective to Mexican history seeking to redress what we might call the "Aztec-centric" bias.[3]

"It is a mistake to study the totality of Meso-american civilization from the *Nahua* point of view (and, worse, from that of its Aztec version)," Paz insists, "because that totality is older, richer, and far more diverse."[4]

The reasons for this imbalance are simple. In the first place, once the Aztecs were settled and entrenched, they set about to destroy whatever chronicles of formative history remained, recasting and legitimizing the story of their heritage in rosier terms. As I described earlier in the story, the Aztecs obliterated all references to their itinerant past, much preferring to claim direct lineage with Toltec "high culture."[5]

The odyssey of the Aztec people

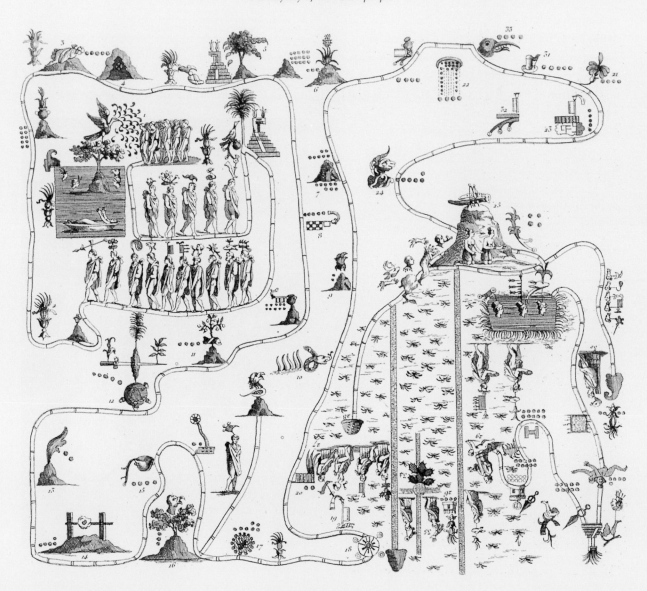

And secondly, by the time the Spaniards arrived in the sixteenth century, the resplendent Aztec version of history was accepted by the conquistadors as gospel. "The Toltecs were truly wise/They conversed with their own hearts" wrote an Aztec scribe in a typical mode of intense identification. He could have been speaking of his own people when he testified, "They guarded the songs in their memories/They deified them in their hearts."[6]

Even understanding that the Aztecs were sophisticated revisionists, their origin stories still appeal to us. The powerful images add permanence to Plumed Serpent as an entrenched being in Mexican folklore.[7]

According to the postconquest history books *Crónicas Mexicana* and *Mexicayotl* (adapted by Hernando Alvarado Tezozómoc in 1878 from *Nahuatl* accounts),[8] the Aztec tribes were precariously led early in their southward journey toward Anáhuac by a shaman named Malinalxóchitl, earthly sister of the god Huitzilopochtli. As Lord of the Sun and Lord of War, he finally had to intercede, warning the wanderers that they would eventually have to rule "by force of arms, not by witchcraft."

Huitzilopochtli set a bellicose tone that became the Aztec way of life: "My orders will be carried out in countries everywhere, and I will stand guard at distant borders to protect the people…glorifying the name of the Mexican nation.… *I will have it all.*"[9]

By the latter part of the thirteenth century, the travelers reached a hilly, wooded area that I visited, now called the Park of Chapultepec ("Grasshopper Hill") on the western edge of Mexico City. They resided there for a generation, "surrounded by strange nations who wished them ill and were only waiting for bad luck to catch up with them." When neighboring leaders conspired to evict the newcomers, the patron god Huitzilopochtli once again reminded his people of their ultimate goal: to become "masters of their own home."

And among the reed grasses—*intollihtic*

The eagle on the prickly pear, Book of the Gods and Rites

inacaitlice, "in the middle of the rushes" — by the shores of Lake Texcoco, east of Chapultepec, the great god's prophecy was at last fulfilled: "*This* is Mexico, *this* is Tenochtitlán, where the eagle screams, spreads his wings, and eats, where the fish flies, where the snake is devoured," whispered Huitzilopochtli, leaning close to the ear of the high priest Quauhcóatl (Eagle-Serpent), speaking to him in a dream. "This is the place. This is Mexico, this is Tenochtitlán. And many things will be done."[10]

The name Mexico comes from the Nahua *met-ztli-xic-co* ("place of the navel of the moon") or *me-xic-co* ("place of the navel of the agave [cactus])." Tenochtitlán is "the place of the cactus (*nochtli*) on the stone (*tetl*)." Hearing Huitzilopochtli's words, "The council of wise men wept with relief and gratitude, realizing they had finally arrived at their rightful home, 'So our town is to be here, therefore, since we have seen those things that Huitzilopochtli told us of.... At last we have been worthy of our god. We are favored. We are blessed.'"[11]

The vision of a noble eagle perched upon a *nochtli* prickly pear cactus at the edge of the water, "punching holes in his serpent prey," has survived to this day as the symbol on the seal of the Republic of Mexico.[12]

When the eagle saw the Aztecs approaching from the distance, he bowed majestically to them. His nest was of precious quetzal feathers, and scattered on the ground at the foot of the cactus — presaging, perhaps, the Aztecs' bloody future — were the bones and remains of all the unfortunate lesser birds this mighty predator had vanquished and killed.

The first temple to be built at the center of Tenochtitlán was an *ayauhcalli*, an oratory consecrated to the public and declamatory worship of Huitzilopochtli. Facing west into the setting sun, it rose upon the same spot where the Aztec patron god had first pointed to the eagle and cactus. Later on, by the sixteenth century, as the small island of Teno-

Aztec Plumed Serpent

chtitlán was gradually expanded and fortified with wooden stakes and mud, two additional towers were placed in the configuration, defining the triangulated leadership of the Aztec pantheon: Tlaloc's temple, He of the Rains, stood just to the left of Huitzilopochtli's. These two edifices were mounted via side-by-side staircases protected at their bases by huge, smiling serpent heads "with single fangs and bifid tongues."

Across the Templo Mayor plaza, at the point of union precisely opposing the notch between the two temple roof combs, once stood the eastward-facing round tower of Éhecatl-Quetzalcóatl. Sixty steps led to the platform under its conical pointed apex, composed of concentric tiered layers "constructed to look for all the world like a throned figure with a distinct head." The entrance to the temple was

Aztec man-serpent

"wide and low, like the mouth of an oven. In order to enter, it was necessary to stoop low."[13] The faint traces of its circular foundation are still visible in the excavated and partially restored Templo Mayor group just northeast of the Metropolitan Cathedral on the Plaza de la Constitución.

Here, too, at discreet distances parallel to Huitzilopochtli and Tlaloc, edifices once stood in tribute to Quetzalcóatl's powerful Toltec alter ego and evil twin, the trickster Tezcatlipoca.[14]

Quetzalcóatl was the patron saint of the *calmécac*, the school where novitiate priests were trained to follow in his sacred ways. From the serpent's-mouth doorway at the summit of the Temple of Éhecatl-Quetzalcóatl, "his priests greeted the new day by blowing on conch shells" and then beat

drums in a steady tattoo as the sun rose, "to mark the triumphant revival of the turquoise prince, the soaring eagle," Xiuhcóatl.[15]

Even though Huitzilopochtli might have epitomized Aztec bellicosity, Quetzalcóatl maintained his role as redemptive hero in the delicate balance among the gods. At the festival of the winter solstice, for example, Quetzalcóatl priests prepared a likeness of Huitzilopochtli out of maize seeds kneaded with penitential drops of blood into a dough. His bones were fashioned with acacia wood. This effigy was set upon the main altar of the Temple of Quetzalcóatl, whereupon one of the priests would hurl a flint-tipped dart into the breast of the dough-god, piercing it: "This was called killing the god Huitzilopochtli so that his body might be eaten."[16]

Starting with the election of their first kings, the Aztecs reinforced the created tradition of Toltec ascendancy, invoking to each new ruler the "fateful warning" that had been an integral part of that earlier nation's investiture ceremony: "Remember, this is not your throne. *It is only lent to you.* One day it will be returned to Quetzalcóatl, to whom it truly belongs."[17]

As Aztec cosmology evolved through three centuries, Plumed Serpent's older characteristics were preserved and emphasized, while new ones added different nuances to his personality. The careful layout of the Tenochtitlán temple complex showed the familiar, intimate relationship between Quetzalcóatl as wind-god, "bringing the violent gusts" and Tlaloc, with the heavy downpours that were his province.

One of the earliest traceable Aztec myths called Plumed Serpent by another name, *Yahualli Éhecatl*, Nahua for "the wheel of the winds." This title might have had earlier roots in northwestern Mexico—the *Occidente* region of Nayarit, Jalisco, and Colima— even before the Chichimecs and Aztecs began the southward trek toward their eventual homeland.

During the last twenty-five years, there have been other notable discoveries in this remote and underappreciated area of Mexico: circular plaza complexes of round, stepped temples and shaft tombs made with mortared stones coated with lime plaster dating from between 1000 and 300 B.C.; and ceramic artifacts and incised panels with bird-serpentine designs representing a "proto-*Éhecatl*" god fashioned in the period A.D. 200–700.[18]

The wind-god identity as an important facet of Plumed Serpent gained momentum in a version of the Aztec creation story in which Ometeotl ("lord of the duality") made a divine couple in the rarefied air of the Thirteenth Heaven. These two new gods, named *Tonacatecuhtli* and *Tonacacihuatl*, brought the last and best of their four sons—Quetzalcóatl—to life by combining their breaths and separating the waters of heaven from the waters of the earth. "And this is why the *breath* of the creators is also *Éhecatl*, god of wind."[19]

Many rounded, caracol-shaped temples, consecrated to Quetzalcóatl, dot Mesoamerica; their design, which imitates the resting pose of the snake's body, permits his unobstructed passage—the

Quetzalcóatl as the Monkey, "El Mono"

"circling hero" whirls by, a restless vortex, into and out of the four cardinal points of the compass.[20]

In the late 1950s in a cave near the village of San Cristobal Ecatepec in the state of Mexico, an almost-obliterated fresco mural in the Aztec style was discovered depicting Quetzalcóatl-as-Éhecatl within a peaked, round temple bearing a striking resemblance to the structure consecrated to his name at Tenochtitlán. The *hombre-dios* appears to have a fleshless body. In one hand, he presents his familiar copal pouch, and in the other he holds maguey thorns for penitent self-mutilation.[21]

Not confined to anthropomorphic and serpentine manifestations, Éhecatl also appeared as a monkey, *El Mono*, wearing a beaklike headdress and standing with slightly bent knees in the transformation-readiness pose we first noticed in the Olmec shaman. To the Aztecs *El Mono* presented the less benign, more destructive character of the wind god. The monkey could be capricious and unpredictable ("*más impredecible*") in his behavior: entertaining, gentle, and domesticated one moment, aggressive and wild the next.

At Cuicuilco ("the place of singing and dancing"), in the area known as the Pedregal—once a volcanic desert, now the site of the University of Mexico in southern Mexico City—a preclassic-period round temple 440 feet in diameter has been dated to between 500 B.C. and A.D. 200. At Calixtlahuaca, ("the house on the plain"), forty-five miles northwest of Mexico City, there stands a round Temple of Quetzalcóatl built and rebuilt no less than four times over a twelve-hundred-year span, from approximately A.D. 300 to 1500; it reflects architectural and iconographic influences spanning from Teotihuacán to this site's eventual destruction by Aztec invaders.[22]

At Malinalco, sixty-six miles southwest of Mexico City, stands the Temple of the Eagle and Jaguar Knights, a circular building carved into the mountainside. Its mouth-doorway entrance, a split ser-pent's head with doubled tongue on the floor, repre-sents Tepeyolotl, the venerated Earth Serpent traced to the time of the Olmecs and even earlier.[23]

At Tamuín, in the southeastern section of the state of San Luis Potosí, about 150 miles due north of Mexico City, Quetzalcóatl-as-Éhecatl was a major figure among the Huasteca peoples who flourished there during the early post-Classic era. "Their characteristic architectural style [is] notable for its many circular structures."[24]

Farther afield lies testimony to Quetzalcóatl's stay-ing power in so many cultures: Zempoala ("the place of twenty waters") on the Gulf Coast, twenty-two miles from Veracruz. It was built by the Totonac peo-ples during the last ripples of the Toltec incursion in the thirteenth century A.D. On the western side of its main plaza is a temple consecrated to Éhecatl that features a semicircular annex at the rear.[25]

According to Aztec legend, the world had been destroyed four times before the creation of the World of the Fifth Sun, *Nahui Ollin*, containing the World of Man within which the Aztecs lived. It was envisioned as a multilayered complex, "a house, a cube, a pyramid, or a cakelike structure of many lay-ers": celestial sky above, terrestrial waters and land masses, and the underworld beneath. These were balanced laterally by "four segments" on the earth's surface, corresponding to the four points of the com-pass. As noted earlier, most of the earthly work of creation fell upon Quetzalcóatl, by decision of the gods gathered at Teotihuacán.[26]

In order to cause the "immobile" new Sun to move through the heavens, the Teotihuacán gods decided to offer their own divine blood. But this self-sacrifice was insufficient to slake "the Sun's ravenous thirst. That is why humans, following the example of the gods, had to sacrifice themselves." And, consequently, according to the rationalization of the Aztecs, that is why man had no choice but to go to war.[27]

The structure and hierarchy of the World of the Fifth Sun, which we still inhabit today, reflects the physical nature of its creator, Plumed Serpent. It is a place where space and time are joined in the same way that the soaring bird—who inhabits the three dimensions of the heavens—and the crawling snake—who inhabits the two dimensions of the earth—appeared together upon the prickly pair cac-tus, marking the place the Aztecs first called home.

The visual sign of the bird consuming the snake also appears dramatically in the preconquest Mayan *Dresden Codex*, where, from the gaping chest of a silently screaming sacrificial victim, the "Tree of the Middle Place" shoots up, supporting the bird in its topmost branches. Joseph Campbell interprets this as an image of renewal. The snake unraveling from the head of the bound victim is his soul, transformed into "a life in the spirit of the next secular age."[28]

Faith in this "Eternal Return," images of perpetu-ation, time rolling forward, and snakelike cycles shedding their skin are, by now, familiar characteris-tics in Mesoamerican spiritual thought. And while the clearly etched example from the *Dresden Codex* makes this return seem salutary—or at least promis-es transcendence of agony in the life to come—most often Aztec "suffering is to be imputed to the divine will, whether as directly intervening to produce it, or as permitting other forces, demonic or divine, to provoke it."[29]

Regardless of what ultimate fate or warrior immortality as a *quauhtecatl*, "companion of the sun," might be waiting in the upper levels of heav-en, the Mexica believed that in everyday life they were all "prisoners of the omnipotent signs." Their present world was created out of four prior cata-clysms, and so only cataclysmic occurrences, daily cascades of hearts and human blood, *chalchíuatl*, allowed them to move forward.

Some day, they prophesied, even the current World of the Fifth Sun will exist no more.[30]

CHAPTER XI

QUETZALCŌATL'S MANY FACES

*I sing the pictures of the book
and see them spread out;
I am an elegant bird
for I make the books speak
within the house of pictures.*
— ANONYMOUS NAHUATL POET[1]

*The metaphors of the feather, the flower,
the gem, with here and there a flash
of water and sun, leave us dazzled.
The mythical allusions,
perhaps deliberately hidden,
and the prophetic phrases
envelop us in their mystery.
The sensibility of [the Aztec] people was keen;
it ranged from tenderness to violence,
moved quickly from laughter to tears,
and revealed itself in a wealth
of exquisite detail.*
— ALFONSO REYES,
The Native Poetry of New Spain

We probe the earliest stories of these Aztecs, island people of mythical *Aztlán*, "place of herons," in search of explanations for their divided nature: cruel and brutal in war, yet so refined and lyrical in the arts.[2] Some legends speak of a primal birthplace deep within seven caves on the island. Others say that the Aztecs, like all their Indian brethren, first emerged from subterranean springs.

Whatever elements formed them, the Aztecs were "the last to leave the caves, by divine command."[3] The exact path they took, bearing Huitzilopochtli's standard to their ultimate home in Mexico-Tenochtitlán, will never be known. Along the way they suffered all manner of natural and supernatural tribulations: war and plague and drought and storm.

The defining theme emerges: triumph over adversity. In barren places inhabited only by vipers, the Aztecs built temples and cultivated fields as they moved toward their ultimate dwelling place by the lake. Over centuries of such progress, the Aztecs accumulated a kind of "chosen people" mentality. "Fairy-tale miracles" infiltrated their history, all the while bolstered by Huitzilopochtli's recurrent promises to succeeding kings who incarnated him that one day all the enemies of the Aztecs would fall.[4]

This self-fulfilling martial prophecy was reinforced at its other extreme by a cultural imperialism dominated by Quetzalcóatl, "the singing master, the teacher of the screenfold scribe," whose "heart lives in the painted page" and who "sings the royal fibers of the book."[5] The legacy of Huitzilopochtli was success in conflict. The gift of Quetzalcóatl—not so much given as appropriated by the Aztecs— was *toltecayotl*: successful craftsmanship in writing and the plastic arts, epitomized by their Toltec precursors.

The Spanish conquistadores were surprised to find many libraries in Mexico—*amoxcalli*, the Nahua called them ("houses of books"). There were three major archives in central Mexico, one in Tenochtitlán and the others in Texcoco and Cholula. All were razed by Tlaxcalan allies of the invading Spanish in retribution against the Aztec oppressors. The unfortunate reality is that only two ritual-calendrical manuscripts from the Central Mexico region bear attributes of preconquest style, and even their dating and provenance are still unclear.

However, pictorial manuscript art was produced in postconquest "New Spain" under the patronage of the conquerors, largely to satisfy the "insatiable curiosity" of the literati back home. These took the form, as we shall see, of "commissioned investigations" into the lives of subjugated Indians. Twenty-one of the most important of these works survive, and Quetzalcóatl in all of his aspects is a noticeable visual personality throughout: as a culture bearer uniting the arts of song and painting, and as a craftsman "casting things as if they were gold" (in the *Codex Vienna*).[6] dressed in full regalia, complete with conical jaguar-skin hat, plumed headdress, body painted black, face painted with a wind design, on his back an array of "flaring red macaw feathers," and white sandals on his feet (in the *Codex Telleriano-Remensis*);[7] as a wandering divinity of the morning star, revered sky bearer, the heavens resting upon his shoulders (in the *Borgia Codex* group); as soul carrier, comrade to the noble dead, surrounded by ritual objects (in the *Codex Borbonicus*).[8]

Returning home from an expeditionary trip to what would eventually be named New Spain,

a judge in the Spanish colony of Darien reported that he had met [an Indian] fugitive from the interior provinces of the West [perhaps Aztec territory]. This man, seeing the judge reading, started with surprise. He asked, through interpreters, "You also have books? You also understand the signs by which you talk to the absent?" [The Indian] examined the book which the judge was studying and saw that the letters were not the same as those signs to which he was used.[9]

Indeed, the "fugitive" would not yet have understood the role of written words within a book. These embellishments came later, when Spanish friars with quill pens and parchment sat down with Nahua elders and debriefed them for weeks and months on end. Assuming the "fugitive" had even been permitted a glimpse inside a screenfold document from his village, he would have seen only a series of pictures. Aztec society was by no means an environment where universal literacy held sway. Reading and writing were the province of an "elite minority, consisting of hereditary rulers with their priests and scribes."

Aztec historical tradition was closely held and portrayed in a manner favorable to the king. Whatever statements came forth from the king were de facto the truth. Only the painting of the mouth of a king could be accompanied by special flowery spirals, *volutas floridas*, signifying sacred songs authorized by his "supernatural descent." His version of history—substantiated by corresponding long-past dates marked on the wheel of time—was gospel.[10]

It was written in the *Libro de los Colloquios* (*The Book of Conversations*): "They who have in their power/the black and red ink, the paintings,/They lead us, they guide us,/they show us the way." The *Cantares Mexicanos* praise "the wise man," with his

*light, a torch, a stout torch
that does not smoke.
His are the black and red inks, his are the
illustrated manuscripts.
He himself is writing, and wisdom.*[11]

The tantalizing notion that the Aztecs were "the last to leave the caves" helps us understand the marginal survival of their *cuicatl*—"songs, hymns, and poetry"—and at the same time the multitude of problems thwarting a legitimate, untainted appreciation of that poetry—and Quetzalcóatl's presence within it.

Their late arrival on the Mesoamerican cultural landscape, relative to other nations, exposed the Aztecs to the Spanish with devastating results. That same sustained interaction with the conquering culture meant that more of their burned pages of poetry were destined to rise again, phoenixlike, although in corrupted ways.[12]

Up to a specific point in their growth as a nation, what we call Aztec literature was an oral tradition, "cued" or "prompted" with the aid of picture books, rigorously studied in the *calmécac* priestly schools and passed down in ritualized memory from generation to generation. The rupture of the Conquest caused a shift in the manner in which this literary tradition was maintained. It was no longer the sole property of the indigenous peoples. It was appropriated by a European culture with its own ingrained way of representing the past.

In defeat the Aztecs built up a history designed to ennoble and legitimize them in their own eyes and, by extension, in the eyes of the Spanish. The decimation of the Aztec people only reinforced their nostalgic desire to be remembered as a dominant force. Even the lime-washed leaves of the sacred codices themselves, in some instances, were covertly "whited out" and then repainted in a desperate effort to cast ignominious events in a more favorable light.[13]

RIGHT: *Quetzalcóatl, (upper left quadrant)* Codex Telleriano-Remensis *(detail)*

Quetzalcoatl.

Capitulo quinto. fo ibidem.

Chicome coatl. es otra diosa ceres

Capitulo septimo. fo. 3.

Cioacoatl.

Capitulo sexto. fo ibidem.

Teteu inna.

Capitulo octauo, fo, ibidem.

The Mexican historian Alfonso Reyes, one of the founding modernist members of the *Ateneo de la Juventud*—a group of upstart social philosophers who began to publish during the first decade of the Mexican Revolution—took a bleak view of the situation in his passionate essays, *Vision of Anahuac* and *Native Poetry of New Spain*. Much of the Aztec "autochthonous [indigenous] poetry…has been irreparably lost," Reyes declared mournfully. In the threatening atmosphere of the Conquest,

this poetry, transmitted by word of mouth, took refuge in the remotest regions; it disappeared or was dissembled by the last bards or priests…it took on a conspiratorial air [against] the engulfing wave of history.… Without a doubt, the Church took a hand in the act of reducing these poems to the Latin alphabet … [and] forbade them to be recited in public, or censored them.[14]

Yet even Alfonso Reyes permitted an ephemeral ray of relief to invade his melancholy frustration: he compared it to straining to hear a symphony by only being allowed to scan the score. He began to read the poems and tease forth their meaning, "restored *a posteriori*, after [they] had ceased to exist, as when the blurred letters of a palimpsest are made legible… blended with authentic texts predating the Conquest and with others of subsequent origin."

He could not help detecting within the stanzas of the *cuicatl* poems, despite the lingering, pernicious odor of Spanish contamination, "traces of an old, unmistakable aroma giving evidence of a non-European aesthetic content and sentience which makes it possible to surmise its flavor."[15]

Let us taste for ourselves.

"Song to the Giver of Life"

Do men have roots, are they real?
No one can know completely
what is Your richness, what are Your flowers,
oh Inventor of Yourself!

We leave things unfinished.
For this I weep,
I lament.
Here with flowers I interweave my friends.
Let us rejoice!
Our common house is the earth.
In the place of mystery, beyond,
is it also like this?
Truly, it is not the same.
On earth: flowers and songs.
Let us live here!

Romances de los Señores de la Nueva Espana, Poesía Nahuatl [16]

Although not about this poem exclusively, Alfonso Reyes's observations on the Nahua lyric were apt:

In the poems designed to be sung at banquets and gatherings [such as this one, we see], the ever-recurring theme of how fleeting is life, and the urgency of enjoying it before death snatches it away…the enigma of death and that which has been so rightly called the emptiness of the heart.…These are emotions which have never been the exclusive possession of any one people, and Mexican poetry merely shares, when it voices them, the bread that is the patrimony of all men.[17]

This is why the "flower" is such a central image in Aztec pictorial writing—sometimes it represents ephemeral speech, at others a sign of the nature of human life: temporary, beautiful, delicate, subject to the "weather" of the gods' whims.

[Poem sung at Teotihuacán cremation rite]

Thus the dead were addressed,
when they died.
If it was a man, they spoke to him,
invoked him as a divine being,
in the name of a pheasant;
if it was a woman, in the name of an owl;

and they said to them:
"Awaken, already the sky is tinged with red,
already the dawn has come,
already the flame-colored pheasants are singing,
the fire-colored swallows,
already butterflies are on the wing."
For this reason the ancient ones said,
he who has died, he becomes a god.
They said: "He became a god there,"
which means that he died.

Codice Matritense [Madrid Codex] de la Real
Academia de la Historia[18]

A subtle, later meaning of Teotihuacán as
"dwelling-place of the gods" (the site where the
gods convened to create man within his new world)
is "the place where men *become* gods" in the
sense that death, as movement into the next world,
was signaled by transformation. This poem
promises the transformation of a human into a
bird. Poised to join others already flying, the ashes
of the dead will drift upward. This either/or state
between being and becoming was a favorite
theme throughout Mesoamerica, from the
Olmec shaman onward.

"Song XX"

The Toltecs have been taken, alas, the book of
their souls has come to an end, alas, everything
of the Toltecs has reached its conclusion, no
longer do I care to live there.
Who will take me? Who will go with me? I am
ready to be taken, alas. All that was fresh, the
perfume, my flowers, my songs, have gone along
with them.
Great is my affliction, weighty is my burden; I
write out a new song concerning it, that some
time I may speak it where I shall go, a song to
be known when I shall leave the earth, that my
soul shall live after I have gone from here, that
my fame shall live fresh in memory.

I cried aloud, I looked about, I reflected how I
might see the root of song, that I might plant it
here on the earth, and that then it should make
my soul to live. The sweet exhalations of the
lovely flowers rose up uniting with our flowers;
one hears them growing as my song buds forth,
filled with my words our flowers stand upright
in the waters.
But the flowers depart, their sweetness is divided
and exhales, the fragrant poyomatl [rose] rains
down its leaves where I the poet walk in sadness.

Cantares Mexicanos[19]

The trailblazing Dr. Daniel G. Brinton, translator
of "Song XX," was the earliest interpreter of Nahuatl
poetry, well before the turn of the century. In the
introduction to *Ancient Nahuatl Poetry*, part of his
Library of Aboriginal American Literature, long out
of print, he wrote,

There is a large body of Nahuatl literature yet
unpublished.... The Nahuatl tongue is one of
the most highly developed on the American
continent, [and] it is greatly to be desired that
all this material should be at the command of
students. The Nahuatl, moreover, is not a diffi-
cult tongue.... I should say it is easier to acquire
than German, its grammar being simple and
regular, and its sounds soft and sonorous.[20]

Because Brinton came early to Aztec translation,
his versions were subject to sharp criticism by later
linguists such as Eduard Seler, who called them
"all-too-sweeping" and rife with "philological
errors." But the German emigré anthropologist and
ethnopoetic writer Margot Astrov leaped to Brinton's
defense, including several of his translations in her
1946 anthology, *The Winged Serpent: American
Indian Prose and Poetry*. Comparing Brinton's texts
with "literal" renditions of the ancient poems, she
found that he had "caught the atmosphere of this
unique literature almost to perfection."[21]

The poem eloquently sings of the Aztec sentiment toward the legendary land of Tula. We can imagine the lamentations of "Song XX" coming directly from the great scribe Plumed Serpent himself as he regrets the loss of his beloved city. A classic example of Aztec "departure oration," "Song XX" also resonates with Plumed Serpent's identity because the day named *Ce Cóatl* ("one serpent") was a propitious one for the commencement of a journey, *cóatl* being another word for "road" in Nahua.[22]

"Hymn to Xipe Totec Iouallauan"

You, drinker in the night,
Why do you insist on praying?
Don your disguise.
Put on your garment of gold.
Oh, my god, your precious-jewelled water
has descended;
he has become transformed, the tall cypress,
into a quetzal-bird;
the serpent of fire
has been transformed into a serpent of quetzal.
The serpent of fire has set me free.
Perhaps I shall vanish,
perhaps I shall vanish and be destroyed, I,
the tender corn shoot.
My heart is green
like a precious jewel,
but I shall yet see the gold
and shall rejoice if the war chief
has matured, if he has been born.

Historia general de las cosas de Nueva Espana[23]

Xipe Totec ("our Lord the flayed one") was the Aztec god of fertility. This poem was recited at the *Tlacaxipehualiztli* ("flaying") festival in the central plaza at Tenochtitlán, a nighttime ritual customarily performed at the end of February, just before sowing, to ensure a rich harvest.[24]

Prisoners were first sacrificed in the traditional manner: their hearts were ripped out and their blood offered as nourishment to the gods. Then, in the vivid symbolism of the necessary renewal of all life, their skins (the "disguise," the "garment" of the first stanza) were stripped from their bodies and worn by the priests like shawls.

Thus garbed, dancing through the courtyards by torchlight, the priests showed that the flesh of the tender maize shoot—the split-tongue of the serpent—would burst through its dried husk "skin." As sure as night followed day, the water serpent would follow the fire serpent. The rain would follow the sun. Golden maize would follow the planting, and all men would be fed.

The priests danced thus for twenty days following the flaying ceremony and distributed cakes of uncooked maize and honey tortillas to the people. At the conclusion of the dancing phase, the skins of the flayed ones were displayed on straw mats in the central plaza, and "everyone paid tribute with song in the center of the city."[25]

[Excerpt from poem to be recited every eight years, when maize is given new youth]

down here on earth
*   you rise in the market place and say*
I am the lord Quetzalcóatl

let there be gladness among the flowering trees
*   and the quechol-bird tribes*
who are the souls of the brave

may they rejoice
*   hear the word of our lord*
the quechol-bird's word

'your brother whom we mourn
*   will never be killed again*
never again will the poison dart strike him'

maize flowers
        white and yellow
I have brought from the flower place

see there is the lord of the jewel land
        playing ball in his old field

there he is the old dog god
                                Xólotl

Cantares Mexicanos[26]

Xólotl was one of Plumed Serpent's several *nagualli*, or animal alter egos—Quetzalcóatl as dog-headed god, descending Venuslike into the underworld of Mictlán to find the bones of the dead and fashion a new race of men out of them. Here the death aspect of Plumed Serpent comes into play in the strictly dualist world of the Aztecs: this identity is relevant here because the poem celebrates a hiatus in the "persecution" or "killing" of the maize plant.

"As we troubled our food to death, thus we revived it," the native informants told Bernardino de Sahagún, pausing in the consumption of their staple food so that it would have an opportunity to be reborn.[27]

CHAPTER XII

THE LIFE CYCLE OF A MYTH

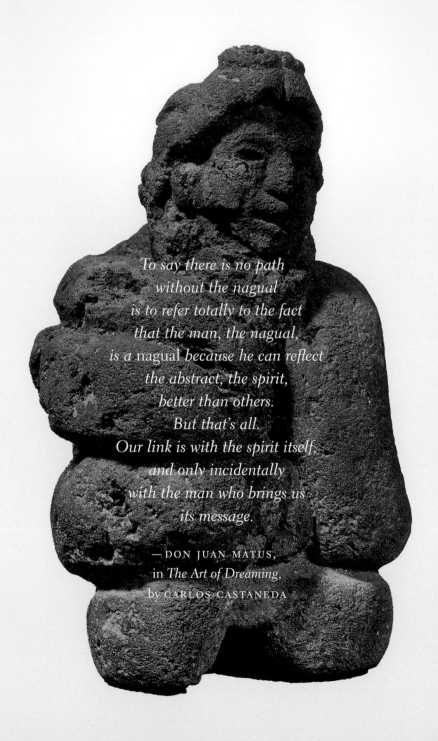

To say there is no path
without the nagual
is to refer totally to the fact
that the man, the nagual,
is a nagual because he can reflect
the abstract, the spirit,
better than others.
But that's all.
Our link is with the spirit itself,
and only incidentally
with the man who brings us
its message.

—DON JUAN MATUS,
in *The Art of Dreaming*,
by CARLOS CASTANEDA

The *nagual* helps us understand who Plumed Serpent was and what he represented in Aztec thought and culture at the eve of the Spanish Conquest.

The *nagual* is the intimate connection of a man with the fate of his personal, magical animal kindred, his "totem." It has been traced back to the Olmec shaman astride his grinning, flying jaguar, and probably existed in prior, as-yet-undocumented Mesoamerican societies. The *nagual* began as a man's "familiar" ally in the animal world, expressing the holistic belief that every thing, every phenomenon on earth was animately fused on a continuum with every other thing.[1]

The *nagual* expanded beyond being a simple alter ego or partner to the man. It could perform a role as protective guardian or companion when the man was tested in moral or religious ways. It could be his mask, or advance "cover" shield, as, through hallucinations brought on by *peyote* or ritual bleeding, he pushed toward the spirit realm.

Ultimately, the *nagual* was the *dios* (god) within the psyche of the *hombre* (man). The Aztec priestly cult recognized this connection when they named themselves after Quetzalcóatl.

The ways that the god Quetzalcóatl was depicted by the Aztecs in sculpture and in the codices is the strongest evidence of his enduring nagualism. Beyond his twin brother *Xólotl*, the dog, and, of course, the snake, Quetzalcóatl derived his protean

Quetzalcóatl hombre merged with his serpent nagual

power from a variety of denizens of the animal kingdom. At the nape of his neck, Quetzalcóatl might wear a bunch of feathers; around the front, a necklace of jaguar's teeth. He bore the jaguar pelt or cloak, representing the stars of the night sky drawn away each morning by Venus. His conical hat (*copilli*) was divided into dark and light parts, "the former sometimes a jaguar skin." The hat was bordered by cactus spines, instruments of bloodletting.[2]

His earplugs and pendants were twisted shells and his pectoral (breastplate) a conch shell, cut transversely to reveal its inner spiral shape, like the eye of a storm or the coils of a snake. This decoration was called *éhecailacacozcátl*, "the necklace of the whirlwind." As Éhecatl, Plumed Serpent could be a monkey wearing a bird-beak mask; or his body might be helical, a snake contorted upon itself.[3]

In the Aztec/Central Mexican tradition at the time of the Conquest, Plumed Serpent's mythic-historical "biography" as creator, Venus god, wind god, culture hero, historical figure, fertility deity, and, always, the only member of the pantheon to assume a human shape encompassed six major "chapters."[4]

He was born in a miraculous way: by some accounts, when his goddess-mother swallowed a piece of jade; in other versions, at the convergence of the breath of the gods. In his youth he sought and retrieved the bones of his ancestors (some said of his father only) and restored human life to the world of the newest sun. Plumed Serpent's enthronement and apogee was "beneficent and theocratic." This dimension became the model for the "chaste and penitent [Aztec] arch-priest" as well as for the "patron of crops."[5]

When the wiles of Tezcatlipoca brought his downfall at Tula, Plumed Serpent as "culture bringer" temporarily lost his heroic status and was forced to take flight. The goal for the journey was nearly always portrayed as Tlillan Tlapallán to the east, with Cholula the most frequently cited "way-stop." Finally came death or disappearance, the fiery transformation of Plumed Serpent's soul into the planet Venus.

The *quequetzalcoa*, "high priests" in Tenochtitlán, maintained the age-old tradition of the *nagual* by assuming the name of their romanticized Toltec precursor. His "fully anthropomorphic form" was linked with his own *nagual*, the "feathered ophidian alter-ego," Plumed Serpent, as well as with a host of other real and imaginary animals added over many centuries.[6]

RIGHT: *Quetzalcóatl as God of Wind*, Éhecatl, Codex Borgia

BELOW: *Quetzalcóatl in penitent blood-drawing pose*, Florentine Codex

In the eyes of the Quetzalcóatl priests, their namesake was the founder of their religion. They were his representatives on earth, "sealed with him forever in sanctity." Their mode of conduct was "supposed to be perfect in all customs, exercises and doctrines. They lived chastely and virtuously, humbly and pacifically, comporting themselves with prudence and tact."[7]

In their spartan *calmécac* schools, a "regime of austerity" dominated. Here, Quetzalcóatl priests trained the *teteuctin*, sons of the elite nobility, in the ways of self-discipline to prepare them for the patron Plumed Serpent's embrace. At night, praying and offering incense to the gods, the young princes used their own bodies as sacrificial altars, drawing blood from legs and ears with agave thorns.[8]

Not every prince was destined to be only a warrior. Some likewise became poets. The prolific Nezahualcóyotl, King of Texcoco, inherited some of the prophetic qualities known to be possessed by serpents. "The sweet-voiced quetzal," he wrote, "there, ruling the earth, has intoxicated my soul,"

I am like the quetzal bird, I am created in the one and only God; I sing sweet songs among the flowers; I chant songs and rejoice in my heart.
The fuming dewdrops from the flowers in the fields intoxicate my soul.
I grieve to myself that ever this dwelling on earth should end.
I foresaw, being a Mexican, that our rule began to be destroyed. I went forth weeping that it was to bow down and be destroyed.
Let me not be angry that the grandeur of Mexico is to be destroyed.
The smoking stars [comets] gather against it; the one who cares for flowers is about to be destroyed.
He who cared for books wept, he wept for the beginning of the destruction.[9]

CHAPTER XIII

FIRST CONTACT

En el 1-Caña nacio Quetzalcóatl
"se cuenta que este año nacio Quetzalcóatl …"
Había prometido volver en al año de su nombre, un 1-Caña,
y el 1-Caña cayó precisamente en 1519,
el año de la llegada de Cortés.
    …Dudaron si tal vez con el capitán Hernando Cortés
        hubiese llegado Quetzalcóatl…
Y porque Moctezuma tenía una mala conciencia.
El imperio había traicionado la doctrina de Quetzalcóatl.…
Un viento cortante como la obsidiana sopló con la conquista.
Pero
    teníanen sus corazones que volvería
    a tomar otra vez su estera, su trono
        El Quetzalcóatl Liberador.

In the year 1-Reed, Quetzalcóatl was born
"it is said that Quetzalcóatl was born this year …"
He'd promised to return in the year of his name, a 1-Reed
and 1-Reed fell precisely in 1519,
the year Cortés arrived.
    …They wondered if perhaps in Hernando Cortés
        Quetzalcóatl had arrived.…
And because Moctezuma had a bad conscience.
The empire had betrayed the doctrine of Quetzalcóatl.…
A wind sharp as obsidian blew with the conquest.
But
    they believed in their hearts that he would return
    to take again his mat, his throne.
        Quetzalcóatl the Liberator.

ERNESTO CARDENAL, *Quetzalcóatl*

The omens began a decade before the Spanish soldiers arrived and were recalled during the 1550s in the vivid *Cantares Mexicanos* and other history songs and performances by the surviving Mexica peoples.

First, a comet shaped like a giant ear of corn began burning in the eastern sky at midnight; it sparked and smoldered until daybreak. When the people saw it, they wept. The temple of Huitzilopochtli burst spontaneously into flame; the fire was so tall it touched the clouds and could not be put out. The temple was reduced to a mound of ashes. Then the thatch temple of Xiuhtecuhtli, the fire god, was struck by lightning on a day when there was very little rain and no thunder. A comet with three tails and a roaring voice emerged from the west in broad daylight. Wind-whipped Lake Texcoco surged over its shores and flooded the city of Tenochtitlán, ruining half the houses. Through the streets of the city, a woman's forlorn lamentations pierced the darkness as she mourned for her lost children. A long-legged, long-beaked, dark-feathered bird was snared in the rushes by the lake. On its crest was a circular mirror. When King Moctezuma II looked into this mirror, he saw a vast army in many ranks approaching over the mountains. But by the time he gathered his wise men to share the vision, the army had disappeared. Two-headed men, *tlacantzolli*, lurked in the streets of Tenochtitlán. But when the Mexica guards brought them before King Moctezuma, the monsters vanished.[2]

Moctezuma II, called Xocoyotzin (the younger), heard the wailing of the people outside the palace walls and was literally petrified, immobilized in the face of such harbingers. "Why should *I* be the one to suffer these visitations?" he complained in agitation to his priests and seers, seeking an explanation and threatening to jail them if they did not provide an answer. "What shall I do? Where shall I hide? If only I could turn into stone, wood, or some other earthly matter, rather than suffer that which I so dread!" The magicians' chilling reply did not provide relief: "A *great mystery, which must come to pass in this land, now comes swiftly.*"[3]

Comet omen vision, Book of the Gods

The prophesied day came full circle toward the end of April 1519, when the dozen ships of Hernán Cortés and his five hundred men dropped anchor off the island of San Juan de Ulúa, less than a mile from shore, near where they soon established La Villa Rica de la Vera Cruz (the true cross) as the first town in New Spain. Word of their arrival came from a crippled beggar who lived by the sea, coming breathlessly to the court of Moctezuma, reporting that he had spotted "towers and mountains moving on the water" from the direction of the House of the Dawn. The light-skinned, bearded creatures, "with hair coming only to their ears," who inhabited these white, billowy "mountains" had left them in small boats and were fishing offshore.

Who were these newcomers? Were they hostile invaders like the Chichimecs of old? Were they emissaries from a foreign country who desired to initiate commerce with the Mexica? Or were they long-lost gods of an ancient era deciding to walk the earth, and who, even as the dream-haunted Moctezuma pondered the possibilities, would gather their power on the beaches?[4]

In Book XII of the *Florentine Codex*, it was written, "For thus [Moctezuma] thought, and it was so regarded, that this was *Topiltzin* [Our Dear Prince] *Quetzalcóatl* who had arrived. For it was held in their hearts that indeed he would come — that he would come to land on and visit his domain. For in truth he had travelled to the east when he first departed."[5]

Beyond fulfilling a promised return, however, we must understand the complex ironies that swirled through Moctezuma's "bad conscience"; they are tellingly described by the Roman Catholic priest and Sandinista poet Ernesto Cardenal in his epic poem *Quetzalcóatl*. Alfonso Reyes, with unerring insight about the Mexica psyche, identifies Moctezuma as "a-tremble with mystic terror…undone by the anguish of presentiment…and morally disarmed before [the presence of Cortés,] the emissary of fate," long before the two leaders had even met in person.[6]

The wheel of history revolved many times in Mesoamerica during the eleven fifty-two-year cycles between the earthly One-Reed birth of Topiltzin Quetzalcóatl, reckoned at A.D. 947, and the first glimpse of Spanish sails on the horizon of the Gulf of Campeche. If it had not been for the Chichimec, Tula would not have fallen. If it had not been for the Toltec, Chichén Itzá would not have been invaded. And if it had not been for the southward-migrating Aztec, the many settled Anáhuac tribes might have continued to live on in peace.[7]

It was, then, only a matter of time and cosmic necessity before the already threatened Mexica, surrounded by tense and resentful city-states in the Valley of Anáhuac, finally received the inevitable retribution. It was their turn. Over the past several centuries, old Toltec books were destroyed, old prayers rewritten, and old hierarchies reversed as Huitzilopochtli's blood-drenched doctrines gained hegemony. It was a far cry from Plumed Serpent's mandate in Tula's glory days, sanctioning the sacrifice of harmless butterflies and the ceremonial taking of one's own blood in single droplets.

Superstitious Moctezuma understood "in his heart" that the Mexica had strayed sacrilegiously from Plumed Serpent's original path. In their "ostentation and vainglory" they had betrayed a spiritual birthright. Plumed Serpent's foundation, upon which ancient Tula had been created, was subverted. The Mexica pantheon claimed Huitzilopochtli's bellicose ideology as its dominant theme. Craving worldly power propped upon the requisites of "ritual slaughter," Moctezuma "claimed to be master of all the riches of the earth." He ruled over a territory the size of Italy. But at what cost?[8]

"He has appeared! He has come back!" thought Moctezuma, "He will come here, to the place of his throne and canopy, for that is what he promised when he departed!" Overcome with trepidation and

Moctezuma receives word of Spanish arrival, Florentine Codex

teca, cempoalteca, injc qujmo
ichteca tlatlanjque: conjtvque
caamoie ichoatl tvtecujoane.
Inm tzioac popocatzin. qujnj
xiptlatica in. Motecuçomatzin:
qujtbuijque. cujx iete intk Mo
tecuçoma conjtv. Canehoatl
in namotechiuh caub in nj Mo
tecuçoma. Auh njma qujtbeuj
que. Nepa xiauh, tleica inti
techiztlacavia, actitechmati
amo vel titechiztlacavis, amo
vel tvca timocaiaoas, amo vel
titech quamanas, amo velti
techix mamatilos, amo velti
techich chioas. amo vel titechix
cuepas, amo vel titechixpa
tiliz, amo vel titech tlacuepi
liz, amo vel titechixpopolos,
amo vel titechix mjmjctiz. a
mo vel titechix coquj viz, amo
veltitechix coqujmatvaz, a
motehoatl cavnca in Mote
cuçoma, amo vel technetla
tiliz, amo vel mjnaiaz, cam
pvias, cujx totvtl, cujxpa
tlanjz, cujnoço tlatlan quj
quehas yiovi, cujx canaca
tepetl coionquj yitic calaqujz

Ni Motecuçoma se nos podra asconder
por mucho que haga, aunque sea ave
yaunque semeta debaxo detierra
nose nos podra asconder de verle
avemos oyde oyr avemos loque
nos dira. Y luego con asienta em
biaron aquel principal yatodos

remorse, Moctezuma was by no means ready to march forth out of the safety of his city to confront Plumed Serpent. Indeed, six more months passed before the Aztec king and the Spanish conquistador came face to face. For now, there was only one thing to do: send Jaguar Knights bearing gifts to his Lord, ordering them to seek some reply.[9]

The emissaries were instructed to present raiments in homage from Moctezuma as Plumed Serpent's self-styled "deputy." They were intentionally made in the form of talismans that could traditionally have belonged to Plumed Serpent or have been worn by him and so were being returned to him. The items included a serpent mask; a breast plate made of quetzal feathers and a shield bordered with them; an ornate, golden collar; earplugs and lip-plugs in the form of serpents; a crooked serpent wand like that used by Éhecatl; a jaguar-skin hat; and sandals decorated with obsidian.[10]

The messengers were gone for many days. Moctezuma agonized, inconsolable, sleepless, and with no appetite. His "heart burned and suffered, as if it were drowned in spices."

The messengers from Tenochtitlán arrived at the shore and were taken in skiffs out to the Spanish ships. With deep reverence, they kissed the prows of the galleons, believing them holy with Plumed Serpent's spirit. The Spaniards called out through interpreters: "Who are you? Whence have you come? Where is your home?" The envoys replied, "We come from Mexico, and the name of our ruler is Moctezuma, and he wants to know where this Lord [Plumed Serpent] intends to go."

"This Lord is your spirit," replied the sagacious Spaniards, "and he says he will go see King Moctezuma."[11]

From 1517 to 1554, the first of the Hapsburgs, his Caesarian Majesty Charles V, Holy Roman Emperor, King of Castile and Léon, reigned as absolute monarch by divine authority; he was the chief defender of the Catholic faith, "bearing the banner of Jesus Christ" over a territory that ranged from Belgium to Naples and across the waters to North Africa. He sought nothing less than the defeat of the infidels and the reuniting of Christendom around the world.[12]

The Spanish knew that God, through His pope, dispatched them to the New World with the responsibility of bringing the Indians over to the side of the church. Theirs was above all a spiritually imperialistic journey, a final crusade to destroy idols, disabuse native peoples of their pagan ways by promulgating the Gospel, and possess and annex new territories in the King's name, making a better world for the "savages."

In Hernán Cortés's opportunistic mind, these highflown, providential reasons for his voyage overshadowed the marginal accomplishments of his two predecessors, Francisco Hernández de Córdoba and Juan de Grijalva, who had touched the shores of the Yucatán. Cortés defied the orders of Diego Velásquez, the governor of Fernandina (Cuba), who had dispatched him simply "to explore and to trade." An ambitious thirty-six-year-old former notary from the Spanish province of Extremadura who had studied law at Salamanca, Cortés believed he bore a holy right of dominion over any and all Indians he encountered, as well as their gold and their women. Even though as the governor's secretary, he was meant to report directly to Velásquez, Cortés intended to write to King Charles, accounting for his martial decisions and subsequent actions in a series of letters designed to establish bold precedents for his expansive trip through alien territory. To Cortés, "Indian resistance *was* rebellion."[13]

Therefore, when Moctezuma's envoys boarded his ship on that warm and humid Holy Thursday in 1519, Cortés was not inclined initially to show his deeper intentions. He was known among his contemporaries as "a wit who affected learning and was circumspect.... He did not reveal that he knew as much, or was capable as he afterward showed him-self to be in difficult situations."[14] His strategy was to speak softly. According to the sanctioned and deli-cately phrased account by his lieutenant Bernal Díaz del Castillo, Cortés welcomed the messengers from Tenochtitlán, fed them a grand meal, plied them with wine, and told them with courtly grace that "he had come to visit and trade with them, and that they should think of [his] coming to their country as fortunate rather than troublesome."

The next day, Good Friday, most of the soldiers disembarked with their horses and armor and built temporary shacks on the sand dunes. On Easter Sunday the Spanish forces set up an altar and chant-ed mass, displaying the cross and "an image of Our Lady." Cortés explained to his visitors that "he wished to be friends" with Moctezuma, at which point the king's elaborate gifts were formally present-ed. As if in reply with a veiled warning, Cortés ordered his men to mount up, dress their horses with breastplates adorned with tinkling bells, and canter along the beach two by two in a cacophonous display that left the visitors awestruck, for they had never seen these snorting, bellowing four-legged beasts before. Then Cortés ordered the cannon to be fired "so that [the ambassadors] might see the shot leave the gun…with a great din," frightening the Indians into prostration and faintness.[15]

Word of this ostentatious panoply and force reached Moctezuma, as the hastily returning mes-sengers made their report, speaking of fireworks and sparks that belched from cannons' mouths and brought down entire mountains with "balls of stone"; of "deer as tall as houses" upon which iron-clad, pale-complected gods rode to and fro; and of tireless, panting, huge, hollow-bellied hounds with bloodshot yellow eyes.[16]

Over the following weeks Moctezuma was con-sumed with efforts to find out more about the strange visitors and to test or appease them. Repeated delegations from Tenochtitlán to Vera Cruz ensued. Perhaps captive sacrifices and blood offerings would be acceptable. On the contrary, the king was per-plexed when the white men turned away in disgust from the obsidian knife; Cortés instead continued his campaign of intimidation, slapping a blood-filled ritual silver cup out of the hand of an Indian priest.

Moctezuma delivered parcels of exotic foods for the visitors. They were received unenthusiasti-cally. In a moment of pique—or curiosity—he sent magicians to conjure up "a harmful wind" against the fair-skinned beings, seeing if it would cause them sickness, but to no avail. Theirs was a different kind of power.

All the while, Moctezuma, a model of passive resistance, held regal ground in his opulent com-pound at Tenochtitlán, two hundred miles distant, while Cortés continued to send word insistently and provocatively of his desire to meet with the great "barbarian" whose imposing Nahua name tantalized him: "He Who Grows Angry Like a Lord."[17]

Moctezuma's reply to Cortés was an attempt to put him off in the conciliatory style of Quetzalcóatl, a god known for resisting conflict: "Humbly beg him to let me die, and when I am dead he may come enjoy his mat and throne, which I have been guard-ing for him." Such outwardly resolute behavior at this time, masking wishful thinking and an ambivalent spirit, calmed Moctezuma's followers temporarily.[18]

The degeneration of the dialogue was due not merely to geographic or linguistic distance. There was a psychological gulf that neither side could have found the words to define. "The inexorable European world of steel and objective reasoning" was poised against "a civilization offering up its very existence in an effort to survive."[19]

In early June 1519, tempted by visions of gold, Cortés decided there could be no more waiting. It was time to march inland toward Cempoala, where he hoped to find allies among the Totonac people in waging war on the Aztec.[20]

CHAPTER XIV

CORTĒS AND MOCTEZUMA

If, for the Spaniards,
the Conquest was a deed,
for the Indians it was a rite,
a human representation
of a cosmic catastrophe.

— OCTAVIO PAZ,
The Other Mexico: Critique of the Pyramid[1]

The friendly Totonac leaders at Cempoala, bearing baskets of plums and exotic cakes scented with rose petals for the Spaniards, resented paying tax tribute to the Mexica. In discussions with the Totonac, Cortés made the canny transition to self-styled ambassador. He realized that the Aztec nation was held together tenuously and that he had an opportunity to fulfill his destiny, to conquer as a latter-day crusader. Citing a verse from the *Book of Matthew*, Cortés wrote in his *Second Letter* to King Charles, "Every kingdom divided against itself is brought to desolation," going on smugly in the next sentence to say that his strategy in dealing with the Indians was to "maneuver one [native lord] against the other."[2]

The Totonac were only one of what appeared to be hundreds of outcast tribes hoping for some god-sanctioned excuse to rise up against their Aztec oppressors at Tenochtitlán.

At this juncture, realizing he would need financial support from the home front to fortify his onward movement, Cortés sent a ship back to King Charles with a huge cache of native gold, mosaics, mirrors, jewels, and shimmering, quetzal-feathered treasures. Cortés then destroyed the remainder of his fleet to underscore that there would be no turning back. In a rousing speech to his near-mutinous men after Sunday morning mass, Cortés reminded them that henceforth "with the help of our Lord Jesus Christ" they would need to "rely upon [their] own good swords and stout hearts."[3]

Accounts vary in telling of the number of Totonacs who willingly agreed in mid-August to accompany Cortés as porters and guide him on the trek westward toward Tenochtitlán, but the Spanish

Totonacs welcome the Spanish, Book of the Gods

had from four hundred to one thousand new allies helping to pull deadly cannons across intervening plains and humid jungles and through the chilly mountain passes to Tlaxcala, "the city of bread," in the Mesa Central.

Here the reception was mixed because commander Xicotencatl and other leaders of the loose confederation of four Tlaxcalan states were aware that Cortés had been in repeated contact with their sworn enemy, Moctezuma. At the same time Tlaxcalan priests bearing tribute gifts sallied forth to talk with Cortés, Moctezuma persisted in warning the Spaniards—via small delegations and messengers who remained in the Spanish camp—to steer clear of them. By the time the Tlaxcalans finally decided to attack, their obsidian-edged wooden swords proved no match for the tempered steel of the Spanish. In defeat, the pragmatic Tlaxcalans willingly joined the Cempoalans, again swelling the ranks of the foreign victors; and they urged them, in another wave of animosity and political intrigue, to take the next step, twenty-five miles farther westward: "This is why …, their souls burning with hatred for the people of Cholula, [the Tlaxcalans] brought certain rumors to Cortés, so that he would destroy them: 'Cholula is our enemy [they said]. It is an evil city. The people there are as brave as the Aztecs and they are the Aztecs' friends.'"

As they spurred Cortés onward, perhaps exploiting him as a wedge against neighboring powerful rivals they would never have been able to subdue alone, the Tlaxcalans also warned Cortés (who by now referred to them in his letters to the king as "faithful vassals of Your Sacred Majesty") that the streets of Cholula could easily present a lethal trap. Why else, they pointed out, would the wily Moctezuma also at this time have asked Cortés to proceed there to receive his final decision about a meeting? The threat of ambush, combined with the exciting prospect of forcing a confrontation, motivated Cortés toward what must have seemed in his inflated ego as a no-lose situation. "Unless the Lord God by His divine mercy were to interfere on our behalf," wrote Bernal Díaz de Castillo, "we had no other way [i.e., except through Cholula] of entering the City of Mexico," which, after all, was Cortés's ultimate goal.[4]

A prosperous city of more than fifteen thousand inhabitants, Cholula was the strategic threshold to Tenochtitlán. Rich in spiritual ambiance, it had been venerated for centuries as Plumed Serpent's first resting place in his fabled exodus from Tula. Here stood Quetzalcóatl's own *monte hecho a mano*, his hand-made hill, the tallest temple in all of Anáhuac, facing two great snow-capped mountains: Popocatépetl, sending his smoky plume "big as a house" (Cortés wrote with awe) directly skyward "by day and by night"; and his sleeping, white-veiled wife to the north, Iztaccíhuatl.

At a reception hosted by the city fathers, Cortés was pelted with rose petals. He then delivered his by-now obligatory speech in which he advised the Cholulans that he had been sent to their land to warn them against worshipping false gods, sacrificing other human beings, eating their flayed flesh, and "committing sodomy and other bestialities."[5]

Cortés was acutely aware that with every passing day, he was closing in. He was now within "twenty leagues" of the place where Moctezuma lived. The second day after his arrival in Cholula, the flow of provisions to his men suddenly stopped. Cortés believed he had found evidence that the treacherous Cholulans were covering up their pre-existing knowledge of a huge army of Mexica warriors "hidden in the thickets and ravines" outside the city, gathering to snuff out the Spaniards. In his memoirs, Bernal Díaz insisted that Tlaxcalan informants had discovered wooden-stake traps dug

beneath the surface of the streets meant to impale Spanish horses.

In one of the most exquisite of many ironies permeating the progress of Cortés's incursion, the agitated conquistador requested a gathering of the Cholulan leadership in the courtyard of the Temple of Quetzalcóatl to bid them farewell properly before departing for Tenochtitlán. After chastising the lords for their duplicity, he locked the gates of the courtyard and ordered his troops, with the assistance of the Cempoalans and Tlaxcalans, to kill all assembled. The massacre quickly moved out into the city streets, where thousands more died, including women and children. "Blood-lust" took over "once the bloodshed had begun." Over the course of two days, the entire city was burned and razed. A cross was triumphantly placed atop the Temple of Quetzalcóatl.[6]

The bloody incident at Cholula, another Cortésian mind game, accomplished its purpose: to send a crystal-clear example of Spanish might to Moctezuma (who strenuously denied any awareness of a conspiracy). "The common people [of Tenochtitlán] were terrified by the news," said the account in the *Florentine Codex*. "They could do nothing but tremble in fright. It was as if… the earth were spinning before their eyes, as it spins during a fit of vertigo."[7]

In early November 1519, Cortés, with four hundred conquistadores and more than a thousand Tlaxcalan friends, began the final leg of his fateful journey, leaving the smoldering ruins of Cholula and heading straight for Tenochtitlán. He followed the trail between the volcanoes, reversing the course of Plumed Serpent's ancient exodus from Tula.

Above twelve thousand feet, snow showers alternated with fine ash drifting down upon them. On the drier downward slopes, clear of the mists, the marching hordes "raised a great dust…the shimmer of their swords was as of a sinuous water course, and their pennons fluttered like bats." Along the way villagers could hear over the wind the distant tinkling bells on the horses' breastplates, faint neighing, and the clatter of armor; and then the ground trembled before the entire mass of men finally emerged into view.[8]

"It was all so wonderful that I do not know how to describe this glimpse of things never heard of, seen, or dreamed of before," wrote Bernal Díaz del Castillo, recalling his first sighting of Tenochtitlán, revealed "like a second Venice" from the summit of the Sierra de Ahualco. "These great towns and buildings rising from the water, all made of stone, seemed like an enchanted vision from the tale of *Amadis* [a romance of chivalry]. Indeed, some of

our soldiers asked whether it was not all a dream."[9]

Surrounded by mountains and connected to the mainland by three broad, bridged causeways, Tenochtitlán was a white and green oval island-jewel in a blue lake setting. Among low white adobe and plaster houses tinted pale red here and there, the tops of pyramids thrust upward, with flat temples at their peaks. Interspersed among the residences were green garden squares, with gleaming canals in a grid pattern threaded among them instead of streets. Around the perimeter of the island, green floating gardens secured by wickerwork were tended by farmers in small dugouts. Lake Texcoco sparkled "in the strange refraction of the sun's rays [through]

Cortés marches toward Tenochtitlán with his Tlaxcalan allies, Book of the Gods

99

the transparent, purified air…the atmosphere so keenly clear…in which everything [stood] out in bold relief."[10]

At dawn on November 8, on the Aztec day named One-Wind, the army, after one night in the outlying city of Iztapalapa, moved westward until it reached the Coyoacán causeway heading north toward the center of Tenochtitlán. Cortés and his men were in the lead, with the mass of Tlaxcalans following. The waters surrounding the road were jammed with canoes crowded with curious and silent Mexica.

To capture the pivotal scene which followed, imagine it filmed by three very different "cameras." The first camera is held by Hernán Cortés, reporting to King Charles in September 1520 as if he were a character in a fairy tale who had finally passed through the looking glass. The second belongs to Cortés's loyal lieutenant, Bernal Díaz, writing indignantly as a corrective for posterity, nearly deaf and blind, forty-five years later. The third is the recollection of native informants, voiced to Fray Bernardino de Sahagún after more than three decades.

Hernán Cortés waited for more than an hour in the sun while dignitaries came one by one to place their hands upon the ground before him and kiss the earth, in a sign of welcome.

Finally, heralded by two columns of more than two hundred barefoot lords, the silver-sandaled Moctezuma walked forward down the center of the boulevard, arm in arm with "great chiefs" on either side of him. When Cortés stepped forward to embrace Moctezuma, these guardians stopped him, for no one but they were permitted to initiate touching the king.

Cortés took off a necklace of pearls and cut glass he was wearing and placed it carefully around Moctezuma's neck. Moctezuma in turn asked a servant

Cortés and the Tlaxcalans enter Tenochtitlán, Histoire Mexicaine depuis 1221 jusqu'à 1594

to put a necklace of golden shrimp around Cortés's neck. Then the king did take the Spaniard's hand and led him into the castle of Axayácatl, his father, instructing Cortés to "sit on a very rich throne" until the rest of his commanders had been properly fed. Another throne was set down directly next to Cortés. Moctezuma, ensconced there, then made a formal speech to him.

The Mexica king knew, "from the writings of [his] ancestors," that his subjects were descendants of "foreigners" who had come from far away. Moctezuma said that a great "chieftain" had brought his people to Anáhuac. This chieftain had "returned to his native land" with the proviso that "those who descended from him" would one day come back and conquer Anáhuac. Therefore, the Lords of Tenochtitlán were merely regents, place holders of the throne until the return of their first leader or his representatives. And, indeed, Cortés had sailed "from where the sun rises," whence that esteemed chieftain had gone. Clearly, Cortés was an emissary of this lord, now recognized as rightful claimant to the Mexica: "In all the land that lies in my domain, you may command as you will," Cortés reported Moctezuma said to him.

Then, Cortés wrote, Moctezuma "raised his clothes" and revealed his bare body, saying in "apocryphal" words oddly reminiscent of Jesus' to his disciples, "See that I am of flesh and blood like you and other men, and I am mortal and substantial."[11]

Hernán Cortés possessed an adept political mind. He knew that Mexica respect was traditionally conferred upon anyone who claimed to be an ambassador. He was aware of the superstitions that preceded his arrival. He had heard the Plumed Serpent tale and knew of "the expected return of the bearded lords from the direction of the sunrise." In the view of Alfonso Reyes, Moctezuma acted toward Cortés as King Latinus of antiquity had faced Aeneas, a similar man of destiny—accepting a *translatio imperii*—an inevitable

transfer of authority: "Moctezuma tells Cortés of those fatal prophecies about Quetzalcóatl," Reyes writes, "and Cortés turns instantly cold, and moves his chess piece coldly. He shuts his eyes, steels his soul, and thinks only of his advantage. The realm of action, or rather the realm of the brain, banishes contemplation. The spirit of conquest assumes full sway."[12]

Bernal Díaz del Castillo (1492–1571) was born in Medina del Campo, Spain, and died in Guatemala, the last survivor of the original conquistadores. Resentful of perceived inaccuracies in earlier accounts of the Conquest by Cortés's official biographers, Bernal Díaz set forth in old age to tell the tale straightforwardly, "singularly free from the temptation to pervert his story in the interests of affections or feuds or personal vanity. To have marched with Cortés was for him sufficient glory."[13]

Underscoring Moctezuma's distinction from his fellows, Bernal Díaz recalled him as shod with golden sandals, descending from a green, feather-canopied litter borne by barefoot lords. They swept the ground before the king as he walked slowly forward, and no one, including Cortés—who reached to embrace Moctezuma and was rebuffed—was allowed to look him in the face or touch him.

After the exchange of necklaces (Bernal Díaz described Moctezuma's gift to Cortés as being made of gold crabs rather than shrimp), offers of hospitality were gratefully received, and the Spaniards were welcomed into the palace of Axayácatl.

Once the two leaders were side by side on thrones, the ceremonial speeches commenced. Bernal Díaz wrote that Moctezuma said "that we must truly be the men about whom his ancestors had long ago prophesied, saying that *they would come from the direction of the sunrise* to rule over these lands." Cortés made it clear (with what seems like a well-timed measure of flattery) that King Charles had sent him to this country to visit

Moctezuma, confirm his mighty reputation, and "to beg [him] to become Christian, so that his soul and those of all his vassals might be saved."[14]

The next day, at Moctezuma's palace, the dialogue resumed with Cortés's repeated insistence that his was a spiritual mission in the name of "Jesus Christ, who had suffered his passion and death to save us," whereas the Indians worshiped "not gods, but evil devils."

Moctezuma countered evenly that Mexica gods were "good" because "they give us health and rain and crops and weather and all the victories we desire." Through omens from the gods and the teachings of their ancestors, his people had long believed in and known of Cortés's eventual arrival. Yet despite these glimmers of self-assurance, submissiveness necessarily and inevitably followed. "As for your great King," Moctezuma said, "I am in his debt and will give him of what I possess."[15]

The native witnesses to the first encounter began their accounts with the symbolically fraught presentation to Cortés of "flowers on a gourd tray… the flower that resembles a shield; the flower shaped like a heart; in the center, the flower with the sweetest aroma." To the Mexica, flowers superseded even gifts of gold and jewels because they represented the powers of "The Giver of Life," "He Who Invents Himself." As set down in the ancient songs, "Only as among the flowers/we might seek someone,/thus we seek You,/we who live on the earth,/we who are at Your side."[16]

However, The Giver of Life will likewise become He Who Takes Life Away: "Man lives in His painted books but some day will be erased from them.… With black ink you will blot out/all that was friendship,/brotherhood, nobility."[17]

Moctezuma's chieftains wreathed the heads of Cortés's lieutenants with flowers. Then the king spoke: "Our Lord, you are weary," Moctezuma said to Cortés in welcome. He continued,

The journey has tired you, but now you have arrived on the earth. You have come to your city, Mexico. You have come here to sit on your throne, to sit under its canopy. I have been taking care of things for you.
This is no dream, [Moctezuma went on, as if speaking to Quetzalcóatl]. I am not sleepwalking, not seeing things in my sleep. I am not dreaming that I see you and look into your face. Indeed, I have been troubled for as many days as there are fingers on my two hands.
I have gazed into the Unknown and have seen you coming out of the clouds, out of the mists. This was foretold by the kings who governed your city, and now it has taken place. You have come back to us. You have come down from the sky.

In comparison to the formal, documentary accounts of the conquistadores, the native version comes across steeped in reverential acceptance of Cortés-Quetzalcóatl and his entourage of strange newcomers: no pretenses of fleshly mortality, no religious preaching, no need to report a balanced exchange of points of view.

For Moctezuma and the Mexica—and for the entire Mesoamerican world—Cortés heralded the beginning of the end.[18]

CHAPTER XV

THE CONQUEST

This is the only example of a Culture ended by violent death.
It was not starved, suppressed, or thwarted, but murdered in the full glory
of its unfolding, destroyed like a sunflower whose head is struck off
by one passing blow.
—OSWALD SPENGLER, *The Decline of the West, Volume II* (1922)[1]

Reading between the lines of Bernal Díaz del Castillo's exhaustive account of his sojourn in the magnificent metropolis of the Aztecs, we gain glimpses into the ambivalent psyche of the invaders. The Spaniards were in the midst of a rich, complex, and decadent court society not entirely alien to their own. The members of Moctezuma's entourage cast their glances downward in humility when he approached. He possessed an armory with every variety of weapon, an aviary with every variety of bird, a treasury with every variety of jewel, a botanical garden with every variety of flower and "sweet-scented tree." He employed *ateliers* full of craftsmen and weavers to design adornments and fabrics for his accessories and garments. There were performers, jugglers, and clowns for his amusement.

The city pulsed with enchanting life. In the central marketplace, merchants who traveled long distances to display their wares set up booths draped with bright canopies. In the closely grouped, pastel-colored stone palaces festooned with hanging gardens, painted jaguar and eagle knights practiced the art of combat. From dawn to darkness broken by torchlight, the streets were awash in the ebb and flow of cosmopolitan life. A woman swept the lintel of her whitewashed house. Little boys, novice priests in training, their heads shaved except for a ponytail tonsure, hurried to class. The occasional *tlatlacotin* slave could be seen, immediately identified by the long pole tied across the width of his shoulders to prevent him from running free. It was indeed a wondrous, strange place.[2]

But all it took was the witness of one ritual sacrifice to transform Spanish awe (even grudging

Diego Rivera, View of Tenochtitlán (detail),
The History of Mexico From Pre-Columbian Civilization
to the Conquest

respect) into revulsion. On the most solemn feast day, dedicated to the supreme deity Huitzilopochtli—"he who set men's hearts on fire and gave them courage for war" — it was necessary to bring forth prisoners of war drawn from tribute-paying nations in the surrounding territories, those same peoples who would eventually tip the balance against the Aztecs and contribute to their defeat.

Six Huitzilopochtli priests were smeared from head to toe with black pigment except for a single circle of white paint around their mouths. They were dressed in white robes and bore little paper shields painted in bright colors. The high priest carried a wide obsidian flint knife. The priest behind him in the procession carried a snake-shaped wooden yoke. The prisoner stood naked in front of the *tzompantli*, the huge, treelike rack adorned with the putrefying skulls of those who had gone before; then he was plucked from the ranks of many to be offered that day and led up the steps of the temple, steeply slanted so that the file of men seemed to be walking up into the heavens. The crowd below craned their necks and observed in silence until they lost sight of priests and prisoner by the time they had reached the topmost platform. Perhaps the unfortunate victim was staggering because he had been offered some intoxicating *pulque maguey* sap brew or *peyote* mushrooms to dull his senses.

Once at the peak of the narrow stairs carpeted with the dried blood of hundreds of others, the prisoner was thrown across a waist-high stone slab one foot wide, "in figure and likeness of the sun." His back was arched bowlike, his chest offered to the heavens. Four priests seized his arms and legs and held them firmly stretched. The wooden yoke was clamped across his neck and yanked downward, to muffle screaming and breathing.

The high priest grasped the knife with both hands, raised it above his head, then thrust swiftly down upon the taut skin at the breastbone, "splitting it open with the ease of a pomegranate." As blood showered forth, the priest reached into the gaping cavity and ripped out the "precious eagle cactus fruit"—the still-pulsating heart.

He stepped forward to the edge of the platform, lifted the heart upward in sight of the assembled multitude, and held it aloft for a few moments, "offering the steam to speak to the sun." Once the heart had cooled, he tossed it into a stone "eagle bowl," where it would later be burned with *copal*. Then the high priest took some blood on his fingertips and sprinkled it to the four points of the compass and in the direction of the sun, which lived in *Cihuatlampa*, its Heavenly House. The priest then exclaimed, "Our Lord, fulfill your duty prosperously!" The prisoner's body, one of fifty to be given over that day to Huitzilopochtli, was rolled down the pyramid steps, borne away to be flayed, dismembered, and partially eaten by the warrior who had captured him.[3]

From one day to the next, Cortés's lieutenants careered from astonishment at the glories of Aztec high culture to revulsion at the unavoidable "stench of a slaughterhouse," from the glittering facets of the Aztec world to its sacred, carnal cruelty—impenetrable, "absurd and pagan." Bernal Díaz's narrative of the first six months of the Spanish occupation of Tenochtitlán is permeated with fears of entrapment and a constant, underlying suspicion of being attacked; pressure and tension fostered a hair-trigger atmosphere. Hernán Cortés, however, was inured to these fearful thoughts. Once he had entered the city, he never thought of departing.

Cortés was biding his time, feeling his way toward the right moment to overcome this Indian nation without further fighting and to convince

Diego Rivera, View of Tenochtitlán (detail)

Charles V that he was capable of ruling the Christianized heathens in this land of gold as their benign sovereign.[4]

As his next move in the chess game, Cortés took Moctezuma hostage. The pretext was an ideological impasse when the King refused to take down his idols, stop worshipping false gods, and allow Cortés to erect in their stead a cross in honor of the Blessed Virgin. Moctezuma reassured his people that he was not a prisoner but rather "living with" the invaders through the will of the gods, even as he had allowed the Spanish into the city for the same reason: "If the gods have allowed this to happen, it is foolish, if not wrong, to resist."[5]

Spiritual nuances aside, native informants decades later recalled the Spanish as motivated

Human sacrifice at Tenochtitlán, Florentine Codex

52.

more by avarice than religious dedication, "grinning like little beasts and patting each other with delight" as they moved unrestricted through Moctezuma's treasure house at Totocalco, "coveting everything, slaves to their own greed."[6]

An unforeseen distraction from the coastal provinces was the next step toward catastrophe. Diego Velásquez, Cortés's former supervisor in Cuba, had been receiving reports all along of the conquistadores's insolent and rebellious progress. In the early spring of 1520, Governor Velásquez sent eighteen ships and nine hundred men to Veracruz under the command of Pánfilo de Narváez with the mission to find Cortés, arrest him, and deport him to Spain. Cortés was driven to respond. He placed the fair-haired Pedro de Alvarado (therefore nicknamed *Tonatiuh*, the Sun, by the Indians) in charge of about 120 men in his occupying garrison at Tenochtitlán, took the other soldiers upon the familiar road between the volcanoes, picked up additional forces at Cholula, marched forth to engage Narváez, and successfully defended his hard-won turf—only to learn that during his three-week absence from Tenochtitlán, the tinderbox had finally ignited.[7]

It was the time of the fiesta of Toxcatl, the feast celebrating the dragon-headed Huitzilopochtli. Alvarado, a "tough soldier, brave but rash, lacking all Cortés's gifts of intrigue," became increasingly nervous to the point of impulsive reaction. Larger-than-life statues of the gods were molded from maize dough, grain, and blood, festooned with ribbons. The *calpulli* priests engaged in ritual bathing and fasting. Ecstatic throngs of thousands in the city center gathered before the Great Temple, Gran Teocalli; all night there was wild, trancelike serpent dancing to continuous, droning, hypnotic music from flutes, bells, and drums.[8]

"At the moment in the fiesta when the dance was loveliest and song was linked to song," say the indigenous texts, "the Spaniards were seized with an urge to kill the celebrants." Chillingly reminiscent of the Cholula massacre, the four corner gates of the temple were closed and locked, and "Alvarado gave the order — *¡Muerán!* Let them die!"[9]

Cortés returned in fury to a permanently ruptured city, his psychological strategy ruined by the bloodthirsty Alvarado. While "clouds of javelins spread out over them like a yellow cloak," the consolidated Spanish forces gathered in the palace of Axayácatl to protect themselves from the passionate uprising led by Moctezuma's brother, Cuitláhuac.[10]

Toward the end of June, after a week of heavy fighting, Cortés, running dangerously low on provisions and ammunition, prevailed upon the proud and protesting Moctezuma, still in chains and heavily guarded, to mount the battlements of the palace and address or "admonish" his people in hopes that he could calm them and bring about a peaceful resolution of the battle. "What more does Cortés want of me?" the dispirited monarch asked. "Fate has brought me to such a pass because of him that I do not wish to live or hear his voice again."[11] According to the Spanish account, as soon as he began speaking, Moctezuma was struck by a rain of arrows and "stones thicker than hail," mortally wounded. According to the native story, the king was stabbed to death or garroted by his captors when they realized his authority had finally run out.[12]

According to Cortés's notes, in the early morning of July 1, six days following John the Baptist's Day, the Spanish leader decided to withdraw from the city in order to regroup and retaliate from a more advantageous position. Under cover of mist and cold drizzle, he chose the western Tlacopan (now Tacuba) causeway as the shortest escape. The Aztecs had destroyed all the bridges spanning the canals, so the Spanish, with Tlaxcalan allies and horses heavily laden with as much gold as they could carry, were forced to rig up makeshift wooden platforms of their own devising.

Moving this way, they successfully crossed the Tecpantzinco, Tzapotlan, and Atenchicalco canals before being discovered. The legend says that an old woman fetching water spotted the Spaniards and cried out in fear: "Mexicanos! Come running! Our enemies are escaping!" The Aztec guards blew upon conch shells and beat melancholy alarms on *teponaztli*, hollowed-out logs, "sounding like accursed instruments of demons"; the vengeful native warriors poured forth, swarming on foot and paddling dugout canoes, screaming in the predawn gloom "like mad dogs without a thought for their lives… giving out the most bloodcurdling shrieks and whistles, dancing and singing, their horrifying yells an excellent weapon that awed the Spaniards" and effectively cut off their retreat.[13]

In the outlying district of Tlaltecayohuacán, the Spanish, at the Canal of the Toltecs (later renamed the Bridge of the Massacre), were overwhelmed on all sides and were forced to take to the water. In his memoirs Bernal Díaz wrote that the canals were

soon choked with the bodies of men and horses; they filled the gap in the causeway with their own drowned bodies. And those who followed crossed to the other side by walking on the corpses…. Even if we had had ten thousand Trojan Hectors and as many Rolands, even then we should not have been able to break through.

More than seven hundred valorous companions of Extremadura and Castile died, three-quarters of the army of the conquistadores; and more than one thousand Tlaxcalans also lost their lives during the infamous *Noche Triste*, the Night of Sorrow.[14]

Cortés now had no option but to retreat to the lands of the Tlaxcalans, Texcocans, Tepeacans, and Huexotzingans, who were united in their resentment of the Aztecs. Then he sent word to Spanish troops at Cuba, Veracruz, and Jamaica to join him with provisions, especially powder, cannon, crossbows, and fresh packhorses to plan a reprisal. The Spanish took a long and laborious path north and then eastward around Lake Texcoco. Passing the sacred ruins of Teotihuacán along the way, they put down a surprise challenge at the village of Otumba by the army of Cuitláhuac, Lord of Ixtapalapa. With his customary blend of reality and romance, Cortés—who received a serious head wound during the combat—wrote to the Spanish King, "We could hardly distinguish between ourselves and them, so fiercely and so closely did they fight with us.… But our Lord was pleased to show His power and mercy, for with all our weakness we broke their great arrogance and pride."[15]

The conquistadores spent three weeks at Tlaxcala. They were crippled, demoralized, and on the verge of mutiny, bickering constantly among themselves over gold, women, and slaves who had been branded to establish ownership. But the Mexica faced a far more grievous challenge: smallpox. "Painful, burning sores erupted on our faces, our breasts, our bellies; we were covered with agonizing sores from head to foot.… No one could walk or move. The sick were so utterly helpless with racking coughs that they could only lie on their beds like corpses. They could not lie face down or roll from one side to the other. A great many died from this plague," laments the ancient text.[16]

The smallpox had been conveyed to the Valley of Mexico two years earlier, from Hispaniola through Cuba and then, in the person of one of the men on Pánfilo de Narváez's earlier expeditions, across the Yucatán, where, it was written, "little by little, bleary shadows and black night enveloped our fathers and grandfathers."[17] On the eve of the Conquest, the population of Mexico was about twenty-five million. By 1600 it was one million.

The Indians could not comprehend the scourge decimating them. They were accustomed to bathing every day, sometimes more than once a day. Keeping to this habit only compounded their casualties. After a reign of barely eighty days, the Emperor Cuitláhuac succumbed to smallpox. He was fol-

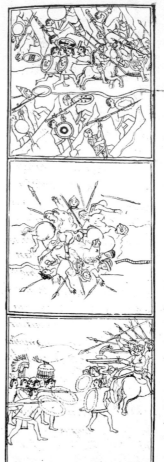

Chaos of battle at Tenochtitlán, Florentine Codex

lowed by his cousin, the young, light-skinned Cuauhtémoc, "descending eagle," his noble name metaphor for the setting sun. Cuauhtémoc was fated to be the last Aztec ruler.

Completing his circuit of the Valley of Anáhuac, Cortés was ready to launch his return by late fall and early winter of 1520. He headed south and west from Tlaxcala, growing in strength all the while, with new warriors from Ixtapalapa, Chalco, and Tacuba whom

The strategy to place the doomed city of Tenochtitlán under fatal blockade in the spring of 1521 was brilliantly executed. Timber, rigging, and parts for a fleet of a dozen small sailing ships—swift, flat-bottomed, and gun-bearing—were cut and amassed at Tlaxcala and then transported by Indian slaves across the mountains, to be assembled there under the supervision of Cortés's expert shipwright, Martín Lopez, in a canal built near the shore of Lake Texcoco. Launched there, the boats would serve well to "clear the Lake of canoes and protect the Spanish flanks as they moved in across the three causeways into the city." By commanding the causeways, the island city would be completely isolated.[19]

Cortés also cut the vital drinking-water aqueducts leading from mainland Chapultepec into Tenochtitlán. The inhabitants, still recovering from the previous conflict, were reeling from disease and miserably low on essential foodstuffs. Starvation was another insufferable burden placed upon the Aztec nation in their last, lean season, even before the Spanish attacked: "The people were tormented by hunger, and many starved to death," cried an ancient *icnocuicatl* (elegy). "There was no fresh water to drink, only stagnant water and the brine of the Lake,"

> *We have eaten branches of linnet,*
> *we have chewed upon salty witch grass,*
> *bits of adobe and ground earth,*
> *small lizards, rats, worms.*[20]

Final fire omen, the spiralling comet, Florentine Codex

he had subdued and then recruited along the way. His force now had a nucleus of six hundred heavily armed Spanish infantry and horsemen surrounded by a cushion of many thousands of Indians.

Cortés wrote, "I am building twelve brigantines with which to cross the lake, and already the decks and other parts are being constructed so that they may be carried overland in pieces and swiftly assembled on arrival."[18]

The viselike siege and ravaging invasion dragged on for three months, into the rainy season, longer than the confident Cortés had anticipated. The Aztecs were in a hallucinatory fight to the death. Every night, Huitzilopochtli priests sacrificed captured conquistadores, pulled out their hearts, and flayed their faces and hands, to the abject horror of their comrades. The hellish stench of death from the corpses of the killed, diseased, and starved hung over the city.

With breezes over the lake in the morning, wind-driven brigantines routed and overpowered the Mexica dugouts. Then Spanish ships pushed hard into the canals themselves, raining cannon fire upon the houses of the Aztecs, reducing them to rubble, and dumping debris and clogging the waterways so that men on foot and horses could follow. Onward the Spaniards plunged, into the marketplace at the center of the city, setting up a huge catapult there, yet another lethal war machine the Aztecs had never experienced before. The Spaniards ransacked and set fire to the Great Temple and its idols, "and the people wept when they saw their temple on fire, they wept and cried out."[21]

The night before the city finally fell, according to the *Codex Florentino*, there was a "final omen." A spiraling comet came with a heavy rain, "blazing like a great bonfire in the sky. It wheeled like a whirlwind and gave off a shower of sparks and red-hot coals. It also made loud noises, rumbling and hissing like a metal tube placed over a fire."[22]

It was August 13, 1521, the feast of Saint Hippolytus, three days before the Assumption of the Most Blessed Virgin, Our Lady. "When the shield was laid down," by the Mexica calendar, it was the day 1-Serpent of the year 3-House.

On the roads lie broken arrows, our hair is in disarray, without roofs are the houses, and red are their walls with blood.... Nothing but flowers and songs of sorrow are left in Mexico and Tlatelolco, where once we saw warriors and wise men.... The cries of the helpless women and children are heart-rending.[23]

Young Cuauhtémoc was captured and brought before Cortés. He placed his hand on the conqueror's dagger and begged him, sobbing, to take his life, for he had "done everything in [his] power to save the kingdom, and [could] do no more." Cortés asked Cuauhtémoc to order his people formally to cease fighting. The city became eerily silent.

The conqueror interrogated the captive king about a huge cache of gold Cortés believed was secreted under Cuauhtémoc's palace. When he vehemently denied its existence, Cuauhtémoc was placed in prison. In abject shame he tried to hang himself. Even after he was tortured and crippled, tied to a stake, his feet burned with hot oil, the "grave and delicate-featured" Cuauhtémoc remained resolute and resistant, claiming that "Cortés had all the gold there was." Cortés kept Cuauhtémoc in captivity during the subsequent Spanish campaign to conquer Honduras—and there, the "descending eagle" was hanged from a ceiba tree.[24]

CHAPTER XVI

PLUMED SERPENT AND THE CHURCH

Hernán Cortés christened the land he had taken New Spain. So it remained for the next three hundred years. In recognition of Cortés's accomplishments, Emperor Charles V appointed him governor and captain-general. The imperialist conquest continued and expanded unabated, south and east through Chiapas and Oaxaca, the Yucatán, and deep into Central America; north and westward into Michoacán, Texas, New Mexico, Kansas, and the California coast.[1]

In the name of the King, the Spanish presence and sovereignty was supported by Indian labor. Upon the ruined remains of Tenochtitlán, the new city of Mexico arose, "a white world set down in a world of color, a small island in a dark sea"; scaffolds teemed with brown-skinned workers who constructed the buildings but were not permitted to reside within the enclave's walled precincts. They were pushed into barrios around the edges and crowded into the depths of silver mines and onto remote, stony, furrowed fields.[2]

The dominant Spanish culture, long convinced of its entitlement to the land and its reputed riches, was confronted with an immense, painful, and perhaps ultimately impossible challenge: to bring stability[3] to a place with two juxtaposed political systems, two races, and two languages. To that end, armies of soldiers were succeeded by the armies of Christ. Cortés, "a devout Catholic and a champion of Christianity," had always portrayed himself as a religious leader, as did the theologians who served in exalted stations in the Spanish government and who had advanced the earliest philosophical rationale for the subjugation of New World peoples.[4]

In the same evangelical spirit, in 1523 Cortés summoned the first three lay brothers to New Spain, led by Pedro de Gante. Gathering his entire court to bear witness, Cortés knelt in the dirt and kissed the hands of twelve mendicant Franciscan friars dressed in humble burlap; they walked barefoot from Veracruz to Mexico City in early 1524 and were followed one year later by the intellectual Dominicans, veterans of the Inquisition. The Augustinian order arrived in 1533 and then, after a forty-year gap, the Jesuits. During the next three centuries of colonial rule, more than twelve thousand churches were built in New Spain.[5]

"Rising in his stirrups and charging into the teeming forest of heresy," the armored conquistador knight had cut his bloody imprint over the past decades, bringing Indian sinners to justice. The new wave of robed conquerors was possessed by a different mission, one they prayed would become more sustained and meaningful. Crucifix and gospel replaced sword and lance. The priests would "harvest the souls" of the Indians, "walk among the dense crowd of pagans, and drench their dark, vanquished heads with a full measure of holy water and exorcism."[6]

During this epoch of his ascendancy, Hernán Cortés was characterized as "the new Moses," who ushered the gospel into the "new Israel," a man "chosen by Divine Providence to open the path for the preachers." Recently arrived friars shared the governor's view that Indians must be segregated from Spaniards, but for different reasons. With a paternalistic tone that became typical of their voluminous accounts over the coming half century, the friars likened the Indians to vulnerable "baby birds" whose wings were not yet strong enough for flight. To be converted, the Indians needed to be dramati-

PREVIOUS: *Church of San Agustín de Acolman*
RIGHT: *Sixteenth-century Franciscan religious instruction in New Spain, after Valades, Rhetorica cristiana, 1579*

cally isolated from all vestiges of corruption remaining in their society. The friars accomplished this protective labor of love—preparing the Indians for receiving the true logos, that is, "the Christian idea of history"—by identifying with their charges, living among them, eating their food, attempting to learn their language, and, above all, destroying the written and visual talismans of their Satanic past—"the picture-books of the Devil."[7]

In flames fueled by this missionary fervor, centuries of priceless "primordial titles" were incinerated by the Christian missionaries in New Spain:

> On these long sheets of bark paper, signs and images spoke. They told of work done and days spent, of the dreams and the wars of a people born before Christ. The inquisitor burns the books. Around the huge bonfire, he chastises the readers. Meanwhile, the authors, artist-priests dead years or centuries ago, drink chocolate in the fresh shade of the first tree of the world. They are at peace, because they died knowing that memory cannot be burned. When its little paper houses are burned, memory finds refuge in mouths that sing the glories of men and of gods, songs that stay on from people to people and in bodies that dance to the sound of hollow trunks, tortoise shells, and reed flutes.[8]

Believing that religious transformation could take root only on freshly cleared terrain, the first friars zealously ordained the elimination of all manifestations of Indian belief: they leveled temples, smashed idols, burned codices (vigorously prosecuting village elders for harboring even one copy of the *tonalamatl*, the sacred ritual-calendrical manuscript), banned celebration of traditional rites and the public recitation of ancient poetry, and often relocated entire villages.[9]

With "subtle, artificial logic" the conquistadores had already succeeded in glorifying "the destruction

of a world." With messianic fervor, the "worthy friars" justified their work: deliberately "tearing out a kaleidoscopic page from the rainbow-colored records of aboriginal America…and bequeathing us broken fragments," disenfranchising a brand of native history many (but not all) of them condemned.[10]

With a clean slate, the Franciscans then set themselves to the monumental, God-given task of retelling the entire indigenous story in their own way, imposing their own systematic methods to interview Indian seers for their memories in order to digest and in some cases reduce or expurgate native accounts. For instance, in the case of one "official Mexica history of the world" called the *Historia de los Mexicanos por Sus Pinturas* (1531), the original pictorial codex upon which it was based was known to have been described and then punitively burned. The *Historia* may not have been a "self-sufficient" text. Like many of its type, it required an accompanying "ritualized, didactic oration" with additional nuances that would have been inspired in the mind of an elder or designated *tlatoani* ("speaker") as he regarded the pictures.[11] The priests likewise taught the Indians for the first time how to annotate pictures with written narratives composed of Nahuatl words using Spanish letters. These Christianized narratives supplanted the native oral histories from which they originated.

In these ways, a new genre of Church-sanctioned ethnography evolved in New Spain. The next incarnation of the Quetzalcóatl story was refracted through a Catholic prism.[12]

Among the first group of twelve Franciscans in New Spain was Fray (Brother) Toribio de Benavente (1500?–1568). He overheard the Indians comment on his bare feet and threadbare appearance, using the Nahuatl word *motolinía*, "the poor little one," and took this as his name.[13] In 1536 Motolinía began one of the earliest colonial books on indigenous life, the *Historia de los Indios de la Nueva España*.

Motolinía celebrated the first mass in Puebla and spent most of his career in New Spain in and around that region, including neighboring Cholula and Tlaxcala. This is significant because, long before the Toltec incursion, it was an area dedicated to the spirit of Plumed Serpent. Motolinía refers to Quetzalcóatl both as "Demon" and "Savior," an appropriate dichotomy for the early ambivalence of the Christian missionaries who confronted this most spiritual of all indigenous gods.[14]

The "Demon" dimension is explicable because the churchmen arrived in the immediate wake of an overwhelming "Aztec-centric" rendition of Quetzalcóatl. His peaceful sanctity had become obscured. He was a demon insofar as he represented an alien spirituality. Motolinía preferred to identify with (and no doubt gained personal solace from) Quetzalcóatl's more benign, even Christlike qualities as an "ascetic" who preached to a "chaste and temperate" cult, who did not tolerate human sacrifice, and who struggled mightily against temptations presented by the Judaslike trickster Tezcatlipoca.[15]

Fray Bernardino de Sahagún (1499?–1590), like Motolinía a Franciscan missionary in New Spain, has been called with good reason "the father of modern ethnography." Among the first of his holy order to master the Nahuatl language, he then went a step further and actually wrote a Spanish-Nahuatl dictionary as an aid to his colleagues. In 1558 Sahagún was asked by the head of the Franciscan order to "undertake a systematic investigation of the native culture" as a step toward "Christianizing the natives of New Spain." Sahagún set up headquarters in the town of Tepepolco, northeast of Mexico City, and for two years exhaustively "interrogated" upper-class Indians on every aspect of their lives, mores, and legends.

He then moved, along with his staff of "indigenous but acculturated" trilingual interviewers, to Tlatelolco, where he spent another several years conducting a similar set of field interviews.

The next decade of Sahagún's labor was spent in Tenochtitlán, where the "final organization" of all his documentation was amassed and consolidated into the twelve-volume classic, *Historia General de las Cosas de Nueva España*, the *General History of the Things of New Spain*. It was transcribed into a Nahuatl-Spanish edition and sent to Spain and then Florence by 1588, where—popularly referred to as the *Florentine Codex*—it is now in the archives of the Biblioteca Medicea Laurenziana.[16]

The *Florentine Codex* has become the most frequently cited postconquest documentary text. With respect to the story of Plumed Serpent, the codex contains a fascinating disclaimer. To Sahagún—who was at great pains to piece together the entire story of his birth, life, death and resurrection—Quetzalcóatl was not a god, but rather

> *a mortal and carnal man, who, despite a virtuous appearance, according to what was told, was only a great necromancer.... What your ancestors tell you [Sahagún wrote, sternly addressing his readers] that Quetzalcóatl went to Tlapallán and that he is to return, and that you must wait for him, is a lie, for we know that he is dead and that his body has returned to earth.*

By vigorously denying Plumed Serpent's viability as a deity, however, Sahagún concedes the likelihood of his historicity, or at least the conviction of such in the minds of his native worshipers: "These—*the ancients*—worshiped an idol called Quetzalcóatl who was a ruler of Tula. And you named him *Topiltzin*. He was a man. He was mortal, for he died. He is no god.... His body died, here on earth it became dust." To Sahagún the Catholic priest, the legend of Plumed Serpent as a deity had to remain just that, a sacrilegious and pagan tale of yet another "false god."

Although it was his sworn duty to recount this pervasive tale and many others, Sahagún also bore in mind his religious responsibility to insist that he did not believe in the Quetzalcóatl represented as a "descending god," coming down from the summit of

Ometeotl, the heavenly mountain, resplendent "beyond imagining, beyond thought…an incarnation of the Inconceivable [on] the axial ladder let down through an opening in the middle of the sky, as though from the golden sun-door of noon to the navel of the earth."[17]

Once his personal Christian credo is laid down, however, Sahagún offers detailed and valuable insights into the identity of Plumed Serpent reaching far enough into the past to establish lines of connection between Olmec and Toltec beliefs. The Nahua described themselves proudly to Sahagún as succeeding from "*la generacion de los Toltecas*," those who stayed in Tula after Topiltzin Quetzalcóatl, the great progenitor, (as *hombre*, not *dios*) carried on eastward to the land of Tlapallán.

Later, in Part X of his massive codex, when discussing the Olmec mother culture of the Gulf Coast, Sahagún reports that even though the Olmec spoke a non-Nahua, "barbarous" tongue, they identified themselves similarly as "*desciendentes de los Toltecas....* Their fertile lands and great wealth are then described, as well as some of their principle customs. It is pointed out that because of their wealth, [the Olmec] were called *hijos* [children] *de Quetzalcóatl*."[18]

The importance of Plumed Serpent representing the exemplary qualities required of the true Quetzalcóatl priest in Nahua culture is strenuously underscored by Sahagún (Book III, Section IX) because once again we are not considering a god but rather a paradigm for morally correct human behavior:

Always the ruler and the great judges elected [i.e., from the ranks of the calmécac *priestly training schools] those who were especially wise and prudent.... Not lineage was considered, only a good life. This indeed was considered. This one was sought out, one of good life, one of righteous life, of pure heart, of good heart, of compassionate heart; one who was resigned, one who was firm, one who was tranquil; one who was not vindictive, one who was strong of heart, one who was of constant heart, one who was of pungent heart, one who made much of another, one who embraced others, one who esteemed others, one who was compassionate of others.*[19]

Sahagún is equally lyrical in the rendition of Quetzalcóatl's decline, fall, and tragic exile from Tula, "climb[ing] between Popocatepétl and Iztaccíhuatl." Even if he must be insisted upon as mere mortal, Quetzalcóatl was larger than life: "And it was said, he was monstrous. His face was like a huge, battered stone, a great fallen rock. It was not made like that of men. And his beard was very long—exceedingly long." In another passage, Sahagún similarly equates Quetzalcóatl with Hercules. His body, symbolizing the "body politic" of Tula, a city in decline, is glorified, so that the story of his removal from grace when it comes in Book III is all the more poignant. As he is drawn to drink Tezcatlipoca's intoxicating potion, Plumed Serpent laments, "Nowhere am I well—my hands, my feet, in truth my body is tired, as if it were undone." Shown the reflection of his transgressing flesh in Tezcatlipoca's mirror, "in a terror of self-recognition" Plumed Serpent cries, "What is this? What thing is my body?" We cannot help but think of Christ's words, and behind them Sahagún's wishful theological thinking, his irrepressible search to find a parallel within a familiar, seductive story he *can* believe. Along the same lines, what are we to make of Quetzalcóatl's crown of agave-leaf "thorns" or of his autosacrifice as "This is my blood"?

These are the syncretistic corruptions and visual slippages insinuated into priestly narratives, attempts—conscious or unconscious—to reconcile and combine different and opposing philosophical and religious principles.[20]

In the preface to the *Florentine Codex*, Sahagún

compared his great literary labor in the midst of the Indians to the task of the doctor in confrontation with his patient. The first thing he needs to do in order to "cure" the sick man is find out as much as possible about what "ails" him. In order to transform the pagans, the inquisitor-priests had first to learn more deeply about them.

Jean Charlot, a French artist and friend to the Mexican muralists of the 1920s, cast the priests' mission in a more ironic light. "Cultural conquest," he wrote, "required as its first step a taking stock of the Indian heritage." This meant transmuting a people of the spoken word into a people of the written word. After the colonization of resources and bodies came the colonization of minds.[21]

Whatever we conclude about Sahagún's ostensible or real (and sincere) motivations, because his work was so lengthy and prepossessing—and still stands as an encyclopedic, formidable, and conveniently orderly gateway to a vast civilization—his field-research methods have been widely questioned in Mexico. For example,

To what degree can the answers [i.e., to the questions posed by Sahagún's colegiales, research assistants] be considered reflections of the ancient culture, rather than merely the personal or class attitudes of the elderly informants [in Tepepolco], since they all belonged to the upper stratum of Nahuatl society?[22]

Furthermore, "Was Sahagún's interpretation of certain of his informant's texts, as presented by him … always the result of an adequate understanding of what the informants had said?"[23]

Ramón Eduardo Ruiz is most outspoken:

Again and again, what purports to be a record of the native viewpoint is actually what the European writers thought the natives were thinking. Rare was the Spanish chronicler, furthermore, who was equipped to report objective-

ly on what was taking place. Even when sympathetic—as the observations of some of the early friars certainly were—their versions display the inevitable bias of writers from one culture looking through the barriers of language and cultural differences at the members of another.[24]

Unlike his Franciscan predecessors, the Dominican priest Diego Durán (1537?–1588) was less concerned with establishing a completely new rendition of the history of the native peoples than he was with a fresh interpretation. Perhaps this shift in attitude came about because, unlike Motolinía and Sahagún, Fray Diego had come to New Spain as a little boy of five years old and had grown up there, in close contact with the indigenous culture and language from a formative period of his life.[25]

"Those who with fervent zeal (though with little prudence) in the beginning burned and destroyed all the ancient pictographic documents were mistaken," Durán wrote. "They left us without a light to guide us." His great work, the *Historia de las Indias de la Nueva España* (1576–1581), possesses an undercurrent of healthy skepticism. Given the persistence of the "heathen" religion even after half a century of mass conversions,[26] Durán believed that Christianization of the Aztecs would remain arduous. He complained that "the whole of their culture is impregnated with the old values." He wrote that the Aztecs must have been descendants of one of the lost Hebrew tribes. Like the Aztecs, the Hebrews considered themselves to be "chosen people." Both suffered lengthy trials and plagues in the desert, wandering for many years until reaching "their respective promised lands." Durán's affinities in this regard may have developed from his family in Spain, who were originally *conversos*, converted Jews.[27]

With respect to Plumed Serpent, Durán begins by taking a leaf from Sahagún's book, referring to

*the probable identity of a great man who lived
in this country, named Topiltzin.... These
people have traditions regarding a great man.
They told me that after he had suffered
many afflictions and persecutions from his
countrymen, he gathered the multitude of his
followers [like Moses] and persuaded them
to flee from that persecution to a land where
they could live in peace.*

Having made himself leader of those people, he went
to the seashore and moved the waters with a rod that
he carried in his hand. As with Sahagún (who had
reiterated that Plumed Serpent "was no god"), Durán
bears personal witness to what he has been told.
There is no doubt in his mind that, variants in content aside, the story of Topiltzin—man, not god—was
linked to an idealized vision of a peaceful future and
had sunk deep roots in Mexica culture.

Much later in the *Historia*, as if to reinforce the
pre-existence of Topiltzin as prince, Durán "quotes"
King Moctezuma I (the father of the Moctezuma
who succumbed to the Spanish invaders) speaking
to his brother, Tlacaélel, about the King's likeness
carved into rock ledges at Chapultepec. "I am well
pleased with these images! They will remain as a
perpetual memorial to our greatness, in the way that
we remember Quetzalcóatl Topiltzin [who] left his
images carved in wood and on stone. *The commoners worship these, but we know that they were men
like us.*"[28]

Diego Durán's boldest theory was that, despite
their sins and abhorrent customs, the natives of
New Spain were, after all, fundamentally "God's
creatures." As such, He would not have allowed
them to exist upon this Earth without a proponent
of His gospel walking among them. Had not the
apostles been sent forth to preach to *all* nations?
Then one of the twelve surely must have reached
these shores. St. Thomas therefore was the *true*
Plumed Serpent.[29]

At first glance, Durán's "diffusionist" theory
devalues the native legend, the underlying assumption being that Plumed Serpent myth was too complex, rich, and sophisticated to have grown in the
arid soil of a "backward" culture. These Indians
must have had "a white-skinned tutor."[30]

Durán backed up his case that the gospel had
already been preached, albeit unsuccessfully, in this
new land by summarizing all the parallels he discerned between St. Thomas and Topiltzin: both had
performed miracles; both had been honored and
revered as holy persons; both had been renowned as
sculptors [Toltec artisan-craftsmen]; both had spent
much time praying, living chastely, and "performing
acts of penance, [and] had abstained from meat, and
fasted"; and both had been followed by disciples.[31]

In the Yucatán, rampant destruction of native texts
was likewise carried forward. Again, one of the
most ardent book-burners became one of the most
diligent historians. Fray Diego de Landa arrived as a
member of the Franciscan order in 1549, with the
charge, as he quaintly put it, "to instruct the Indian
children." Thirteen years later, in July 1562, at Mani,
he presided over a pyre of twenty-seven picture
books he determined were "works of the Devil,"
"deluding" the Indians and distracting them from
understanding the true word.

Upon his return to Spain in 1566, Landa composed the *Relación de las Cosas de Yucatán*, translated into French by the Abbé Brasseur de Bourbourg
and published in Paris three hundred years later.[32]

Here is the familiar story of Kukulkán, [or Kukul
Can], a man who came from the west in a second
wave of Itzá immigration after the original peoples
from the region of Chiapas and who had significantly "wandered for forty years." Kukulkán was "rever-
enced as a god," before returning to Mexico, where
he was worshiped as Cezalcohuati [Quetzalcóatl].
The movement of a person may have been blurred
with the movement of an entire people. Kukulkán's

classic attributes remained embedded in Mayan culture. He—or his imported ethos—was seen as responsible for the growth of organized religion and for the introduction of hieroglyphic writing in the Yucatán region before the Conquest.[33]

Every year, on the evening of the sixteenth day of the Mayan month *Xul* (November 8), a great festival, resembling the "New Fire" ritual of the Aztecs, was celebrated in worship of Kukulkán. The chiefs and fasting priests sat for five days and nights, burning incense and making offerings. It was believed that on the fifth day, Kukulkán descended from heaven and accepted the penance of his people.

At the relatively late period when Landa composed his history, the belief persisted in the area of Chichén Itzá that the men from the land to the west had originally come "to rule in great peace, and with justice." Landa describes the main Temple of Kukulkán at Chichén Itzá with its serpent-mouth foundations; consecrated to closely held ideals of purity, it was subsequently perverted and dissolved when this Great Man became "absent."[34]

I remember stopping on Highway 132D heading out from Mexico City to Teotihuacán to pay a visit to the airy, gothic monastery of San Agustín de Acolman, one of the finest examples of the blending of Indian and Christian iconography. It was built and intricately adorned between 1539 and 1560 by indigenous carvers under the supervision of European designers.

Across the road from the main door of the atrium, behind a wrought-iron fence, stands the *Cruz Atrial*, the Indian rendering of the Passion of Christ. The dun-colored cross is proudly out of doors in full sunlight, an innovation inspired by native ritual practice, moving the tradition of Catholic worship from

darkness into open air. Its shape reminds me of two rounded, hewn logs fused together. Only Christ's head appears at the crux, surrounded by flowers and skulls eerily reminiscent of the racks where flayed heads of sacrificial victims were mounted.

A full fifty years after the Conquest, Diego Durán told the story of encountering an old Indian man "persisting in his pagan practices. I reprimanded him for the foolish thing he had done, and he answered, 'Father, do not be astonished, we are still *nepantla* [in the middle].'" Durán observed that his "converted" flock came to celebrate Mass only on days corresponding with holy days in their ritual calendars. And he surmised that those who entered the new cathedral—built by Indian labor—in the center of Mexico City did so in order to continue to worship their old gods. The stones of destroyed temples had been used in its construction, and "the columns of the Cathedral actually [stood] on the plumed serpent."[35]

By the end of the sixteenth century, the art of pictorial manuscript painting among the Indians had died. But "under the slight veneer of Christianity, the ancient religion was still thriving." It was "like a plant caught beneath the ruins of a building that has collapsed, which—after a painful struggle—manages to push its leaves through the ruins."[36]

Despite "all the terrors of Spanish ecclesiasticism," the old ways reappeared, stubbornly and secretly: in the faces of ancient gods incised into church niches; behind altars consecrated to the body and blood of Christ, where little idols lay buried; in local spirits, *santos*, honored in village and field; in patrimonies of poetry preserved within well-trained and stubborn memories of old men; in *las grutas*, the subterranean caves of Mayaland, where the wraith of Ix Chel, Moon Goddess, floated above the Virgin Mary.[37]

The Indian rock was a very large one,
but the Spanish hammer,
though small, was wielded
with terrific force.
Under its quick reiterated blows,
the strangely sculptured monolith
of American civilization broke
into fragments.
The bits are still there, indestructible,
but no longer a shapely whole.

— ALDOUS HUXLEY[1]

CHAPTER XVII

CREOLES

No matter who writes about the Conquest and its aftermath, the images are consistently violent. Octavio Paz refers to a "clean and deep slash line" separating the old society from the new, the tribal culture from New Spain.[2]

Cortés was not Quetzalcóatl.

How to imagine the sixteenth-century worldview of the Mesoamerican Indians, whose ancestors engendered Plumed Serpent three thousand years earlier and who had no choice but to move on — if only temporarily — from the unfulfilled dream of a "foreign redeemer"?[3]

Despite military defeat, religious suppression, the denial of history in their terms, the accompanying degradation of their languages, and slavery under new masters, the emotion of what we call "disillusionment" would have had no meaning for the Indian people of New Spain. There was a reason for what had happened to them. As surely as day followed night, the end of a cycle always triggered the advent of another. New gods of Christianity had arrived; hence the appearance of a new Plumed Serpent in a different guise was inevitable. The stones of new Christian churches stood atop foundations made from the ruins of old Indian temples. New Christian gods had eclipsed but not eradicated the old Indian gods. Idols lay temporarily vanquished but not dead. Baptized Indians still followed the old ways:

The Indians parade the Virgin on feathered platforms. Calling her Grandmother of the Light, they ask her each night that tomorrow may bring the sun; but they venerate more devoutly the serpent that she grinds underfoot. They offer incense to the serpent, the old god who gives a good corn crop and good deer hunting and helps them to kill enemies. More than Saint George, they worship the dragon.[4]

The Spanish Crown's bureaucratic representatives sent over from the mother country — aristocratic viceroys, beginning with Antonio Mendoza — shared the paternalism of the friars and viewed the Indian-*peónes* of New Spain as inhabiting their own inferior, segregated, one-class society, separate from the colonists. It was a feudal pyramid with an exclusive, light-skinned summit and a broad, dark-skinned base. The authority of village leaders with traditional higher status was no longer recognized. The Indians were seen as all one kind, legal minors "upon whose brown shoulders the white world rested." Wards of the state, they no longer worked only for the benefit of their communities. They labored in hazardous silver mines for Spanish employers and were poor chattel slaves *sui generis*. "They spoke their own language; they lived in huts; they hardly ate at all." They were organized into gridlike rural communes outside burgeoning cities.[5]

Pedro Antonio Fresquis, The Virgin of Guadalupe, ca. 1780–1830

Toward midcentury the power of Charles V waned, and at last he abdicated. With Charles's departure came a decline in the vestiges of imperial "conquistador mentality" and the rise of *criollos* (creoles), a breed of so-called new men with a new version of national character. These were the first Spaniards born in the New World, a proud group, children of conquerors and descendants of first immigrants; they cherished their unique lineage while taking pains to distinguish themselves from their parents, like any rebellious generation. They set themselves apart disdainfully from the Spanish-born *peninsulare* immigrants and from the much-maligned *mestizos*.

Sharing the lowest rung on the caste system of New Spain with Indians, blacks, and mulattoes, the mestizos were the predominantly illegitimate children of Spanish men and Indian women, habitually abandoned by their fathers to grow up in impoverished Indian villages.[6]

How to imagine the colonial creole mentality, beginning in the middle of the sixteenth century, trying to cope with an Indian society relegated to subservience but with no intention of disappearing? In fact, the native population began to grow again by the end of the eighteenth century after the ripples of the smallpox and famine years had finally faded. How could the "pervasive, secret presence" of the Indian society be legitimately "negated" by the creoles, placed at the outermost fringes except for one purpose, to support the master class? Could the colonists truly and cleanly claim New Spain as their own, with a new consciousness as "distinct people," emphatically not European, without assigning any value to the Indian past?[7]

These questions formed the core of an important struggle seizing the imaginations and testing the faith of the clerical scholars and university intellectuals of New Spain. The struggle to articulate—to construct—a creole identity evolved over the ensuing two hundred and fifty years.

The primary touchstone for this debate was the identity of Plumed Serpent, the most sustained and therefore most unavoidable indigenous entity of all. The process of revisiting and revising Plumed Serpent's lineage dovetailed with the effort to confer integrity upon New Spain.

The Dominican priest Diego Durán had already set the theological wheels in motion with his daring supposition that Plumed Serpent might very well have been St. Thomas, preaching (without success) in the new land. The historian Fernando de Alva Ixtlilxochitl (1578–1650), a direct descendant of the revered lords of Teotihuacán, concurred gingerly that "in the epoch of Christ's incarnation," the Olmec people, which he situated prior to the Toltecs, were visited by Quetzalcóatl-Huemac.

The baton was carried one step farther along by Antonio de la Calancha (1584–1654). He was an Augustinian in Peru who believed that America could not possibly have been entirely overlooked by "the Twelve" and who stated, again with some obliqueness, that "seventy-two years after Christ's birth, the Gospel had been taught in the West Indies."

The underlying motivation behind these informed if hesitant speculations was to impart a Christian basis to New Spain through the person of "Quetzalcóatl-as-Saint-Thomas" or the "Phoenix of the West," freeing New Spain from any hint of spiritual debt to the mother country.

Nevertheless, the Franciscan Juan de Torquemada (1562?–1624), in his massive history of Anáhuac, *Monarquia Indiana*, adamantly rejected the absurd supposition that Toltec high culture emanated out of "an early Apostolic mission to the New World." Quetzalcóatl the man, on the contrary, was expelled from Tula in the eighth century A.D. because he was a demonic necromancer and a coyotelike trickster. It had been sheer "folly" for the Toltecs to believe in his return.[8]

With the efflorescence of the last priestly order to reach the New World, the Jesuits, Plumed Serpent's identity crystallized in the conflicted search for roots obsessing the minds of creole New Spain. The poet and historian Don Carlos de Sigüenza y Góngora (1645–1700), a Jesuit until his expulsion from the Puebla order in 1688, significantly appropriated and fashioned for his major works the name Mexico from the original Mexica peoples, signaling it as a predestined homage to his present homeland—"no mere adjunct of Spain," he declared, "but a country with a rich heritage of its own."

Although he looked down upon the contemporary Indian, Góngora criticized the conquistadores for having been so cruel to those he deemed spiritual forbears, the noble Aztecs. In 1680 Sigüenza was commissioned to design the traditional welcoming arch in Mexico City for the newly arrived Viceroy, Don Tomas Antonio de la Cerda. He incorporated portraits of Aztec rulers and the god Huitzilopochtli, who led the original Aztecs to Anáhuac. His didactic purpose was to show a causal relationship between the Mexico-Tenochtitlán of yore and the Mexico City of his time.[9]

Composing his *Historia antigua de Mexico* while exiled in Italy—more than two thousand Mexican-born members of "the Sons of Loyola" were expelled from New Spain by the government of Charles III in 1767—the criollo Jesuit and professor Francisco Xavier Clavijero (1731–1787) was the man who stringently divorced the indigenous past of the unknown continent from any connection with the preaching of the gospel.

Ancient Mesoamerican beliefs possessed their own inherent validity, he said. There had never been a need for apostolic creeds. The serious, unfettered study of classical (dignified) Indian society, with its valuable documents and customs, revealed once and for all a magnificent, moral civilization, akin to that of ancient Rome (in this perspective he agreed with Góngora), with a wealth of "natural virtues" and "true faith."

The bias of Jesuit-influenced creole history tilted

Virgin of Guadalupe

gradually away from the no-longer-irreproachable motives of the conquistador invaders toward sympathy for noble savages of antiquity. It was not Hernán Cortés but Moctezuma and the brave martyr Cuauhtémoc who had laid the groundwork for the promised land in which the creoles now lived.[10]

A decade after the Conquest, in early December 1531, a poor Indian named Juan Diego was

125

walking in the mountains near the town of Tepeyac, four miles north of Mexico City, when he heard what seemed like celestial music. In a splash of light he saw a gleaming, dark-skinned Lady hovering miraculously above a nopal cactus, just as the eagle had appeared before Juan's Aztec forefathers when they came upon the place called Tenochtitlán. The Lady told Juan Diego to go to Bishop Juan de Zumárraga and ask him to build a shrine in her honor. The Bishop rebuffed the Indian several times, until poor Juan at last appeared with his cape strangely full of roses in midwinter, provided by the Lady. When Juan opened his cloak before the Bishop and the "holy forest" of flowers fell to the ground, they left Her likeness painted in the coarsely woven cactus-fiber cloth. At this sight the bishop was overwhelmed, and a chapel was built at Tepeyac, rebuilt nearly one hundred years later, and rebuilt yet again as a great basilica on the same site at the end of the seventeenth century.

The story of the Virgin of Guadalupe, as she came to be known—retold and enhanced by criollo priests in the middle years of the seventeenth century and spread throughout the country—became powerful testimony to the spiritual autonomy of New Spain: "The private ecstatic experience [was] translated over the years into a communal experience whereby a whole people [was] blessed."

There is a link between the developing cult of the Virgin and the swirling, contradictory stories making up the accumulated biography of Quetzalcóatl. The village of Tepeyac was known before the Conquest as the site of feast-day veneration of the white petticoat-clad Tonantzin, sacred "snake-Earth Mother-goddess" and "wife of the Serpent" in the Aztec pantheon. She was often portrayed decorated with flowers and seashells and carrying a broom, a female complement to Quetzalcóatl the road sweeper.[11]

When Juan Diego spoke excitedly in the Nahuatl tongue of his sighting of the Virgin, he could well have said *coatalocpia*, the phonetic equivalent of the Spanish place-name Guadalupe, a combination of *cóatl* (serpent), *tealoc* (goddess), and *tlapia* (watch over): "protective serpent goddess." As a convert to Catholicism, Juan Diego would have learned from his clerical teachers of the Immaculate Conception of the Virgin. In any case—as with so many Indian gods and Christian figures—the Virgin's familiar story was conflated with the underlying female force of Tonantzin, whose ancient name is still referred to in Tepeyac, now a suburb of modern Mexico City.[12]

For the creole priests who refined and tailored aspects of this epiphanic tale to suit the evolving identity of their "Western Paradise" of Mexico, the Virgin of Guadalupe's revelation was a clear statement. The Lord was treating the Mexican people differently than any other on earth by giving them, in the person of this brown-skinned Mary, "their own patroness...the mark of [their] favor with God."[13]

A detailed account of the entire viceregal period—absorbing as it would be—is beyond the scope of this book. However, to remain true to our

Miguel Hidalgo y Castilla

biography of a myth, it is necessary to scan the accumulation of nationalistic currents that flowed out of New Spain's indigenous past into the highly charged personalities of the insurgent uprising.

The late eighteenth century was an unprecedented boom time for New Spain. This prosperous economic situation aggravated tensions between a colony that felt it was being exploited and an increasingly watchful landlord across the sea. With more than two-thirds of its entire colonial revenues derived from New Spain, the Bourbon mother country imposed higher taxes and ever more stringent trade-outflow requirements.

For the first time since the Conquest, royal troops were sent over to New Spain. The viceroys in residence were selected on the basis of their military experience. A new governing structure divided the recalcitrant colony into twelve regional departments. The expulsion of the Jesuits was another symptom of growing tensions and was especially hurtful to the Indians; the measure was taken because of King Charles's suspicion that activist priests were encouraging revolt.

The victorious struggle of the thirteen English colonies in North America and the Haitian slave rebellion against seemingly impossible odds made an impression on the criollos. "The Mexican, a Mexican without a Mexico, a Mexican of New Spain…[felt] that he was living on borrowed time." Four years after the "Conspiracy of the Machetes"—the first quelled creole rebellion in New Spain—the scientific traveler Alexander von Humboldt was acutely sensitive to the precarious atmosphere as he ranged outward in all directions from Mexico City during an eleven-month stay in 1803–1804. He observed,

Mexico is the country of inequality.… Since the peace of Versailles, and in particular since the year 1789, we frequently hear proudly declared, "I am not a Spaniard, I am an American"—words which betray the workings of a long resentment…The mother country foments incessantly the spirit of hatred among the castes and constituted authorities.[14]

When France invaded Spain in 1808, Napoleon Bonaparte installed his brother Joseph as ruler, forced Ferdinand VII to abdicate the throne, and imprisoned him in France. The government of New Spain, already on shaky ground, was thrown into confusion. Juntas arose immediately in most other South American colonial territories. Secret criollo grievance groups in New Spain, the last to take action, coalesced all over the country, trying to organize and seize their moment as chaos reigned overseas. Had the time for rupture finally come, and were they capable of stepping into the breach?

The leader of the New Spain Independence movement was Miguel Hidalgo y Costilla (1753–1811), a descendant of the founders of the city of Valladolid in Michoacán. The son of a criollo hacienda manager, Miguel was schooled by Jesuits and then taught at the Colegio de San Nicolas in his hometown for more than two decades. He was a classical scholar who spoke French as well as several native tongues, including Mixtec and Nahuatl. An expert farmer and builder, he liked nothing more than to roll up his sleeves and work side by side with his flock. Hidalgo had the popular touch and pleaded for the abolition of Indian servitude.

Yet with typical criollo ambivalence (and after all, unlike the Indians, the creoles, self-styled loyal vassals, were never economically disenfranchised) Hidalgo believed in the sovereignty of the king and favored Ferdinand's eventual return to power. He wanted New Spain to become a free, independent *patria* and was an enemy of bad government; yet he praised the king and did not bear him any personal animosity.

"Long live *America*! My children! Will you free yourselves?" These were Hidalgo's ringing words as the bells chimed from the steeples in his parish of

Dolores. "Will you recover the lands stolen three hundred years ago from your forefathers by the hated Spaniards? The present movement attempts to regain the holy rights conceded by God to the Mexicans!"

Hidalgo marched toward Guanajuato in late September 1810 under the banner of the Virgin of Guadalupe tied to a spear. He instinctively understood that Her sacred image, a "badge of favor," would galvanize and inspire the people to act with a sense of divine mission: "Long live Our Lady of Guadalupe! Death to the *gachupines*— the Spanish dogs!" Hidalgo gathered an army of tens of thousands of mestizos, Indians, miners, and farmers. Pelting a rain of stones, they descended upon the city and set fire to the Corn Exchange building at the center of town.[15]

Emboldened by their victory, the insurgents overran Spanish forces in territories north and west of Mexico City and then headed south toward the capital itself. There, on the brink of an invasion that surely would have brought the struggle to an immediate close, Hidalgo had a change of heart and chose to retreat north toward Guadalajara and Texas.

Hidalgo had come face to face with the ultimate test of his resolve, and then criollo inhibitions won out. After all, he was a clergyman by training, not a soldier. Not able to confront such an extreme of violence, he collapsed. By the early spring of 1811, his ranks were depleted and divided, and Hidalgo was captured near Chihuahua. He was judged guilty of treason, defrocked, shot by a firing squad, and beheaded.

José María Morelos

Hidalgo's idealistic intentions and his ability to inspire the rank and file with fiery rhetoric ultimately clashed with his moderate, intellectual side. Even his military colleague, the young Ignacio Allende— also executed at Chihuahua—was unable to control the passions of the masses once Hidalgo had set them in motion.

When Hidalgo died, the peoples' impulses as well as their confusion remained his legacy. But criollo faith was greatly diminished. The desire for an end to the old order was real, but the means to that end seemed objectionable to those in New Spain who had aspirations toward a new order.

José María Morelos (1765–1815) learned this lesson quickly when he assumed command of the uprising. Like Hidalgo, he was a devout Catholic and a native of the mountains of Michoacán. Like Hidalgo, he was a parish priest concerned with the needs of the poor. But there the likeness ends. Morelos was a mestizo. Ill-educated, stocky of build, he had spent his younger years as a mule driver and still took to wearing a handkerchief across his sweaty brow.

Morelos understood how to win back criollo sympathies. In September 1813, he convened a Congress of Independence at Chilpancingo, south of Mexico City in the province of Guerrero. He pointedly made reference to long-past generations of indigenous heroes—the familiar names of Moctezuma and Cuauhtémoc—who, during the great era of Anáhuac, had paved the way with their lives so that their modern "sons" could "free themselves from the claws of tyranny." The memory of Miguel Hidalgo was invoked as a link in the chain of this tradition of Mexican heroism. All the rhetoric in the world accompanied by seemingly inexhaustible parades of guerillas were not enough to withstand the sophistication of Spanish forces under the expert and merciless command of Viceroy Félix Maria Calleja del Rey. Within two years, Morelos was captured and killed.

Independence, when it finally and wearily arrived in Mexico, was anticlimactic after the constant pendulum swings of the preceding decade. It came in the person of Augustín de Iturbide, a criollo who had established and built his career by joining the Royal Army in New Spain and battling both Hidalgo and Morelos. With expedience and the sense that a more enduring victory might lie on the other side, Iturbide crossed over to the insurgent forces and led a campaign in 1820, succeeding in overthrowing the same viceroy who had employed him.

In February 1821, Iturbide presented his *Plan de Iguala*, a manifesto for independence, to the Spanish Crown. It differed from the manifestos of 1813 with its moderate language guaranteeing status quo to both dominant white classes in Mexican society—peninsulares born in Spain as well as criollos. The Church hierarchy remained in place, as did the rights of the gentry to hold on to their lands.

Mexico, a colony no longer, would henceforth become a "constitutional monarchy." The tactically sophisticated representative of the crown, Juan de O'Donojú, recognized the right of Iturbide, with his grip firm on the military, to ascend to the role as the new nation's first emperor.

It had been a strange, attenuated revolution animated by appropriating as its models the indigenous peoples of Anáhuac against the blackguard oppressors from Spain. It was perpetuated by exploiting the raw strength of the disenfranchised and concluded—or compromised—by reaffirming the authority of vested interests who reconciled their resistance to change with the craving for autonomy.

Plumed Serpent had been an undying symbol of hope and renewal throughout the prehistory of Mexico. The early Toltec hope for deliverance was transmuted by the Aztecs (to their perception, justly in the cycles of time). Cuauhtémoc had been a brief flash in the darkness. His spectre would rise again.

The *dios* dimension of Quetzalcóatl had long since become recast to *hombre* in the years of upheaval we have surveyed. There remained a need for a national hero who could forge an emerging Mexican sensibility that was attempting mightily to become "revolutionary."

Heroes have a way of remaining entrenched in the collective imagination of Mexico especially when they fail.

CHAPTER XVIII

THE INDIAN PROBLEM

*The Noche Triste will occur again,
because the blood of the Mexican people
is mostly Aztec and by tradition
and conviction they hate
the murderers of their fathers.*

— *El Monitor Republicano,*
Mexico City, January 9, 1862[1]

Struggling to find words and symbols to define their new republic, writers and artists of nineteenth-century Mexico found a mythic image in the romance of old Anáhuac. To confer dignity and order upon the rampant social disorder of their day, poets gave voice to an imagined past informed by "the soul of the Amerind child of nature." They vaulted over three intervening Spanish colonial centuries as an intrusive aberration, a parenthesis separating the true and present Mexico from its originating spirit, the proud eagle on the cactus bush. They resurrected and idealized the ancient culture, remaking it in their own "severely righteous" style.[2]

The lyricist who exemplifies the Romantic flowering of Mexican letters is Ignacio Rodriguez Galván (1816–1842). In the *Profecía de Guatimoc* (*Prophecy of Cuauhtémoc*), an homage to the last Aztec martyr, the poverty-stricken poet waxes nostalgic, looking to Mexico's Edenic past and yearning for a better future:

Was it reality or dream?…Vain question…
A dream assuredly, for a deep dream
is the voracious passion that consumes me;
it was a dream, no more, the joy that touched
my cheek with faint caress; a dream the accents
of that voice that lulled my grief to sleep;
a dream that smile, a dream that blandishment
and that soft gaze…I suddenly awoke;
and the fair Eden vanished from my sight
as the wave that rides in from the sea
and scatters; there is nothing left to me
except the cruel memory that wrings
my soul and without ceasing gnaws my heart.[3]

Manuel Vilar, The Tlaxcalan General Tlahuicole, 1851

With equal measure, Galván issues a stern warning invoking the shattering debacle of the 1520s. The *Profecía*, written in 1839, was an acerbic, protective reminder of hard-won freedoms composed ten years after the Spanish attempted to reinvade the Mexican republic, only to be repulsed at Tampico by General Santa Anna and his troops:

The barbarous European pardons nothing;
He breaks, he devastates, he annihilates
With furious arm.
His delight is to turn into desert wastes
All inhabited places (Honorable exploits, indeed!)
His sleep is not serene if on dead bodies
He does not pillow his head.....
He who draws the tears of grief from unhappy eyes
Will weep the bitter tears of anguish;
He who tramples on the helpless shall
*   be trampled.*
He who kills wantonly shall reap the harvest
*   of death.*[4]

The reassuring combination of hazy dream with grand, patriotic gesture was echoed in the visual arts of the republic. In midcentury at the Academy of San Carlos in Mexico City, the sculptor Manuel Vilar (1812–1869) concentrated on a series of larger-than-life, Hellenic portrayals of the "noble savages" of yesteryear, such as Moctezuma and Tlahuicole.[5]

Vilar and his teaching colleagues were influential in encouraging a new generation of Mexican painters to concentrate on glorifying the timeless landscape of their *patria* and portraying symbolic scenes from history. Like Galván, the artists sought solace in past triumphs, "rescuing the ancient indigenous world from undeserved oblivion" to meet the challenge of defining their current social identity.[6]

For example, José Obregón could not have chosen a more typically "indigenous" subject than *The Discovery of Pulque* (1869), the native drink distilled from the maguey cactus. There is solemnity and reverence much in evidence through the elegant pose of the maiden bearing her offertory beverage as she is led to the throne of the monarch, perhaps by her proud parents. The courtiers stand in the shadows, quietly gossiping, and the respected Old One sits close by the king's left hand. The classical style of the work "bears no resemblance to Mexican reality."[7]

Similarly, the artist Rodrigo Gutiérrez of San Luis Potosí imagined *The Senate of Tlaxcala* (1875), the governing body of the Tlaxcalan Indians, arranged like the Roman Senate, with sun-drenched orators holding forth as if given breath from above. "This fancy was widely accepted" in romantic and then *Renascimiento* Mexican art of the latter half of the nineteenth century. It left an imprint of reassuring validity on the *cultura* of the republican era. In the dim background idols of the gods can be discerned, although the wall paintings resemble Egyptian hieroglyphs more than indigenous signs.[8]

The true situation of the predominantly rural Indian in nineteenth-century Mexico was in stark and paradoxical contrast to these inspiring images concocted from antiquity. Although the Indians still made up more than 60 percent of the population, *Neoaztequismo*, the revival of pre-Columbian cultures, remained an invention of the intellectuals. The contemporary Indian was silent,

José Obregon, The Discovery of Pulque, 1869

ruled by harsh policies subjecting him to corporal punishment and exploitative labor. The *hacendado*, the supreme authority in the countryside, continued to impose limitless work obligations and abuse the laborer-peons.[9]

"Independence from Spain ushered in no new dawn of liberty" for the Indian. The increasingly bourgeois criollos of Mexico, especially in the cities which were their domain, continued to get richer still. "Equality under the law" was a catch-phrase proclamation of the post-Empire movement. The Estados Unidos Mexicanos Constitution of 1824 emulated the democratic tone of that of its northern neighbor, but it contained no paragraphs itemizing the rights of the poor, whose average daily wage (2.5 *reales*) had remained the same for a century.

As a matter of fact, José María Luis Mora, a liber-al (and pointedly anti-Spanish) "doctrinaire" historian and one of the conveners of the 1824 Congress, moved that the word *indio* (Indian) "be abolished from public usage."[10]

To the governing powers of federalist Mexico, the melancholy, stolid, backward, and degraded Indian was a "problem." He professed indifference to the dominant white society. He refused to learn Spanish and retreated whenever possible to closed communal property—his patch of land, his village. He was a psychological mystery and a moral burden who did not fit in to the abstract picture of ideal, progressive nationhood.[11]

When these Indian *bárbaros* did take it upon themselves periodically to rise up and rebel against

Rodrigo Gutiérrez, The Senate of Tlaxcala, 1875

their oppressive conditions—as, for example, the Yaqui and the Maya did—such revolts only perturbed and confused liberal and conservative alike, prompting them to propose, at various times, revocation of political rights, relocation and colonization, or even extermination of this "dangerous class."[12]

The century following independence was a violent one, a time of rapid change, ceaseless internal and external warfare, and a goodly measure of anarchy. There was no organized, national economic system in this still mostly agricultural country. The Spanish had been expelled, and the creoles who defeated them dominated the most exalted levels of government, the military, and the clergy. Meanwhile, the mestizos also continued to grow in numbers and ambition, intensifying the class conflict that had fragmented the country for so long.

Benito Juárez

The United States went to war against Mexico in 1846, claiming more than half its territory, occupying Mexico City, and intimidating an already unstable society into questioning the validity of its existence when it failed to mobilize to defeat the external threat. The feeling among Mexican liberals was that as long as vestigial colonial-era standards prevailed, particularly an overbearing central government, their nation would never achieve self-definition.

Conservative thinkers believed the exact opposite, advocating both the restoration of church authority and a return to the monarchy, the glory days of Iturbide. After 1824 Mexico's internal turbulence had caused forty-six changes of government, so conservatives welcomed the authoritarian regime of Antonio López de Santa Anna; it was a sporadic remedy, as he was in and out of power for two decades and finally ousted and exiled in 1855.[13]

With the Revolution of Ayutla, the pendulum swung back toward the liberal camp under the ideological leadership of secretary of justice Benito Pablo Juárez (1806–1872), who was later appointed Chief Justice of the Mexican Supreme Court. The orphaned son of Zapotec Indians, Juárez was "born in the mountains, amid the rocks that resemble him, on the shores of Lake Guelatao … without smile or speech, always in frock coat and high collar, always in black." He had been schooled from the age of twelve in the Royal Academy at Oaxaca. He was a man of letters whose well-intentioned Reform Laws aimed at curtailing the authority of the Church. His utopian contributions to the new Constitution of 1857 included, ironically, the endorsement of the removal of Indian-held lands. Juárez was still a nationalist, intertwined with the establishment, and thus could never wholly represent the interests of the people from whom he had sprung.[14]

For three years, from 1858 to 1861, the Civil War of the Reform pitted the liberal splinter government in "exile" in Veracruz against conservative forces centered in Mexico City. The battleground was the Constitution—"the law, and only the law"—the direction in which the country should be heading. Juárez's army prevailed. He was elected president in 1861, but at the expense of severely bankrupting and fragmenting the nation again, leaving it vulnerable to foreign predators.

Spanish and then British forces were repulsed late in 1861, but the French surged through Mexico during the ensuing five years. Napoleon III installed the Austrian archduke Ferdinand Maximilian as Emperor of Mexico. The *Juárista* pariahs eventually ended up far away from Veracruz, biding their time in El Paso del Norte until the winter and spring of 1867, when they seized their moment in Maximilian's weakening regime. "The old Indian Benito Juárez was inexorable," rejecting the captured Maximilian's pleas for clemency and authorizing his execution for the crime of "nationcide" on June 19, 1867. In October, the isolationist Juárez was reelected to the presidency of a country in disarray. More than three hundred thousand people had perished during the "tragic decade."[15]

"The Indian problem" persisted, even during the *Republica Restaurada* period under the nationalistic and controlling Indian president. Juárez's constitutional government espoused universal voting rights, but in fact wealth conditioned democracy. He advocated obligatory education for the young, but in fact schools were predominantly concentrated in urban areas. Juárez spoke in generalities for the right of proprietorship over ancient land plots, but in fact he suspended civil liberties when tenacious Indians in the countrysides of Chiapas, Tabasco, Michoacán, Zacatecas, and Nayarit were driven to burn the haciendas of the *arriviste* new landowners, and when the Maya of Yucatán, where one of every three Indians was a slave, rose up on the *henequen* plantations. During the Juárez years, trying to reclaim what meager communal property they believed was theirs by long-lost birthright, the native peoples of Mexico, unprotected by any liberal laws, were in a state of restlessness verging on revolt. They were constantly trying to break through from a subterranean layer of suppression to the fresh air of recognition.

Mexican "reform" made large ideological strides toward defining what it meant to be Mexican among a mainstream minority.[16]

The masses of Indians, however, continued to live in a diminished, separate economic and cultural reality that provided fertile if only symbolic nourishment for the progressive, highflown sense of self-conscious *mexicanidad* that remained the exclusive province of the urban (and urbane) middle and upper classes and their cultural arts. The new historical novel and the landscape painting of the Academy especially drew their sustenance from the pre-Hispanic era.[17]

Despite all Mexico's pretensions of readiness to join the world community of full-fledged, sophisticated nations, it still felt as if the country had been on a feudal treadmill when the Oaxaca-born mestizo Porfirio Díaz was elected to the presidency in 1876. Although he acted as if he were donning the mantle of liberalism, Díaz was destined to become over the ensuing three decades "the most illustrious dictator in Spanish America," "a born politico but not a statesman," presiding over a society that relinquished none of its stratified character.[18]

Díaz set out forcibly to realize economic expansion in Mexico even as he assumed greater control over all institutions. He instigated the proliferation of telegraph wires and, with them, added thousands of miles of new railroad lines. He accelerated textile manufacturing, petroleum drilling, and silver and mining production. He launched a major drainage project in the Valley of Mexico. He welcomed foreign investments in the Bank of Mexico. He established favorable treaties of trade and commerce with many European nations. He encouraged immigration coupled with larger and larger land grants, especially to foreign farmers and middle-class Mexicans who wanted to become landlords because their presence helped further weaken the Indian presence on traditional *ejidos* (village lands). He returned money and power to a strengthened and centralized federal government and placed sympathetic allies in provincial governorships. He tightened up the justice system and added to the capacity of prisons. He curtailed freedoms of speech and the press.

The *Porfiriato* regime routinely put down border skirmishes and internal uprisings by the perennially troublesome Indians, who continued to protest their conditions of squalor and servitude. Indians of Mexico gave increasingly audible voice to an eternal debate that was growing more extreme in post-Colonial society. The direct consequence of progress and modernity for the few at one end of the spectrum—*hacendado* and capitalist—was festering discontent by peons and laborers on the other.[19]

From Díaz's point of view, the Indians were intellectually benighted. They did not share a perspective on the political life of the whole nation, caring only for their immediate if rapidly diminishing plots of communal soil. Untouched and unmotivated by the industrial revolution, circumvented by the almighty thrust of the locomotive, they would never be able to comprehend the importance of modernizing Mexico. The counterproductive protests of the Indians were quelled by Díaz's elite, hardened *rurales* forces: "It was better that a little blood should be shed [so] that much blood should be saved," the President reflected to James Creelman, interviewing him for *Pearson's Magazine.* "The blood that was shed was bad blood; the blood that was saved was good blood."[20]

This intractable attitude inevitably became untenable as the gulf widened between rich—and even middle class—and poor in Mexico at the turn of the twentieth century. Broad social forces at work

José Guadalupe Posada, The Soul Alone,
La anima sola, ca. 1911

weighed against the racially biased grip of Díaz and his seemingly eternal administration. A new, younger generation of liberal intelligentsia established meeting groups throughout the country. Their primary issue of discussion was inordinate growth in the influence of the Catholic Church, symptomatic of the *Porfiriato*'s overall doctrine that bigger was better.

A series of alternative manifestos and tabloid newspapers vilified Díaz as a "devil" and a "beast" who fed the appetites of his "cronies" in provincial bureaucracies and in the central government, seeking to find the greatest good for the smallest number.[21]

Hand in hand with the natural disenfranchisement of the *campesino* who was forced to seek employment as a lowly day worker on the hacienda—because he no longer possessed enough farmland to remain economically self-sufficient—was the rag-tag but effective growth of a union movement among the industrial laborers. Stagnant wages, inhumanly long hours, and terrible working conditions led to increasingly frequent strikes throughout Mexican railways, factories, mills, and mines—there were hundreds of job actions from the 1890s to the tinderbox years in the first decade of the new century.

The chaos and polarization in Mexican society during these careening years of prosperity and depression on the eve of revolution found distinctive expression in the artistic work of José Guadalupe Posada (1852–1913). Graphic arts of the new century overwhelmed the romanticized aura of earlier Renaissance years. As befitting the pressure-cooker tension of the times, Posada's rich black zinc-engraved prints—done on cheap, pastel-tinted broadsheets sold on street corners—were sardonic snapshots documenting the rituals, customs, and upheavals in daily life during the waning *Porfiriato*.

Posada was born north of Mexico City, in Aguascalientes. He moved to the heart of the metropolis and worked at the open window of his workshop on Calle de Santa Iñez, just behind the teeming zócalo. He created more than fifteen thousand engravings over twenty-five years. Diego Rivera and José Clemente Orozco praised Posada as "a daring skirmisher with broadsides." He was a contributor to the many periodicals that sprang up in opposition to the Díaz regime.[22]

Death imagery plays a prominent role in Posada's work—whether it be the *tapatia* (gangster) defiantly gulping down his tequila; a mob of students amassing in the streets to protest Díaz's reelection as riot troops gather ominously; the assassination or execution of yet another political figure; sombrero-clad skeletons gleefully dancing on the Day of the Dead; or the soul amidst flames in purgatory, gazed upon dispassionately by an all-male Trinity, which—although considered heresy by the Pope—remained an icon in early twentieth-century Mexico.[23]

Posada's imagery, an intoxicating brew of *mexicanidad*, folkloric wisdom, and death, captured the mood of a country unable to find relief from contradiction.

CHAPTER XIX

ZAPATA

And in broad day the quetzals' tails
soar and whirl like Catherine wheels,
like showering stars, flying flowers,
fountains of emerald, gushing, falling
in sprays of willow.
The great anaconda writhes
like sinuous water,
and the thicket quivers
its vast bulk, cold and chill,
inlaid with flowers, encrusted with stars,
in strict geometry.

—JOSÉ JUAN TABLADA (1871–1945),
The Idol in the Porch[1]

If the myth of Quetzalcóatl has retained
its vitality throughout its successive avatars,
in colonial and independent Mexico alike,
it is because he is the symbolic expression
of the Indian past…the new incarnation
of the Indian messiah come from the depths
of the ages, a Phoenix who is reborn with each
new "sun" from the ashes of the preceding sun.
Like the aspiration for justice, Quetzalcóatl
is imperishable.

—JACQUES LAFAYE,
Quetzalcóatl and Guadalupe[2]

THE FALL OF DÍAZ AND THE RISE OF
FRANCISCO MADERO — A HORSEMAN FROM
MORELOS MAY BE THE NEW PLUMED
SERPENT — EMILIANO ZAPATA, DREAM OF
THE CAMPESINOS — THE PEOPLE FIGHT
FOR THEIR BELOVED LAND

Summarizing the multiple, complex causes of the Mexican Revolution—as with *any* modern revolution—it is easy to be seduced by the traditional class-struggle argument, assuming that there were elements in the society so at odds with each other that they could no longer coexist, leaving violence as the only solution.

The four centuries since the Spanish Conquest were marked by the continued oppression and alienation of the Indian peoples and *campesinos*. However, the tenacity of their grip on the old ways and their organic connection to the land did not spark an intensity of conflict sufficient to lead to lasting reform. How and why did *both* "socially conservative" (i.e., middle-class *mestizos*) *and* "lower-class" (i.e., agrarian, indigenous peoples) groups seek to overthrow the Díaz government?[3]

The regime of the by now nearly deaf Porfirio Díaz presented a progressive and, above all, orderly face to the world. Its habituated leaders, the self-styled *Científicos*, (Díaz's Kitchen Cabinet reformers), grandly promoted economic expansion and industrial strength. But as the years of the *Porfiriato* wore on, this inner sanctum became a tired echelon of elderly men, "rheumatic antiques" and Francophile snobs out of touch with the restless, rapidly growing middle class longing for more power and blocked

LEFT: *David Alfaro Siqueiros, Zapata, 1931*

139

from social advancement. Arrayed against this entrenched elite was a phalanx of radical critics chafing for legitimate balance within the culture.[4]

This inflammatory ideological effort at the turn of the century was publicly spearheaded by the notorious Flores Magón brothers. Jesus, Ricardo, and Enrique founded a weekly newspaper in Mexico City symbolically entitled *Regeneración* (*Rebirth*) in which they wrote systematic critiques of local-level political bosses, many of whom, in office for two or even three decades, gave the lie to any semblance of democracy in the provinces.

In retaliation for these left-wing transgressions— especially the assertion of rights of public speech against all manner of vested interests—the military, prosperous *jefe* landholders, privileged foreign financiers (including the "*yanquis*") who owned pieces of the Mexican economy, and the Church— the brothers were summarily arrested. This repressive measure only increased attention to the Flores Magóns' outspokenness. They resurfaced in exile as public enemies with bounties on their heads, warning (from St. Louis, Missouri) that "the day of liberation" was coming.[5]

That day was hastened by an economic crisis in 1907, brought about in large measure by a succession of droughts that caused severely curtailed harvests, runaway inflation, widespread unemployment in the countryside, and the virtual collapse of the vital *henequen* industry in the Yucatán. There was also an epidemic of willful unemployment as itinerant tenant farmers grew weary of selling themselves to the eight hundred *hacendado* families that owned 97 percent of all the farm and ranch land in Mexico; they simply stopped reporting for work.[6]

Díaz's mixed political signals proved to be the death knell for his long rule. During the infamous 1908 interview with the reporter James Creelman, the President announced he would not seek public office again after his current term, which happened conveniently to coincide with his eightieth birthday

and the centennial of Mexico's War of Independence from Spain. "I welcome an opposition party," he magnanimously declared.

It was as if Díaz had tapped into a latent national fantasy. An anti-reelection movement instantly sprang forth, framed by two important thinkers. In 1909 Andrés Molina Enriquez published his manifesto, *The Great National Problems*, advocating "the continuity of the [next generation of] *mestizos* as the preponderant ethnic group" and as the key to the future success of a mature nation in which "creoles no longer counted as an historical force capable of embodying Mexican nationality." Indeed, at the time of Enriquez's book, mestizos made up nearly one-half the population.[7]

The Coahila-born spiritualist Francisco Madero, a "virtuous son of the Constitution," who was schooled in France and America—a man who had originally

Porfirio Díaz

anticipated running for office with Díaz—criticized the dictator in his book *The Presidential Succession of 1910* and decided to run in opposition to him. A political pragmatist, the wealthy Madero was a moderate clothed in idealistic rhetoric. Traveling widely throughout the country, he delivered inflammatory speeches denouncing "this autocratic, violent, and illegal system" and preached the need for free elections. Infuriated, Díaz—who insisted that his remarks to Creelman were speculative, that he never really intended to step down at such a symbolic juncture in the Mexican story—had Madero and many of his associates arrested and jailed.

Turnabout was fair play. Not surprisingly, the *Porfiriato* declared a sweeping victory. Francisco Madero was able to escape to San Antonio, Texas, to regroup and compose his call to arms in the fall of 1910. After six months of sporadic guerilla pressure,

Porfirio Díaz submitted his resignation. The following November Madero was finally sworn in as president.

At that very moment, south of Mexico City, among the sugar plantations in mountainous Morelos province, Emiliano Zapata, an ambitious mestizo from the palm-thatched adobe village of Anenecuilco, announced the *Plan de Ayala*, the clarion call for agrarian reform and entitlement.[8]

All of thirty-one years old, he had lost his parents as a teenager and had experienced run-ins with the law. But even in his restless twenties, Emiliano, a modest farmer of the property he had inherited, was inclined to get involved in local politics and redefine the biased real estate laws. During dry periods he resourcefully turned to mule driving. He bought, sold, and broke in horses, earning a reputation as a deft livestock handler whose few indulgences

Emiliano Zapata (front row, center) and his men, 1914

included fancy, embroidered riding garb and a silver-adorned saddle for his prancing white horse— proud signs of the *métier*.⁹

Zapata was an introspective, muscular "man of silences," compact of stature, with high cheekbones, a face the color of oak, "as if carved out of obsidian," with a thick, waxy black moustache curling to fine points on either side of a tautly set mouth. The tall, broad-brimmed, black-felt sombrero he favored cast Zapata's brow in a shadow from which his eyes gleamed with inner light.¹⁰

Sweeping with his companions on horseback into the villages of Morelos to round up support and mold what were, during the early period of the Madero reign, sporadic protests into unified revolt, Zapata quickly became a charismatic symbol of hope for the local leaders of the *campesinos* and *proletariados* seeking a champion for their cause. Surrounded by white-garbed Indians wearing traditional *huaraches* sandals on their feet and .30-.30 cartridge belts across their chests, Zapata strode to the center of town and read manifestos to the people in the ancient Nahuatl tongue: "*Notlác ximomanaca!* Join us! Our flag belongs to the people. We will fight together. This is our great work which we will achieve before our revered mother, called *Patria*! If we work for our unity, we will fulfill the great command: Land, Liberty, Justice.... We will not rest until we come to possess our lands, those that belonged to our grandfathers, and which the greedy handed thieves took from us! We will fight for the land and not for illusions that give us nothing to eat!" Emiliano Zapata's inspirational speeches were the last preserved public documents in Mexican history written in Nahuatl.¹¹

Zapata's *Plan de Ayala*, named after the Morelos village where it was drafted, was the militant populists' embittered and dogmatic response to Francisco Madero's "inept" federal and judicial policies, which they believed did not go far enough toward truly "redeeming" the inalienable "fatherland" and recovering ancestral property. To the Zapatistas, the reformer Madero was—like Porfirio Díaz before him—a fickle, condescending "false man and a traitor" who had "defaulted on his promises to the Mexican people," "tricked the will of the people," and "tried with the brute force of bayonets to shut up and to drown in blood the *pueblos* who ask, solicit, or demand from him the fulfillment of the promises of the revolution, calling [us] bandits and rebels, and condemning [us] to a war of extermination."¹²

The Zapatistas gave unequivocal notice in their plan: the fields, woods, and waters, which the monopolizing syndicates and holding companies run by *Científicos* and *jefes* had brutally usurped from the simple citizens who held titles or right of inheritance, must henceforth be returned. There was the thinly veiled threat that any resistance to the revolutionary juntas in each state carrying out wholesale repatriation of these communal *ejidos* would be met with "immense misfortunes." Bureaucrats and generals would no longer be permitted to make decisions for the community.¹³

The ensuing "Great Rebellion" in Mexico was "the epic of a people searching for its soul"¹⁴ and grappling with longstanding grievances against labor oppression, land hoarding, and government favoritism. It was a severe and tragic epic, renewing a bloody pattern woven permanently into the fabric of Mexican life, pitting (at first) Madero's federal forces against flare-ups in the provinces, both nearby and as far away as Veracruz.

With the pillaging of Mexico City came the downfall and murder of Madero. His presidential successors, Victoriano Huerta, Francisco Carbajal, and Venustiano Carranza did not fare any better. The stakes were simply raised higher. The ranks of federal troops swelled, and more peasant blood was spilled in all-out, anarchic civil war, aggravated by American intervention.

More than half the population of Morelos province lost their lives during the bleak and fractured decade, but the Zapatista forces persisted. Symbolizing revolution throughout Mexico, they became an embarrassment to the weak Carranza government, which ominously branded Emiliano as "beyond amnesty." He could no longer be allowed to "roam brazenly around the countryside."

Through a ruse perpetrated by a government officer posing as a turncoat, Zapata was lured to an early-afternoon meeting on April 10, 1919, in a hacienda at the town of Chinameca, thirty-five miles south of Anenecuilco, the place of his birth and familiar territory. As the tribute bugle call sounded, heralding Zapata's entrance into the courtyard, two shots rang out, and he crumpled to the ground. Federal troops seized Zapata's body and took it to the police station in Cuautla as night fell.

Thousands of *campesinos* descended upon the village to view the body. Many refused to believe their assassinated hero was dead. The body was not his, they said. Their friend 'Meliano had moles and scars in different places—and besides, that suit he was wearing wasn't familiar. He had been seen in the hills surrounding the town. His horse was glimpsed, too, a white blur against dun-colored mountains. Last night, wasn't that Zapata atop his steed, galloping fiercely southward toward the safety of Guerrero province, to hide and then return

another day, to complete the unconsummated work of revolt he had begun?[15]

In the rugged terrain around Cuernavaca, the capital of Morelos state, four hundred years after the Conquest, the people still tell you that when the wind blows, they hear the mournful cry of the soul of Zapata, brought down through betrayal. Emiliano had spoken to the people in the ancient tongue of *Éhecatl*, the wind.

His spirit continues to do so today. The legendary horseman's name has been adapted by modern-day Zapatista namesakes in rural Chiapas who—as of this writing—marched directly into the *zócalo* at the center of Mexico City to dramatize their demands. "Like Morelos and Cuauhtemoc, [Zapata] is one of our legendary heroes," Octavio Paz declared in his landmark essay "The Labyrinth of Solitude." "The 'eternal return,' the will to return, the search for our own selves, the cult of the leader, is one of the implicit assumptions of almost every revolutionary theory." Twenty-five years later, Paz addressed the point more directly: "As a political myth ... in the popular imagination, many of our heroes are only translations of Quetzalcóatl. They are, in fact, unconscious translations.

"This is significant, because the theme of the Quetzalcóatl myth is the legitimation of power."[16]

CHAPTER XX

LOS TRES GRANDES: DIEGO RIVERA

Mexican art of our own time, especially mural painting, is closely linked spiritually and ideologically with the social and political movement that brought about a renewed life in the second decade of the century: the Mexican Revolution.

—JUSTINO FERNANDEZ,
Arte mexicano de sus origenes a nuestros días
(A Guide to Mexican Art, 1961)[1]

Alvaro Obregón was elected president of Mexico in the year after the murder of Emiliano Zapata. He faced the task of enacting at least some of the civil liberties required by the Constitution of 1917. He did this with more restraint than fervor. To avoid what he delicately called "an unbalanced state," he slowly redistributed a fair measure of land from the *hacendados* back to the villagers' *ejidos*. To demonstrate his affection for the working man, Obregón supported the expansion of Mexican labor unions, except those he believed inordinately left-leaning—such as on the plantations of the Yucatán, where conflict continued unabated between the Socialist Workers Party and the International Harvester Company. Obregón's approach to the rights of the military were clear cut: "There's no general who can resist a salvo of fifty thousand pesos."[2]

But in the less-threatening realms of education and the arts, Obregón made an inspired appointment to his cabinet, choosing José Vasconcelos (1889–1959), Rector of the National University in Mexico City, to become Secretary of State for Public Education. Vasconcelos had been the youngest member of the Generation of the Centenary, a sophisticated group of essayists and philosophers including Alfonso Reyes, Pedro Henriquez Urena, Antonio Caso, and Martín Luis Guzmán. During the waning years of the *Porfiriato*, these men had founded a lecture and debating society, the progressive *Ateneo de la Juventud* (the Athenaeum of the Young). With an idealistic, populist outreach campaign in their many *conferencias* in Mexico City and around the country, they expressed the desire to bring the humanities beyond the aesthetes—themselves included—out of the

Edward Weston, Portrait of Diego Rivera, 1924

Academy, and directly to the people.[3]

Obregón immediately gave Vasconcelos the authority and the financial means to establish a network of rural schools and public libraries throughout Mexico and to distribute books and periodicals across the land. The infrastructure that fell into place so rapidly during Vasconcelos's brief, three-year administration was driven by a nationalistic and sensitive man with the bureaucratic clout to enact his ambitious plan for a new Mexican identity to match the "new" Mexican state—even if Vasconcelos's vision of it surpassed the reality.

The advent of the 1920s inaugurated the two-decade cultural Golden Age, the "constructive" or "second phase" of the Mexican Revolution.[4] In the aftermath of the carnage of civil war, more ink was spilled than blood, into all manner of manifestos and declarations invoking the country's autochthonous character—*Mexicanidad*—shedding "the burden of the colonial past" and calling for a wholesale re-examination of native history from pre-Columbian times.

This exercise in national self-knowledge was accomplished through literature, poetry, dance, music, and, most demonstratively, in the visible, "fighting and educative" public art of the mural. Perhaps this is what Joseph Campbell meant in his last published work when he observed that "the final and most essential function of mythology is *pedagogical*."[5]

José Vasconcelos, the prime mover and teacher in this enterprise, sounded the call to dispel the nation's artistic inferiority complex and "slacken the cord that held Mexican art in abeyance to Europe." Now was the time, he said, to glorify Amerindian traditions and raise up aboriginal values within a "universal society." Mexico required "an art saturated with primitive vigor, new subject matter, combin-

145

ing subtlety and intensity, sacrificing the exquisite to the great, perfection to invention."[6]

The looming role of *hombre-dios* Quetzalcóatl was reimagined and reborn in many works of major muralists of the Mexican modernist period (as well as succeeding generations). It was truly a vital renaissance—"the heart of Mexican history beat[ing] with its diastole and systole."[7]

The new public art created by the fair-skinned mestizo now condemned the genocidal invader Cortés and his traitor-mistress, Malinche. The goal of this art was to take back the identity of the country. Like the Mexican art of earlier periods, the new art made allegorical use of Aztec and Mayan motifs. But this time, the aesthetic themes were "in the service of the Revolution and the people at large."

This statement by "we Mexicans" floated ironically upon the surface of the culture. In everyday practice, did these heroic representations—lime-resistant, earth-nuanced pigments of the brown man garbed in white, larger than life on hundreds of square meters of walls—raise the consciousness of his oppressors? Did the enhanced image of the Indian as a participant in the new Mexico, placed side by side in the foreground with European and mestizo faces and revolutionary slogans, bear any resemblance to his authentic contemporary impact?[8]

Alfonso Reyes, one of the original *Ateneo* members from 1909, reminisced about that intoxicating time of the 1920s: "It was like discovering again the

Courtyard of Palacio Nacional, Mexico City

patrimony once forgotten, like digging out of the earth the hidden gold of the Aztecs—so we had all this in our house, and we never knew it?" Much about the modern Mexican "renaissance" revivified the past in a paean to the primitive rather than as an anthem to an imagined future.[9]

Mural painting in 1920s Mexico drew upon a centuries-old tradition. Remember the three sophisticated and seamless vaulted Mayan rooms at Bonampak in the Chiapas jungles (Late Classic era, ca. A.D. 790), or the Temple of the Frescoes (also known as Structure 16) by the Caribbean Sea at Tulum, or the multicolored walls at the painted city of Teotihuacán. The difficult, demanding technique of "true fresco" is in evidence in all these places: painting done rapidly upon a wet, freshly prepared lime-plaster wall with pigments ground in water or lime-water, so that when dry, the colors are locked in place between plaster particles. The paintings become an integral part of the wall (and, for that matter, of the entire building), as permanent in intention as any artistic expression could be. And, most important to the narrative of the mural, the paintings are designed and laid out in an array, anticipating that the spectator will move back and forth across the length of the work and not remain limited to a fixed point as he would in observing an easel painting.[10]

The Mexica had journeyed to the Teotihuacán Valley in sacred pilgrimages to revere the spirits of their Toltec forbears. So, too, the Mexican modernist artists of the 1920s, led by José Vasconcelos, took field trips to Teotihuacán to view the archaeological revelations of Manuel Gamio, Alfred L. Kroeber, and others; they also journeyed to the Isthmus of Tehuantepec and to Uxmal and Chichén Itzá in the Yucatán to make sketches from life, meet the native peoples, and study the "plastic possibilities" in the colorful *buon fresco* practices of their ancestors. The modernist message would be embedded in a time-honored method.[11]

In pursuit of aesthetic authenticity, Diego Rivera prepared his fresco surface with a mixture of nopal cactus slime and lime putty as an added layer over fresh plaster. He further mixed the resinous, fermented liquid with pigment for use in painting. "I am not merely an artist," he said, "but a man performing his biological function of producing paintings, just as a tree produces flowers and fruit."[12]

This larger-than-life, infamous, and charismatic exemplar of Mexican mural art, the *discutido pintor* ("much-discussed painter," as he was constantly referred to in the press),[13] was born in Guanajuato in 1886. Rivera's father was a schoolteacher, chemist, and newspaper editor, and his mother owned a candy store. The family moved to Mexico City, where young Diego was schooled at the eminent San Carlos Academy from the age of ten. There he met the engraver José Guadalupe Posada in his street-level studio nearby. Initially funded by a scholarship from the governor of Veracruz to study art in Madrid, Diego lived and traveled widely through Europe for fourteen crucial years, 1907–1921, painting his way enthusiastically across every phase of modernity, from symbolist easel portraiture to fauvism to impressionism to Dada to futurism to more than two hundred cubist canvases.

Ending up, inevitably, in Paris, Rivera met David Alfaro Siqueiros, and the compatriots had many conversations about the necessity "to produce a truly Mexican art."[14] They traveled to Italy to study Renaissance frescoes. Rivera spent almost a year and a half there and became intrigued by the potentialities of "public, socialized art."[15] The two were recalled to their homeland to meet with José Vasconcelos and sparked the movement to transform the buildings of Mexico into a vast and vibrant palette of *Mexicanidad*.[16]

"The true novelty of Mexican painting," Rivera announced with characteristic fervor in an interview in 1923, "in the sense that we initiated it with Orozco and Siqueiros, [is] to make *the people* the hero of mural painting.... Our hope is based on the fact that *all personages*, positive as well as negative, of this as yet minute movement, are impelled by a deep force: the aspirations of the masses, which shake the surface of the country as does an earthquake."[17]

The entire east side of the Plaza de la Constitución in Mexico City—extending 675 feet—is occupied by the three-story Palacio Nacional (National Palace), which contains the offices of the President, the Treasury, and the National Archives. Before the Spanish Conquest, this site housed the court of Moctezuma II, which was razed by Cortés. He erected in its stead a home with a large inner courtyard of pink volcanic *tezontle* stone, vestiges of which remain. It was used as the viceregal palace, partially destroyed in 1692, rebuilt again, and has been the location of the seat of Mexican government since 1821.

As we face the palace, we see three entryways. The farthest to the right is the *Puerta de Honor*, reserved for the president and members of the diplomatic corps. The farthest left, nearest the cathedral to the north, is the *Puerta Mariana*, made during the administration of President Mariano Arista (1851–53). Above the *Puerta Principal* is the Bell of Liberty struck by Miguel Hidalgo at Dolores on the night of September 15, 1810, as the call to revolution. We walk through the Central Doorway and present our identification to the soldier at his desk, comrades standing close by, machine guns at the ready. Beyond an archway, in the central courtyard, a replica of the original colonial fountain stands bathed in sunlight at the middle of eight flagstone paths emanating from it like spokes of a wheel. Immediately to our left is the Main Staircase leading to the second-floor—there, on the north wall, Diego Rivera's vision of Quetzalcóatl is revealed.

Commissioned during the presidency of Emilio Portes Gil, Rivera began work on *The History of Mexico* fresco in July 1929, one month before his civil-ceremony marriage to the twenty-year-old painter Frida Kahlo in Coyoacán. He labored on the huge epic for six years, eventually covering 275 square meters. During the early 1940s and for the ensuing decade, Rivera returned to the palace to execute eleven more nostalgic panels bordering the second-floor corridor, *From Pre-Columbian Civilization to the Conquest*. Interrupted by the artist's death in 1957, the work was to have been brought completely around to the top of the staircase, where it would have climaxed with an image of "the contemporary world."

By midsummer 1929 Rivera was well into the first panel of his *History* triptych, *The Ancient Indian World,* working round the clock and falling asleep on the scaffold. He spent so little time at home with his new wife that Frida began to accompany him to the palace, bringing midday meals in a basket. In the fall the obsessive, chronically overweight Rivera collapsed from nervous exhaustion. There would be no honeymoon for "the elephant and the dove" (as Frida's parents named the couple) until late December.[18]

My first impression of Rivera's *Ancient Indian World* viewed from the top of the staircase is of the "simultaneity" of the story, the contemporaneous quality of the images. During Rivera's time in Europe he explored with the futurist Gino Severini "the representation of a fourth dimension…the extra factor of time movement" in three-dimensional work (i.e., painting). His sustained involvement with Cubism led Rivera to portray multiple points of view in one plane. Claude Lévi-Strauss cautions that the significance of myth is not put forth in a sequence of vignettes but rather by what he calls "bundles of events … appearing at different moments in the story." It is preferable (he says) to "read" myths "exactly as in a musical score," as an array of tones or a shower of impressions. By so doing, we move away from the "civilized" linear narrative of Western stories to which we have become accustomed and toward the cyclic, rhythmic mode true to ancient belief.[19]

Quetzalcóatl as presented by Rivera has a fourfold self. His fiery birth with bifid tongue erupts from the mouth of the earth in the form of the Plumed Serpent we already know. The bearded, pale, earthly *Topiltzin* prince, attired in ritual garb—including conch-shell breastplate and plumed helmet—presides beneath the shelter of his peaked temple at the top of the pyramid. He magisterially regards the multitude of men, instructing them in his ways. His departing avatar glides off into the heavens on a serpent raft, to be metamorphosed into Venus, *Tlahuizcalpantecuhtli*, the Lord of the House of the Dawn.

In his incarnation as the setting (upside-down) sun (who falls head first) *Tzontémoc*, at the top of the panel, Quetzalcóatl does not disappear but is only half obscured, because he will arise for many tomorrows.

Upon closer scrutiny, the primordial world of Quetzalcóatl is not entirely ordered and idyllic. How could it be? Although Quetzalcóatl sits with cross-legged dignity and Buddhalike calm in the safe circle of his acolytes, beyond that charmed center

Diego Rivera, Quetzalcóatl in The Ancient Indian World, 1929

spreads a hubbub of many forces: horn and drum clamor, heralding the harvest; the industriousness of weaving; the slow work of craftsmen; the traditional molding of tortillas; children instructed in the ancient ways. These comforting, everyday rituals slowly degenerate as our glance travels left and downward toward the forced labor of building stone temples, and the bloody conflagrations of tribal war and human sacrifice.

This gradual movement from major into minor tones, a tumbling river of darkness, prefigures the dark panel illustrating the "external violation" of the Conquest[20]—adjacent, but separate at the lowest site of the mural, the first of five inner arches. The theme of outside corruption introduced to the pure native society is taken up again with depictions of the arrival of evangelizing monks in the sixteenth century and the later French and American occupations. History repeats itself in a series of mutations. The martyrdom of Cuauhtémoc culminates in the eagle with the serpent in its mouth—Mexico's national symbol of identity—first seen by the wandering Aztecs when they arrived at the site of Tenochtitlán.

The eagle with the serpent—Quetzalcóatl's components in modern guise—stands as a bold visual and thematic base for the slogan of revolutionary generations to follow: *Tierra y Libertad* (Land and Freedom). From the glories of Hidalgo and Morelos we move on to Benito Juárez and the reform movement; then the opposition to Porfirio Díaz, represented through the armed forces of Emiliano Zapata (one of Rivera's favorite subjects) and the intellectual ideologies of José Vasconcelos. Following the five arches, there are the final images on the south wall of *The Worlds of Today and Tomorrow*, "outer flanking scenes" balancing the first pre-Columbian panel, populated by a fairer-skinned, modern mestizo society. Zapata's bywords *Tierra y Libertad* are supplanted by a proud red banner proclaiming *Huelga* (strike). And Quetzalcóatl, the first teacher, is mirrored by Karl Marx who (Rivera believed) points toward a better future.

Rivera was possessed with an encyclopedic vision. The totality of *The History of Mexico* is egalitarian, an exhaustive enactment of the artist's faith in the dignity and primacy of the masses. Each of the countless individuals depicted, beginning with the earthly person of Plumed Serpent, possesses a similar visual weight.

However, only *hombre-dios* Plumed Serpent displays additional, multiple identities across the span of the entire work—beginning as deity, returning here and there as a revolutionary hero, as an angry eagle in the sky, and as the fiery sun erupting again at the top of the picture frame, behind Marx's head, illuminating an idealized future for Mexico.

CHAPTER XXI

OROZCO, SIQUEIROS, AND TAMAYO

*In every painting,
as in any other work of Art,
there is always an* idea,
never a story.
*The idea is the point
of departure, the first cause
of the plastic construction,
and it is present all the time
as energy creating matter.*

—JOSÉ CLEMENTE OROZCO,
handwritten manuscript,
The Frescoes[1]

*El tema inicial era
el de Quetzalcóatl.*
The first subject
[for the murals]
was Quetzalcóatl.

—JOSÉ CLEMENTE OROZCO,
Autobiografía, 1945[2]

TAKING PLUMED SERPENT INTO AMERICAN TERRITORY — HE BECOMES
THE KINDRED SPIRIT OF OTHER SAVIORS — JOSÉ CLEMENTE OROZCO'S VISION
AT DARTMOUTH — YOUNG CUAUHTÉMOC LENDS A SPARK TO THE LEGEND

In his native land José Clemente Orozco is known as "the Goya of Mexico." He was born in 1883, in the town of Ciudad Guzmán (also called Zapotlán El Grande), Jalisco. His father was a printer and soap manufacturer. From his strong-willed mother he received a love of music and the fine arts. When José was six, the family moved to Mexico City, where, the following year, his family obliged his request to enroll in evening drawing classes at the Academy of San Carlos. Like Diego Rivera, he eventually became fascinated with José Guadalupe Posada's engraving work, "the push that first set [his] imagination in motion."[3]

After a practical, career-oriented course in agricultural engineering, the seventeen-year-old José entered the National Preparatory School to study mathematics and architecture. An explosion during a chemical experiment (reported in some accounts as "an accident while playing with gunpowder") caused the boy to lose his left hand at the wrist and badly shattered his right hand.

He also suffered permanent hearing loss and serious vision impairment, which required him to wear thick bifocal glasses for the rest of his life.[4] "My first thought," Orozco casually told friends years later, was one of relief "that my accident had made me unfit for architecture.... *Now, at last, I can be a painter!*"[5]

He returned, this time with even more joy, to the Academy of San Carlos and then set up a studio in Illescas Street, an impoverished neighborhood near the red-light district. He became immersed in the gritty ebb and flow of street life, especially at night. As Orozco's palette edged gradually into darker realms, his senses of line and caricature became more convoluted and sardonic as he lived through — bearing witness, but not fighting — the most intense

and bloody years of the revolutionary period.

Orozco's political cartoons and acerbic sensibility caught José Vasconcelos's eye, and the Minister of Education asked him to illustrate a new edition of the classics. Orozco received his first major mural commission in 1923: to decorate three floors of walls around the patio of the National Preparatory School, the former Jesuit College of San Ildefonso on the Avenida Justo Sierra in Mexico City.[6]

But this was Diego Rivera's time in the limelight. The public reaction to Orozco's work ranged from disappointment to outright antagonism. The two artists were at opposite ends of the spectrum, and there was no love lost between them. Rivera, the extrovert populist, romanticized Indian heritage with rainbow hues. Orozco, the surly misanthrope, gloomily surveyed the ruin bourgeois Mexico had brought upon itself. Rivera, the optimist and chronic mythologizer, imagined a bright — if undefined — future for Mexico. Orozco, the unsparing pessimist, painted swirling bodies of faceless, shirtless revolutionaries draped over each other in futile death. Rivera was obsessed with the surfaces and panoplies of events in Mexican history. Orozco wanted to penetrate and search beneath them: "Rivera paints sensualities.... Orozco paints desperations."[7]

Bitter, disgusted, on the verge of financial ruin toward the end of the 1920s, Orozco temporarily left his wife and three children at home in Coyoacán and headed for the United States, which he had briefly visited a decade earlier. He joined the Delphic Studio Circle in New York, a Greenwich Village cultural and literary salon headed by the beautiful journalist, critic, and art patron Alma

PREVIOUS PAGE: *Edward Weston, Portrait of José Clemente Orozco, 1930*

Reed. She took Orozco under her philanthropic wing, introduced him to the New York gallery world (where he presented two one-man shows soon after arriving), quietly underwrote his public works, and became a tireless advocate for the artist in America.[8]

During the 1930s Orozco created a triumvirate of immense, ambitious masterworks on the walls of three American institutions. The first, in Frary Hall at Pomona College in Claremont, California, was *Prometheus:* the upward-gazing, fiery-hued figure strains to break through the top of the arch that shelters him. The second, in the dining room at the New School for Social Research on West Twelfth Street in New York City, was a somber and rigorous tribute to workers around the world oppressed by various species of imperialism and totalitarianism: *A Call for Revolution and Universal Brotherhood.*

And the third, *American Civilization–The Epic of Culture in the New World,* took up three thousand square feet, the walls of the entire Reserve Reading Room at Baker Library on the campus of Dartmouth College in Hanover, New Hampshire.

In the treasure trove of journals, manuscripts, sketches, newspaper clippings, and photographs making up the Orozco Murals Archive in the Dartmouth College Special Collections of Baker Library, there is a typewritten transcript of a letter dated May 22, 1932, from Alma Reed to Professor Artemas Packard, the chairman of the Dartmouth College art department. Written after Orozco had received his commission to begin work on what he called "the walls of my dreams … my epic of America" at the college, the letter sheds valuable light on the artist's original intentions.[9]

Reed refers to the planned mural as

the Quetzalcóatl project…. As Orozco pointed out, there is enough material in the Quetzalcóatl myth, as he already conceives of it, to fill every wall in the college. It really will

be an epic of civilization on the American continent, bringing us into the present and pointing out the responsibilities of the future.[10]

Enclosed with Reed's letter is an outline on the Delphic Studios letterhead presenting a thematic and visual plan for the entire mural, entitled, in all capital letters at this early date, *Quetzalcóatl.*

The accompanying one-page manifesto composed by Orozco with Reed's help—*New World, New Races and New Art*—states his unequivocal position regarding the life cycle of the emblematic hero; it is a useful prologue to the work itself. Deliberately unlike Diego Rivera at the *Palacio Nacional* three years earlier, Orozco will not draw so directly upon "aboriginal traditions." It is time, rather, for a "new cycle," he says, and to forego "looting indigenous remains … however picturesque and interesting these may be."

Orozco's "Epic of Civilization" will be

developed in terms of the American myth of Quetzalcóatl (the symbol of the Power of Good in the Universe)…. It is to be understood that there is no literary or other record of the exact implications of this ancient myth of Quetzalcóatl and that this interpretation grows out of the inspired idealism and creative imagination of Orozco.[11]

Three days later Dartmouth College formally announced José Clemente Orozco's two-year residency on campus, quoting the artist as emphasizing "the great American myth of Quetzalcóatl [as] a living one … pointing clearly by its prophetic nature to the responsibility shared equally by the two Americas of creating here an authentic New World civilization."[12]

Eighteen months later, heading into the concluding phase of the work, Orozco reiterated the significance of his new Quetzalcóatl in a statement drafted for the *Dartmouth Alumni Magazine* of November 1933:

The important point regarding the frescoes of Baker Library is not only the quality of the idea that initiates and organizes the whole structure, it is also the fact that it is an American idea.... It seems that the line of Culture is continuous without shortcuts, unbroken from the unknown Beginning to the unknown End. But we are proud to say now: This is no imitation, this is our own effort, to the limit of our own strength.

Orozco painted the entire mural by himself, without the help of apprentices, finishing on February 13, 1934. In the summer of 1968, all twenty-four panels were carefully restored and then coated with protective polyvinyl acetate.[13]

The drama of Orozco's mural is enhanced by the way I come upon it, downstairs to the silent lower level of the library, entering the Reserve Room at its narrow western end. Suddenly, there it all is, extending 150 feet straight ahead on parallel walls. To my immediate right the narrative begins with a prologue, the panel "Ancient Human Migration": naked Indian men of many hues, fists clenched, and jaws set in determination as they stride across the Bering Strait, down the western edge of North America, and purposefully toward their eventual home in the Valley of Mexico. Moving as close to the surface of the wall as I dare, I make out the incised line in the plaster distinguishing one area of color from the next, "the sign of true fresco."[14]

To my immediate left is the familiar image of human sacrifice in the Aztec ritual: four priests holding the yoked, splayed, naked victim while the masked Huitzilopochtli high priest, representing his "chosen people," opens the man's chest with an obsidian knife.

The Quetzalcóatl saga appears on the long northern wall. Actually, it is the *array* in mythological terms, because Orozco is not troubled with dynastic accuracy. As a muralist, he wants to create a *gestalt*

in the viewer's mind, not a mere tale of events flowing from A to B.

Quetzalcóatl seems startled rather than angry. He springs up, white-robed, backlit by a flash of lightning, between the Pyramids of the Sun and Moon of Teotihuacán, and over the downcast, benighted, sombre (and somnolent) Toltecs. To these people "the benign, Blakean" Quetzalcóatl brings two gifts for which he will forever be renowned: maize and art.[15] I note the familiar conch-curled stela, adjacent to which a distinctively Maya-profiled man raises his hand in a universal gesture of triumph. It is a short-lived victory of the spirit.

In the following panel, the elevated fist is translated into a gesture of defiance. Quetzalcóatl, his earthly reign as Topiltzin-Prince having come to a cruel end, is cast out by the same people to whom he had delivered faith. The exile is ambivalent—some men are waving, some recoil in fear, and one has his back turned and is bent in dejection as

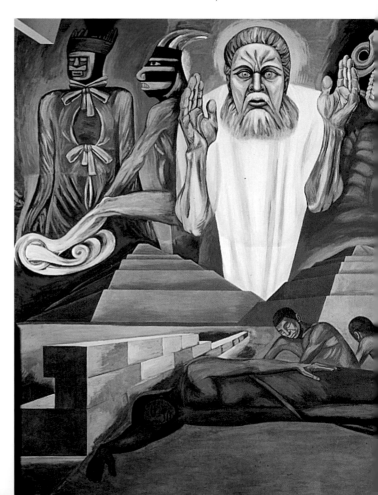

Plumed Serpent sets forth amidst the snakes who will bear him across ominous and turbulent waters.

Plumed Serpent's arrow-straight pointing hand—the tip of his index finger is the fulcrum of the mural's narrative force—and his half-opened mouth articulate the intention of his departure and also prophetically touch upon the Conquest as a holocaust waiting in the wings to redress the grievance of Plumed Serpent's betrayal.

Anonymous, helmeted Spanish soldiers bear their bulky cross as a lethal mace to bludgeon the New World. The consequences of Quetzalcóatl's hoped-for return are vengefully represented in the stock-still person of Cortés, standing on the threshold of a cruel, hellish future populated by machines.

In radical contrast to Diego Rivera's image, Orozco's Quetzalcóatl is a timeless symbol, rushing like a rocket up and out of the primordial period with the introduction of itinerant primitive peoples onto our shared American-Mexican continent. The

formative years of civilization are pervaded with suffering because of mankind's ruined potential for greatness.

Even as portrayed in the twentieth century, Quetzalcóatl bears the still-living spirits of kindred saviors—Hernán Cortés, Emiliano Zapata, Jesus Christ, and other rebellious figures not yet named—forward and back in time. Orozco's Cortés was welcomed by the Aztecs and then demolished their culture. Orozco's Zapata is on the verge of being stabbed in the back by the government forces of Díaz. Orozco's Christ, destroying his cross, recalls the seventeenth-century conflation of Quetzalcóatl and Saint Thomas. These "Plumed Serpents" arrive in hope and depart in despair. Orozco believes the fault lies in the society of man.

In tranquil if temporary counterpoint to these fire-and-brimstone allegories is "Modern Industrial Man," reclining in dark and pensive splendor at the center of the south wall of the Reserve Room, directly opposite the book-return desk. Dressed as a classic proletarian with a peaked cap, he has set aside his sledgehammer, donned spotless white gloves, and is reading, lost in thought. Is this a cautionary message to the Dartmouth students at their study tables below? Or is it a sign from Orozco that the destiny of the Americas might not become a complete loss if we are capable of bearing in mind the universal (not only Mexican) lessons of history?

T he youngest of *Los Tres Grandes*, José David Alfaro Siqueiros (1896–1974), was consistently the most politicized and outspoken in expressing the mission of the Mexican mural movement. Born of a well-to-do Catholic family in Chihuahua, José was raised by his paternal grandparents in Guanajuato. At the age of sixteen he led a student strike at the Academy of San Carlos demanding the dismissal of

José Clemente Orozco, The Epic of American Civilization: The Coming of Quetzalcóatl (Panel 5), 1932–1934, Dartmouth College

its conservative director. For throwing stones at Antonio Rivas Mercado, Siqueiros the young revolutionary was jailed; he remained proud of his "[self-styled] act of pedagogical-political rebellion" for the rest of his life.[16]

Unlike his colleagues Rivera and Orozco, Siqueiros saw action during the Revolution, rising to the rank of captain in the Constitutional Army. Just before leaving the country for a three-year stint in Europe, Siqueiros became affiliated with the *Centro Bohemia*, a group of radical artists in Guadalajara. During their convocations, he first came to terms with the idea of "the social purpose of a national art" dedicated to articulating the aspirations of the people.[17]

Arriving in Paris in 1919, Siqueiros met Diego Rivera, moved on to visit Italy, and lived in Barcelona, where he founded a magazine called *Vida Americana* (*American Life*). In the issue of May 1921 (the first and only number to appear), Siqueiros published an "exhortation to his compatriots," a manifesto widely considered to be the cornerstone of the birth of modern Mexican mural painting—*Tres llamamientos de orientación actual a los pintores y escultores de la nueva generación americana* (*Three Appeals for a New Direction to the New Generation of American Painters and Sculptors*):

As regards ourselves, let us come closer to the work of the ancient settlers of our valleys, the Indian painters and sculptors (Maya, Aztec, Inca, etc.). The geographical proximity we share with them will help us to absorb the constructive vigor of their work, in which there is a clear and fundamental knowledge of the elements of nature that can certainly serve us as a point of departure.... Let us adopt their synthetic energy without, however, settling for the lamentable archaeological reconstructions ... which are currently so fashionable and which are leading us toward ephemeral stylizations.[18]

The following year, after repeated insistences from José Vasconcelos, Siqueiros agreed to come home and join the painters working at the National Preparatory School in an ambitious program for a Mexican "plastic renaissance." With characteristic flair for the dramatic, Siqueiros told Vasconcelos,

The enthusiasm that your letter breathes intensifies my great desire to return to the patria, there to collaborate with all my resources to the common task.... I am in total agreement with your basic idea to create a new civilization extracted from the very bowels of Mexico, and I firmly believe that our youth will rally to this banner![19]

Once again together on native grounds, Siqueiros and Rivera, the galvanizers, followed in the tradition of the laborers they idealized and formed their own union, the Syndicate of Revolutionary Painters, Sculptors, and Printmakers of Mexico. Their statement of purpose was drafted by Siqueiros as an extension of themes he had been promoting for the past decade. The artists of the new epoch in Mexico dedicated their imagery to

the Indian race, humiliated for centuries; to soldiers made into executioners by their officers; to the workers and peasants scourged by the greed of the rich; and to the intellectuals uncorrupted by the bourgeoisie.... The art of the Mexican people is the most important and vital spiritual manifestation in the world today, and its Indian traditions lie at its very heart. It is great precisely because it surges from the people and is therefore collective.[20]

In the years that followed, Siqueiros became a full-fledged labor organizer and an integral player in the Mexican Communist Party—from which he was later expelled. He traveled and exhibited widely in the United States during the early and middle 1930s, founding an experimental workshop in New York

City to explore the use of new techniques and materials in large-scale painting. One of his students was the young Jackson Pollock. After exile in Chile that resulted from his involvement in an abortive attempt to assassinate Leon Trotsky, Siqueiros once more returned to Mexico City, where, in 1944, he painted the first of three murals dedicated to the struggle, torture, and apotheosis of Cuauhtémoc.

We remember that following the deaths of Moctezuma and his brother Cuitlahuac, the Aztec throne was assumed by their cousin, Cuauhtémoc. The brave "Descending Eagle" was to be the last Aztec ruler. Defending the city of Tenochtitlán against the Spaniards through a debilitating blockade and onslaught by ship and catapult, Cuauhtémoc was finally captured in August 1521

José Clemente Orozco, Study for the Departure of Quetzalcóatl (1930–1934), Dartmouth College

and brought before Cortés. The young king was interrogated about a cache of gold Cortés believed was hidden under Cuauhtémoc's palace. This he vehemently denied, and thus was imprisoned, and in despair tried to hang himself.

Cuauhtémoc was gruesomely tortured, and his hands and feet were burned with hot oil, yet he remained resolute in his innocence. After the fall of Tenochtitlán was complete, Cortés took the captive Cuauhtémoc with him on a campaign into Honduras, where he was hanged from a ceiba tree.

The symbolic appeal of Cuauhtémoc to Siqueiros resided in the brave king's opposition to the seductive belief that had felled his predecessor, Moctezuma—that Cortés embodied the returning spirit of Plumed Serpent. Because of this conviction, emphasized by the high priests, the compliant and indecisive Moctezuma had "lost his will" and invited the Spanish forces into the Aztec city, triggering the downfall of an entire nation. Siqueiros's painting *Cuauhtémoc Against the Myth* glorifies all that the artist loved—everything "anti-imperialist" about the proto-Mexican people of four hundred years ago, now represented by the timeless, heroic figure of Cuauhtémoc rising up against the Spanish oppressor.

The Spaniards are symbolized by the immense, rearing figure of a centaurlike horse bearing a cross in the shape of a sword. In opposition to this fantastic threat, perched upon a templelike structure, Cuauhtémoc stands poised with an obsidian-tipped spear aimed at the horse's jugular.

In smaller counterpoint in the background, Moctezuma's open-armed stance embraces the conqueror. The most compelling element of the composition is the painted and fanged stone Feathered Serpent head. At Cuauhtémoc's feet, Quetzalcóatl has been transposed photographically from the walls of the temple consecrated to his name at Teotihuacán. Siqueiros issues a corrective to the Quetzalcóatl tale, placing the glaring, hollow-eyed ancient god's mystique on the side of indigenous peoples who resisted the Spanish enemy.

It gives us pause to realize that (in harmony with Siqueiros's expressed ideology) Cuauhtémoc exploited Plumed Serpent's legacy to justify revolt. "The value of the Mexican hero is rooted in history as a symbol of the struggles of all the oppressed peoples of the world," the artist commented seven years later.[21]

The following two panels in the Cuauhtémoc triptych were made in 1950–51 on the third floor of the Palacio de Bellas Artes in Mexico City—the art nouveau/art deco white Carrara marble concert hall and arts center at the eastern end of the Alameda Central. *The Torment of Cuauhtémoc* depicts flames licking at the feet of the naked, tight-lipped martyr-king and his companion in arms, Tetlepanquetzatzin,

Jean Charlot, Portrait of David Alfaro Siqueiros, 1933
RIGHT: *David Alfaro Siqueiros, Cuauhtémoc Against the Myth, Tlatelco, Mexico City, 1944*

King of Tacuba, surrounded by anonymous Spaniards, their halberds erect. The women of Tenochtitlán wail in despair.

In a stunning reversal, *The Resurrection of Cuauhtémoc*, the slain monarch has donned the armor of his torturers, and the forbidding centaur from the first panel lies vanquished and impaled on his side. The sad and pitiful expression of Cuauhtémoc's eyes in *Torment* has been replaced with a vengeful glint as he strides forward, obsidian mace in hand—Siqueiros's realized dream of the peoples' triumph.[22]

One year later, and one floor below Cuauhtémoc's saga in the Palacio de Bellas Artes, Quetzalcóatl was reborn yet again in the apocalyptic masterpiece by Rufino Tamayo, *Nacimiento de nuestra nacionalidad*. Soon after leaving the academic environs of the San Carlos Academy of Fine Arts in Mexico City, in concert with his muralist comrades before him, Tamayo met and fell under the ubiquitous spell of José Vasconcelos, likewise a native son of Oaxaca. The artist recalled that "Vasconcelos wanted to draw upon Mexico's own heritage, instead of on themes and techniques borrowed but not assimilated from foreign cultures. He also felt that people needed the propaganda message that would be contained in the murals."

While in his twenties, Tamayo was appointed head of the department of ethnographical drawing at the National Museum of Archaeology. He went to work every day in a small, cubiclelike office at the center of the huge pre-Columbian collections. "I was surrounded by objects that were a revelation to me," Tamayo told an interviewer a half-century later. "They made me realize that everything I had been taught in school was useless…. I absorbed a new influence, almost subconsciously, in emotional, spiritual, intellectual, and technical ways."

Over the years, Tamayo came to believe that all the peoples who created art and artifacts in the

Nickolas Muray, *Portrait of Rufino Tamayo*

LEFT: *Rufino Tamayo, Nacimiento de Nuestra Nacionalidad (detail), Palacio Nacional de Bellas Artes, 1952*

epochs before the Spanish Conquest, and "not the Zapotecs [i.e., of Oaxaca] alone," were his forebears. "Tamayo could hardly discard a racial heritage that was not for him a cerebral option but a biological fact," observed his friend, the critic and artist Jean Charlot. "His colleagues had picked the most gigantic of antiquities as touchstones against which to assess their muscles—the monolithic moon-goddess

from Teotihuacán, the geometric serpent-heads dug up in the Zócalo [of Mexico City], the colossus Coatlicue girded with snake-rattles."[23]

The first factor I take into consideration when standing in front of the mural *Nacimiento de nuestra nacionalidad* (aside from its immensity—it is thirty-six feet long and sixteen feet high) is the title, *Birth of our Nationality* [or *Nationhood*]. In Spanish the word *nacimiento* has three additional layers of meaning beyond "birth" in the conventional sense: "sprouting," as in the plant or the corn seed; "origin"; and "nativity," with direct reference to Jesus Christ—all of which, throughout the history of Mesoamerica, converge upon Quetzalcóatl.

And what a swirling mass of confused yet coherent identities *Nacimiento* truly is! Behind the white pillar of Greco-European tradition holding up the left-hand side of the painting sits a temple which could be Egyptian or Teotihuacán. Coursing across the sky is a direct visual descendant of Orozco's wide-eyed prophet and Siqueiros's centaur. But this rider is portrayed as the feared yet welcome visitor: the white-garbed, bearded Plumed Serpent. The hooves of his howling steed crush holy temples into broken stone ruins. Among them lies the familiar, staring serpent, fanged jaws agape, sliced into sections eerily reminiscent of the fragments sitting today in the dust around the temple-bases of Chichén Itzá.

The wild rider points one avenging arm downward toward the serpent—is it disavowing a former self or beckoning to it? The moon eclipsing the sun in the upper right quadrant brings to mind the two great pyramids of Teotihuacán, the dual core of Plumed Serpent's life cycle.[24]

CHAPTER XXII

PRECIOUS TWIN

*The Indian, the Aztec, Old Mexico—all that
fascinates me and has fascinated me for years.
There is glamor and magic for me.*

— D. H. LAWRENCE at Taormina, Sicily,
(letter to E. H. Brewster, November 16, 1921)[1]

*Americans…must catch the pulse of the life
which Cortés and Columbus murdered.
There lies the real continuity….
We must start from Montezuma,
not from St. Francis or St. Bernard.*

— D. H. LAWRENCE, "America, Listen to Your Own"[2]

D. H. Lawrence, always in transit, was seeking what he hoped would be "the next *real* thing… probably here, in America (I don't say just the U.S.A.)." Accompanied by his German wife, Frieda, he finally arrived in Mexico City for the first time in late March 1923 via Santa Fe and El Paso, "in an unkempt Pullman trailing through endless deserts." One week later, at the Hotel Monte Carlo, a modest establishment near the National Library on the Avenida Uruguay, he was met by two American acquaintances: the poet and translator Witter Bynner, and his former writing student from the University of California, Willard "Spud" Johnson. On a bright morning after Easter in early April, the foursome hired a car and, following a stop at the Acolman Monastery, drove to the Teotihuacán ruins.

Their sightseeing began with a climb to the top of the Pyramid of the Sun to photograph each other—the dark-suited Lawrence, at thirty-eight, appeared pale, green-eyed, slight and bearded, his straw hat removed, revealing a shock of red hair.[3]

He was overwhelmed by the expansive Pyramids, finding them "far more [impressive] than Pompeii or the Forum" in beloved Italy.[4] But Lawrence's imagination was indelibly captured southward, below the San Juan riverbed, at the huge Ciudadela ("citadel") quadrangle, where he strolled slowly around the inner boundaries of the one-square-mile plaza, encompassed by walls seven meters high. It was big enough to embrace the Aztec Templo Mayor and, it was said, to hold the entire population of Teotihuacán at its height. He lingered for a long time, hesitantly touching the smooth, enameled stones and "brooding" before the forbidding

D. H. Lawrence (right) and Spud Johnson descending the Pyramid of the Sun, Teotihuacán

snake heads at the Temple of Quetzalcóatl, the last major structure and first sculptured building in Teotihuacán.[5]

It had been four years since an archaeological team under Manuel Gamio, first director of the Department of Anthropology at the *Museo Nacional*, had picked up where the earlier digging of Leopoldo Batres left off and cleared away centuries of accumulated shrubbery, vines, and unquarried rubble on the inner walls at the Citadel's easternmost edge. There they unearthed the polychrome, petal-necked serpents, some with still-glittering obsidian eyes, ascending for seven levels in a palatial facade twenty-two meters high, bisected by a broad stairway.[6]

Mindful of Lawrence's volatile, impulsive disposition, standing at a respectful distance from the English writer, Witter Bynner watched his "half-frightened, half-fascinated" friend pace back and forth, approaching and withdrawing from the serpents. Bynner wondered if it was at this point that "the germ of a theme" for his new "American novel" came to Lawrence through the vision of "this animal of all animals, this snake of all snakes, this creature part snake and part bird, Mexico's natural god and in many ways his own."[7]

In an essay called "Au Revoir, U. S. A.," written soon after the Teotihuacán visit, Lawrence revealed the depth of his obsession with the Plumed Serpent as it took over the center of his restless mind and became the motif for the imminent book he described as "the most important" he ever produced.

It's a fanged continent. It's got a rattlesnake coiled in its heart, has this democracy of the New World [Lawrence wrote of his new (although temporary) home]. I admit that I feel bewildered [he recalled of the still-fresh experi-

ence at the ruins]. There's nothing amiably comic in these ancient monsters. They're dead in earnest about biting and writhing, snake-blooded birds.... And out at San Juan Teotihuacán where are the great pyramids of a vanished, pre-Aztec people, as we are told—and the so-called Temple of Quetzalcóatl—there, behold you, huge gnashing heads jut out jagged from the wall-face of the low pyramid.... But look out! The great stone heads snarl at you from the wall, trying to bite you: and one great dark, green blob of an obsidian eye, you never saw anything so blindly malevolent; and then white fangs.... The anthropologists may make what prettiness they like out of myths. But come here, and you'll see that the gods bit.[8]

In November 1921, at the time D. H. Lawrence and Frieda received the invitation from Mabel Dodge Sterne to visit her estate in Taos, New Mexico—to live with all conveniences provided in an adobe cottage built and furnished just for them—this irascible coal-miner's son, high school dropout, and lapsed schoolmaster from Nottinghamshire was already known (and notorious) as a poet, painter, short story writer, and as the author of the sensuous novels *Aaron's Rod, Sons and Lovers, The Rainbow,* and *Women in Love.* But the wealthy Mrs. Sterne was attracted to Lawrence's atmospheric travel essays. She "decided that he was the one to describe her beloved Taos." After marrying the Pueblo Indian Antonio Luhan, Mabel Dodge became "Lorenzo's" devoted admirer and patroness.[9]

Ever peripatetic, Lawrence took up her generous request eagerly and, in his first adventure outside Europe, headed from Sicily to Naples and then, by roundabout way of Ceylon and Australia, arrived in Taos from San Francisco almost a year later. In a place the native peoples called "the heart of the world," he avidly immersed himself in the "animistic...dark and impersonal" cultures of the

Pueblo, Navajo, and Apache.[10]

"One must somehow bring together the two ends of humanity," Lawrence wrote in immediate reply to Mabel Sterne, "our own thin end, and the last dark strand from the previous, pre-white era. I verily believe that. Is Taos the place?"[11]

His friend, the English writer Richard Aldington, pointed out that the journey to New Mexico, and from there to the true goal, Mexico itself, was the fulfillment of Lawrence's drive to find antiquity below the modern landscape, a quest that mirrored his penetration of the human psyche. Soon after the First World War, Lawrence had read C. G. Jung's *Psychology of the Unconscious* (published in German in 1912, in English in 1917). He discovered the provocative idea of the archetype: within the mind of contemporary man slumbered vestigial "memories" of the myths of primitive man's "old, far-off, far-off experience."

"The dark underworld meadows of the soul" Lawrence sought were accessible only when modern rational man liberated himself to come into contact with the "ancient beauty" of the landscapes of forgotten ancestors. Wading through the high grass of these rough meadows in search of hidden secrets was hazardous but necessary training for his literary and spiritual odyssey. Lawrence confided in Frieda that he wanted to write a novel on every continent, and thus his steady pilgrimage, which continued with the composition of *The Plumed Serpent.*[12]

However, this was not merely an impressionistic writer depending upon exposed nerve endings to provide mystical flavor for his novel. Once he set himself to the task of taking on the saga of Mexico, Lawrence undertook a meticulous self-education from the early to middle 1920s. Mrs. Lawrence, Mrs. Luhan, and Witter Bynner recalled the omnivorous author on many evenings curled up on his bed in the hotel room or sitting in a rocking chair after dinner in the Taos cottage, oblivious to noisy, brandy-inspired conversations and cigarette smoke swirling around him, reading and taking notes from—among others—many of the classic works mentioned throughout this book: Sir James George Frazer's *The Golden Bough*; Lewis Spence's *The Mythologies of Ancient Mexico and Peru*; L. Gutierrez de Lara's and Edgcumb Pinchon's *The Mexican People: Their Struggle for Freedom*; William Hickling Prescott's *History of the Conquest of Mexico*; Adolph Bandelier's *The Gilded Man*; Cortés's *Letters to the King of Spain*; Bernal Díaz del Castillo's *The Conquest of New Spain*; Baron Alexander Von Humboldt's *Vues des Cordillères*—and T. Philip Terry's tourist *Guide to Mexico*, which Lawrence's American publisher, Thomas Seltzer, mailed to him from New York after repeated requests before his friend left the states.

On three occasions during the frenetic sight-see-ing tour of Mexico City and environs in the spring of 1923, Lawrence, not settled into a concentrated writing regimen, brought his wife along on a visit to *Casa Alvarado*, the suburban Coyoacan home of the American expatriate archaeologist and author Zelia Nuttall. Here, after lunch or tea, while other guests took advantage of siesta, Lawrence absented himself for hours at a time to dip into her vast col-lection of scholarly literature on Mexico. He had read and admired Mrs. Nuttall's major work, *Fundamental Principles of Old and New World Civilizations* (1901).[13] The particular attraction of *Fundamental Principles* resided in Mrs. Nuttall's descriptions of the polarities in Plumed Serpent's identity as "Precious Twin," spirit of the soil and of the air, crawling snake and soaring bird, the god who probed the world beneath the surface of the earth as easily as he became the fiery planet Venus—the ever-renewing and Phoenixlike spirit of the heavens.

"I am the living Quetzalcóatl!" was Lawrence's incantation in *The Plumed Serpent*. "The serpent sleeps in my bowels, the knower of the underearth. And the eagle sleeps in my heart, the strength of the skies. I am Lord of the Two Ways, star between day and the earth.... I am the spiral of evolution."[14]

By the end of April 1923, Lawrence was growing increasingly irritable. Brief excursions to Puebla, Orizaba, Cholula, and Atlixco interested and distracted him, but he urgently needed a place of his own to settle down and get to work. If such seclusion proved unattainable, he announced (more to himself than anyone else) that he would have to return to England. *Terry's Guide* sang the praises of a village called Chapala, five thousand feet above sea level and reachable by the train that ran north-west of Mexico City to Guadalajara ("a burnt, dry town"), Jalisco, and two more hours—thirty-two miles—of a two-peso bus ride south and east of that city to the sixty-mile-long lake deriving its name from the Nahuatl word *chapalal*, the sound of waves splashing upon the beach. Encircled by mountains, Chapala was home to thousands of southward-bound birds at the beginning of the Mexican winter, "a mingling of feathered nations in a land of perpet-ual summer."[15]

Lawrence went to "reconnoiter" the possibilities of the idyllic site ahead of Frieda, Bynner, and Johnson. At the edge of town he quickly found a one-story, L-shaped bungalow on Zaragoza Street (no more than an unpaved lane), which was bordered by mango trees on two sides. The house featured an iron gate; a wide porch; a red-tiled, shadowy, white-pillared patio with pots of geraniums around it; cas-cades of brightly colored oleander, hibiscus, and bougainvillea; and a servant maid. "I can begin a novel now," he wrote with relief to Thomas Seltzer on May 2, "as soon as I can take breath."[16]

The writer's daily routine was steady. He awoke early, before the "eternal sun" was high, and walked alone to the lakeside beach. Massive willow and pep-per trees stood at the end of a narrow peninsula. Lawrence sat in the sand with his back against a tree trunk, took out a blue-bound composition notebook, and started writing, pent-up, fast, and furious. In the intervals between these bouts of creativity, Lawrence shifted to marking the final proofs for his forthcoming book of essays, *Studies in Classic American Literature*, scheduled to be published by Seltzer that August.

The first piece was still giving him trouble. It was called, appropriately enough, "The Spirit of Place." Lawrence had been reworking it in one form or another over the previous five years. Reflecting on the origins of the Pilgrim Fathers, Lawrence could easily have been writing about himself: "To get *away*—that most simple of motives. To get away. Away from *what*? In the long run, away from them-selves. Away from everything. That's why most peo-ple come to America, and still do come."[17]

Finally, in the white heat of creation, oblivious to the sun glare off the water, the shouts of fisher-men in white boats approaching the jetty, the shrieks of playing children, and the splashing wash-erwomen, Lawrence churned out a 415-page first draft for the novel he called *Quetzalcóatl* during the five weeks between May 10 and June 15. "Or will people be afraid to ask for a book with that name?" he wondered.[18]

At the center of the first version of the story is Kate Burns, a young and strong Irish widow on her first trip to Mexico. She is a transparent composite of Lawrence and Frieda. Much of what happens to Kate is a barely altered replica of the couple's early experiences in the foreign land: a trip with two writer friends to a repulsive and bloody bullfight in which the picador's poor horse is eviscerated; tea in the suburbs with Mrs. Norris (a caricature of Zelia Nuttall); and visits to museums and outlying ruins to absorb the spell of the old, dark gods.

In typical Lawrentian fashion, just beneath the atmospheric, exotic skin of the tale ripples a heated, turbulent theme—the descent of resistant, civilized, and Western Kate through the looking-glass, into a pagan culture. She is drawn to visit Lake Chapala (the very same, since at this early stage Lawrence's

thinking is not yet thoroughly fictionalized), where a strange man has recently emerged from its depths, claiming to have "spoken with the God Quetzalcóatl."[19]

Perhaps recalling the *Cenote de los Sacrificios* at Chichén Itzá, Lawrence equates Quetzalcóatl with all that conspires to "pull Kate down" in the most complete way and drown her in the swirling, ancient mythologies of death and rebirth that were for so many centuries exemplified by the ubiquitous Mexican deity Plumed Serpent. She feels his pres-ence when she sits every morning under the droop-ing willows by the shore of Lake Chapala "in the early light," gazing at "every wrinkle in the great hills opposite, already covered with green sheen."[20]

Kate's painful struggle to settle into life at Chapala and come to terms with Mexico is a barely disguised version of Lawrence's conflict, an unspar-ing representation of what it feels like for a modern traveler in unfamiliar territory, one who is willing to open up to sensations stranger and more novel than those available from conventional tourism (in Europe, for example). Rather, "in this country, it did not seem a disaster to be cut off as she was cut off. It seemed inevitable. Something strengthened her, something unknown and rather grim…."[21]

Quetzalcóatl's ancient pledge to come back to his people has put the peons of the village of Chapala into a stir of anticipation, placing "something dark and cognizant in their souls all the time." Is this the second coming, the deliverance so long awaited? In the course of answering the question, Lawrence introduces a different kind of revolution, a religious rather than a social upheaval, led by two charismatic men: Ramon Carrasco and Cipriano Viedma. The tale is driven by Kate's rapport with them. Don Ramon desires to see the triumph over daily oppres-sion by "the dark-eyed men of his own Mexico" who "had waited so many centuries outside the gates of their own being."[22]

Ramon is the ruminative, philosophical power

behind the raw and aggressive energy of his friend Cipriano, who fervently hopes to "see Mexico become himself" rather than continue down a path that would force it "to become cornered by the great world of industrial mankind."[23]

D. H. Lawrence, manuscript page from first draft of the novel-in-progress, Quetzalcóatl

The scales fall from Kate's eyes and we readers likewise bear witness. Quetzalcóatl-Ramon (the mestizo ideologue) pushes Huitzilopochtli-Cipriano (the Indian nationalist) to place faith in the snakelike "spiral of evolution." First they must resurrect and unify the indigenous antagonist-gods of the past.

Reincarnated, Quetzalcóatl and Huitzilopochtli will fight together as brothers. Then, in their name and under their banner, the Mexican people will turn away from the white spectre of the Church of "gringo" Jesus and march to true autonomy.

Virtuous Kate's descent from studious learning about Mexico into spiritual-erotic love with the noble, brown-skinned Cipriano is vintage Lawrence. At the same time, this skillful writer takes pains to remind Western readers of the pitfalls in romanticizing

the terrible difference between [Cipriano's] blood and [Kate's] own.... She remembered the story that he had serpent's poison in his blood and that his bite was venomous.... When Cipriano was really worked up...something seemed to be starting out of him...some strange, invisible, dark-feathered demon.

In tenuous approach to Cipriano, Kate acts the same way Lawrence did when he reached to touch the forbidding serpent-snout at Teotihuacán. Both fear—yet are exhilarated by—the threatening "bite" of Mexico.[24]

In the end, Kate cannot withstand the magnet of her past. She "get[s] on with her packing" and prepares to return to "pale, almost ghostly" Europe, despite Ramon's pleas that she marry Cipriano and join their idealistic fight.[25]

The first draft of Quetzalcóatl completed, Lawrence endured two weeks of ambivalence about his next step. He took a boating trip along Lake Chapala, ostensibly seeking a *hacienda.* Then he decided to "give up." "It's no good," he told his friend the Danish painter and writer Knud Merrild. "If I can't stand Europe, we'll come back to Mexico."[26] By the middle of July, Lawrence and Frieda were in New Orleans and then New York City, where they quarreled bitterly when he refused to sail back to Europe with her. Instead, he forged onward to Los Angeles and then southward to Guadalajara and Chapala again—but this time in disillusionment. "Somehow it is unreal to me now. I don't know why." Finally, in exhaustion and loneliness, Lawrence retreated to Frieda in London ("Gloom—yellow air—bad cold—old house—tea in old cups").[27]

"England is only one end of the broken rope. *Hay otro*. There's another.... I am like a wild beast in a cage," he complained, away from the unforgettable and sultry land he left behind.[28] Nagging in the corner of Lawrence's feverish imagination was his resolve to take another pass at the Mexico novel. He knew his compositional requirements well enough to be aware that it could only be revised *in* Mexico.[29]

The tug of that invisible rope was compelling. By mid-November 1924, after a reviving stay in Taos and a two-day narrow-gauge train ride from Mexico City, the Lawrences were in Oaxaca. He wanted to come closer to the "pure Indian" lands of the south, the Zapotec and Mixtec, for the three-month "hard fight" with words which lay before him now. Chapala and the Aztec Central Valley region no longer signified the profoundest spirit of Mexico. Oaxaca, predominantly Indian (as it remains today) was more "*simpático*." Instead of sitting under a tree by a lake, Lawrence—craving total seclusion—walked from his rented house in town on the Avenida Pino Suarez and out into the desert, pencils and copybook in hand; he found a spot facing the mountains and the austere ruins of Monte Albán beyond, and worked in the shade of a giant bush over which he propped a big, black umbrella.[30]

At the insistence of his agent, A. W. Barmby, and his new publisher, Alfred A. Knopf, both "in a sort of a panic" over the unpronounceable title, Lawrence reluctantly changed his new book to the less exotic *The Plumed Serpent*, insisting, however, that the old name, *Quetzalcóatl*, be printed in parentheses below.[31] The final version, almost twice as long as the Chapala draft, was completed in February 1925 despite the fact that Lawrence was

suffering from influenza and had retreated to his bed, critically ill with malaria.

Kate Burns becomes Kate Leslie, and Chapala becomes Sayula. Beyond these and other cosmetic changes, the book flowers from within. Kate's "oppressed" alienation from "the black, serpent-like fatality"[32] of Mexico is sharply etched from the start, making the final reversal denied her in the first draft more dramatic. Don Ramon's profile is toned down, and Cipriano, the full-blooded Indian, is brought to the foreground. Thanks to Lawrence's stay in Oaxaca, including an enthralling trip to "the carved courts of Mitla...where a wind blows the dust," the legend of Quetzalcóatl is fleshed out, his attributes elaborated to include Éhecatl, "the wind that whirls from the heart of the earth." The poignant Virgin of Solitude, Oaxaca's patron saint, hovers in Cipriano's memory.[33]

The terrain—Octavio Paz's "symbolic geography"—assumes deeper contours through Lawrence's enhanced sensitivity to the ever-present Mexican mountains, which haunted him in Oaxaca as they had at Chapala, the "blue, ribbed, corrugated, secretly beating heart of the earth."[34] He even manages to include rural details such as cocks crowing all night long.

However, the most significant creative advance in the published version of *The Plumed Serpent* is its extended, poetic liturgy, the ritual basis for a new religion Lawrence always dreamed about: an ideal, spiritual society celebrating, once and for all, the triumphant fulfillment of man *and* woman, and their origin in nature, "down on the dark, volcanic earth."[35] "Who sleeps—shall wake! Who sleeps— shall wake!" sings the Indian drummer heralding Quetzalcóatl's resurrection "with a new body, like a star," to conduct his people on the path to this ideal way of life:[36]

D. H. Lawrence (second from left) and Frieda at Mitla

Someone will enter between the gates,
Now, at this moment, Ay!
See the light on the man that waits.
Shall you? Shall I?

Ramon shares with Cipriano his fantasy of a "natural aristocracy" made up of every man in an "organically united" world, promulgating the egalitarian doctrine of eternal comrades represented by Quetzalcóatl "of the blue sky" and Huitzilopochtli "red at the gates."[37] Kate, by yielding to the men— and with her adopted names of Itzpapalotl and Malintzi, through eventual marriage to Cipriano— will complete the dream. Bathed in rainwater, anointed with fragrant oil, dressed in a white chemise, she represents the capitulation of the white world to the primal state of Mexico.

Lawrence, seriously ailing and only four years from death by tuberculosis, conjured up the courage during his second sojourn in Mexico to complete the passionate vision of Quetzalcóatl. The gods remake Mexico into the society it was, long before the advent of Olmec, Toltec, Mixtec, or Aztec nations and long before the Conquest—a place imbued with the spirit of "the old prehistoric humanity…before the glacial period":[38]

Hola! Hola! Mexicanos! Glance away a
moment towards me.
Just turn your eyes this way, Mexicanos!…
Let us have a spring cleaning in the world.

D. H. Lawrence, Quetzalcóatl Looks Down on Mexico[39]

CHAPTER XXIII

THE QUETZAL BIRD

VISIONS OF QUETZALCÓATL PERSIST IN TODAY'S MEXICO — FORGING A LINK
WITH THE STUBBORN INDIAN WORLD — ELUSIVE LEGEND, EVANESCENT BIRD

New generations of Mexico's modern artists continue to search for the *alma nacional*, the national soul. As a result, Quetzalcóatl, "the secular image of a lost Golden Age," is still visible as the most prevalent symbol in public art works throughout Mexico City.[1]

A dramatic example is Juan O'Gorman's immense mosaic facade (1950) covering the four exterior walls of the ten-story library at the National Autonomous University on the Avenida Insurgentes. The north wall depicts "the American culture of Anáhuac," dominated by darker forces in Aztec cosmology, as well as the "beneficent" Quetzalcóatl and Tlaloc, hovering high above the eagle of Tenochtitlán. To O'Gorman, the pre-Hispanic era, before the "intervention of Europe," was "the only true American phase" in the long history of his nation.[2]

Elsewhere in the university complex, at the great courtyard of the Science Faculty, looms a glass mosaic by José Chavez Morado, completed in 1952, *The Return of Quetzalcóatl*. The artist has taken a conciliatory view of Plumed Serpent as the great unifier of mestizo culture. A "boat of entwined serpents" carries representatives of various races, offering themselves to the New World: idealized Mexico, in melting-pot, mixed-race harmony.[3]

In 1956 Raúl Anguiano executed a mural in oil on masonite for the Mexican Chamber of

Raúl Anguiano, Mexican Labor and Commerce, 1956

Commerce on the Paseo de la Reforma, *The Story of Mexican Labor and Commerce*. Crouched among the intertwined roots of a ceiba tree, a subterranean Indian woman, eyes gazing upward, gently cradles in her curved fingers corn sprouts that represent the beginning of all life. In the topmost branches, a Teotihuacán plumed serpent grins, displaying his bifid tongue to the heavens.[4]

Federico Cantú's eleven-by-eight-foot fresco on the tenth floor of the Social Security Building, *Quetzalcóatl Dispensing His Gifts to the Toltecs* (1959–60), reprises a timeless theme, the creator god conferring the blessing of fire upon his chosen people.

Ritual has the reassuring power to bring forth religious feelings born in ancient times, allowing us to experience them in endless cycles as if for the first time. Plumed Serpent, the snake shedding his skin, can still be found in rituals of Indian Mexico. In Chiapas province to the east, Tzotzil Maya dress up as Quetzalcóatl and dance in circles.[5] Across the country, in Puebla province, near Mexico City, during the festival of the *Quetzales*, dancers wear huge, wheel-shaped headdresses more than five feet in diameter decorated with colored paper, silk ribbons, and, in front, a painting of the head of the quetzal bird. The costumes are red, the primary color for the east, whither Plumed Serpent went and whence he may return.[6]

Throughout this century the writers and thinkers of Mexico have struggled to define the proper degree of connection to the Indian psyche. To Alfonso Reyes, at the beginning of the modern age, "unity with yesterday's race" was not something about which Mexicans had any choice. The patrimony was compulsory, composed of raw nature, of the air breathed in the realm of Éhecatl, "the gods circulating in the vital space surrounding [the contemporary Mexican]." And with every new ruin the archaeologists uncovered in their fervor to keep digging, a stronger rapport with the past was welded.[7]

Octavio Paz took this insistence a step further: "Otherness is what constitutes us," he said. "The *other Mexico*, submerged and repressed, reappears in the modern Mexico." Especially now—in the final years of our century—"many ghosts have come back to life." The result is the simultaneous existence of multiple pasts in unresolved conflict.[8]

Carlos Fuentes fears darkly that the world of the Indian "has become the secret repository of all that we have forgotten and disdained." Fuentes's humanist concern is that today's Mexican, victimized by progress (in this respect sharing the dilemma of all contemporary cultures), ignores the past at his peril. Fuentes employs the strong image of the "buried mirror" to warn that "we [the Mexicans of today] do not wish to see our own reflection" there—because it may too much resemble the Mesoamerican face.[9]

During the years I followed the legends of the Plumed Serpent, I was heartened by this ambivalent, impressionistic language. For centuries so many fine minds, within Mexico and without, have grappled with the essential nature of the land and its myths. I, the latecomer, was not alone. After all, I found out, many others in the field came to Mesoamerican studies as "talented amateurs and individualists" from various disciplines.[10]

Even the great Claude Lévi-Strauss humbly conceded that on his lifelong "road toward the understanding of man"—an anthropological road, it seems to me, he built so that an entire discipline could follow—there were frustrating spells of "ignorance" about the lifeways and culture of peoples he studied. Lévi-Strauss realized he would "probably never achieve chronological certainty" about the "itinerary" of one culture leading into another.

Lévi-Strauss found solace, however, in the conviction that regardless of the background or heritage we bring to bear, "a myth is still felt as a myth by any reader anywhere in the world." I was encouraged by Lévi-Strauss's belief that ultimately "myth is language, functioning on a very high level."[11] Although the complicated legends and mysteries of Plumed Serpent, with their twists and turns and variations, at times

Dance of the Quetzales, Puebla

confused me, I kept the faith. Constructing this mosaic, working as an open-minded "good traveller,"[12] I believed I would eventually find a way in.

On one of my later trips to Mexico, still the self-conscious professional stranger, I arrived at the airport after the quick flight from Newark, eased through customs, leaped into a cab, and told the driver to take me directly to Teotihuacán—"*las pirámides*." We started chatting in a fragmentary way once we reached the toll road heading north and the crowded urban world faded away.

The resplendent quetzal

He asked me why I was going straight to the ruins without even stopping in Mexico City to see the sights. I told him I was writing a book. What was the book about? "Quetzalcóatl," I replied, looking at the back of his head. He nodded immediately and gave me a warm glance in the rearview mirror. "Ah, sí, *Quetzalcoat*'" he said with a smile, the last letter trailing off in a guttural sound. There was immediate recognition, the same kind of warm acknowledgment I received wherever I went: three-hour luncheons in the "las Lomas" district of Mexico City, late nights in cafés near the University, or research visits at regional archives.

These conversations, limited by my halting Spanish but helped along by newfound friends' attempts at English, began to follow a predictable pattern. There were grudging admissions that "all was not well" in Mexico. Then followed indecisive reasons that dwindled to inconclusive, gloomy, and awkward silence. There was no money to stimulate economic incentives. There was no real democracy,

only authoritarianism. The increasingly militant Zapatistas in Chiapas seemed unable to marshal enough support to effect permanent shifts in the political system. Mexico was politically and socially instable, and fated to remain so. A somber pause. Then brightening again, "But please—tell us more about your book on Quetzalcóatl!"[13]

In the misty, damp mountain cloud forests of Chiapas and Guatemala, down into northern Nicaragua and Honduras, lives the fabulous and threatened quetzal bird, taking its name from the Nahua *quetzalli*, "precious tail feather." The scientific classification, *Pharomachrus mocinno*, means "long mantle."

The Maya trapped and temporarily caged the revered bird, plucked his tail feathers for ceremonial headdress attire and ritual shield decoration, and then released him so that the tail would grow back. To kill a quetzal was to risk being executed.

The resplendent male is a short-distance flier with brown eyes, yellow beak, red breast, green "shoulder cape," and an iridescent, green-blue-gold-flecked, four-plumed tail covert up to three feet long. He reclusively prefers the highest treetop reaches, making a nest hole in the soft sides of mulberry and oak trees, more than 150 feet above the leafy jungle floor.

The quetzal travels in impulsive bursts like a woodpecker, grabbing berries while in motion and sipping dewdrops from lofty leaves. On occasion, however, the lively bird will break into spiral flight, straight upward—singing while he circles away beyond the trees.[14]

Acknowledgments

Even though the act of writing must always be a solitary pursuit, whenever I arrive at the conclusion of labor on a book, I am invariably astonished by the amount of support I have received during the years along the way.

For research guidance, hospitality, and friendship during my visits to Mexico, I am deeply grateful to Federico Mendoza Aguirre; Arturo Garcia Bustos; Barbara Eurard; Patricia Segues de Barrios Gomez; Jorge and Aura Hernandez; Antonio and Maria Eugenia Lopez de Silanes; Maria Teresa Franco y Gonzalez Salas, Directora General, INAH; Gerardo Estrada Rodriguez, Director General, and Norma Rojas Delgadillo, Directora, Instituto Nacional de Bellas Artes; Alberto Ruy Sanchez Lacy, Director General, *Artes de Mexico*; Cecilia Urbina; Eleazar Lopez Zamora, Director, Fototeca del INAH; and Luis P. Zarate.

For institutional and scholarly assistance with access to innumerable rare books, special collections manuscripts, art works, and photographs, I thank Barbara Mathé, Department of Library Services, American Museum of Natural History; Luisa Orso, Art Resource; Timothy Troy and Dianne Nilsen, The Center for Creative Photography; Peter Howe, Director, Corbis Corporation, and Norman Curry, Researcher, Corbis-Bettmann; Rebecca Fawcett, Kathy Hart, Diane Miliotes, Timothy Rub, Hood Museum of Art, Dartmouth College; Anne Ostendarp, Special Collections, Baker Library, Dartmouth College; Jeffrey Quilter, Director, Precolumbian Studies, Bridget Toledo, Librarian, Precolumbian Studies, and the Fellows of Dumbarton Oaks; David Wilcove, The Environmental Defense Fund; Kathleen Hammond, Chuck Koch, and Luis Anthony Lugo, Jr., Hammond, Inc.; Ricardo Gutierrez Vargas, INAH; Kimberly Kostas, Rights and Reproductions, Los Angeles County Museum of Art; Ross Day and Virginia Webb, Robert Goldwater Library, The Metropolitan Museum of Art; Jeri Wagner, The Photograph Library, The Metropolitan Museum of Art; Juan Garcia de Oteyza, Mexican Cultural Institute of New York; Christine Barthe, Photothèque, Musée de l'Homme; Grace de Almeida, El Museo del Barrio; Kathleen Curry, Virginia Dodier, Thomas Grischkowsky, The Museum of Modern Art; Susan Henry, National Geographic Society; Gail Persky, The New School Library; Sharon Frost, Wayne Furman, John F. Rathé, and Julia Van Haaften, The New York Public Library; Martha Labell, Photographic Archives, Peabody Museum of Archaeology and Ethnology, Harvard University; Clayton C. Kirking, Parsons School of Design Library; Douglas Wechsler and William Matthews, Visual Resources in Ornithology, Philadelphia Academy of Natural Sciences; Kathleen Ryan, Rights and Reproductions, Philadelphia Museum of Art; Heather Chalcroft, Lawrence Pollinger Limited; William L. Joyce, Rare Books and Special Collections, Princeton University Library; David Coleman, Department of Photography, Harry Ransom Humanities Research Center, The University of Texas at Austin; and Alison Gallup, VAGA.

Several authorities in the Mesoamerican field were patient by telephone and in person with my queries and clarifications: Keith F. Davis, Hallmark Collections, Kansas City; Philip A. Dennis, Department of Anthropology, Texas Tech University; Susan T. Evans, Department of Anthropology, Pennsylvania State University; Mildred Kaplan, *Arte Primitivo*; Balaji Mundkur, University of Connecticut, Storrs; and Robert B. Pickering, Chairman, Department of Anthropology, Denver Museum of Natural History.

There is always a cadre of knowledgeable, receptive and empathetic people whose help defies categorizing; but each of you knows why your name appears here: George F. Andrews; Philip A. Berry; Claudia Carr; Charles Cantalupo; Nicholas Clapp; Sandra Dijkstra; Bob Fein; Constance Folz; David C. Groves; Robert O. Groves; Kathryn Harrison; Irene Hunt; O. Aldon James; Nellie Kearney; Susan and Michael King; Fred Kobrak; Agnes Krup; Suzanne Jill Levine; Gregory Long; David McCullough; Mimi Muray; Jonathan Newcomb; Walter Oliver; Jonathan Plutzik; Robert D. Rubic, Precision Chromes, Inc.; Flo Silver; Christine and Roger L. Stevens; Mel Stuart; Beth Gates Warren; and T. H. Watkins.

My intrepid and determined agent, Philippa Brophy, and her assistant, Nichole Britton, kept me moving forward whenever I was struck by that particular brand of authorial anxiety. Peter Osnos, Robert Kimzey, and the dedicated staff of PublicAffairs seized upon the inherent story in this book and brought it to life with unflagging energy and devotion.

Final gratitude, of course, must go to my family — Roberta, Nicholas, and Allegra — because when there is a moody writer in the house (even if he is in isolation on the third floor, behind closed doors) no one can ever be completely at peace.

Notes

CHAPTER I

1. Charlot, 1972, p. 99.
2. Von Humboldt, 1995, pp. xv, 11.
3. Batalla, p. vi.
4. Mesoamerica is an area of Mexico and Central America in which the common presence of certain pre-Hispanic cultural traits permits the classification of separate cultures within the area as one civilization. The concept was first proposed, geographically and culturally, by Paul Kirchhoff in 1943. Muser, p. 99.
5. Sahagún, cited in Thomas, p. 186.
6. Batalla, p. 38.
7. Nicholson, 1967, pp. 78–113.
8. Lévi-Strauss, 1963, p. 218.
9. Lafaye, p. xi.

CHAPTER II

1. Bloch, p.27; pp.54–55.
2. Wilford, p.1.
3. Campbell, *The Way of the Seeded Earth*, 1988, p. 48.
4. Vaillant, p. 169.
5. Saenz, p. 29.
6. Ignacio Bernal, in *Cosío Villegas*, p. 17.
7. Boas, pp. 406, 455.
8. Jung, 1978, pp. 71ff.
9. Luckert, p. 27; and Mundkur, p. 255.
10. Campbell, 1981, p. 300; and Henderson, p. 36.
11. Wilson, pp. 360–61; and Paz, 1993, p. 76.

CHAPTER III

1. Brotherston, 1992, p. 13.
2. Paz, 1972, p. 88; and Lévi-Strauss, 1977, p. 287.
3. Léon-Portilla, 1980, p. 11.
4. Wauchope and Nash, 1967, p. 5.
5. Franco, p. 15.
6. Brotherston, 1992, p. 125.
7. Bernal, 1969, p. 18.
8. Cosío Villegas, p. 21.

9. Coe and Diehl, p. 392.
10. Coe, 1965, p. 14.
11. Franco, p. 30.
12. Panofsky, pp. 5–17. I am grateful to Susan T. Evans for directing me toward Panofsky's works.
13. Coe, 1965, p. 17.
14. Markman and Markman, 1989, p. 72; and 1992, p. 289.
15. Bernal, 1969, pp. 60ff.
16. Sweeney, n.p.
17. Richard A. Diehl in Paz, 1990, pp. 56–58.
18. Bierhorst, 1990, p. 24.
19. Coe and Diehl, pp. 22, 308.
20. Coe et. al., 1995, p. 27.
21. Mundkur, p. 127; and Franco, p. 78.
22. Pina Chan, p. 13.
23. Coe, et. al., 1995, p. 69.
24. Portillo et. al., p. 12, citing Roman Pina Chan.
25. Mundkur, p. 147.
26. Bernal, 1969, p. 67.
27. Coe, 1995, p. 129.
28. Grove, pp. 112ff.
29. Brundage, p. 29.
30. MacLachlan and Rodriguez, p. 27.

CHAPTER IV

1. Léon-Portilla, 1964, p. 37; and Berrin and Pasztory, p. 51.
2. Brambila, pp. 27–34; and Fiedel, p. 282.
3. Valades, p. 27.
4. Eliade, 1959, pp. 90, 119.
5. Eliade, 1991, pp. 62, 88.
6. Evans and Berlo, p. 8.
7. Gruzinski, p. 231.
8. Bierhorst, 1984, p. xii; and Scully, pp. 5, 6.
9. Brambila, p. 38.
10. Arnold, p. 40.
11. Campbell, 1981, p. 187; and Paz, 1990, p. 37.

12. Berrin and Pasztory, p. 202; and Townsend, pp. 144–145, citing Esther Pasztory.

13. Valades, p. 56.

14. Ibid., pp. 17–18.

15. Berrin, p. 26.

16. H. B. Nicholson, cited in Markman and Markman, 1992, p. 171. Nicholson's ground-breaking 1957 Harvard doctoral dissertation was the first study to trace the origins of Quetzalcóatl the man.

17. Evans and Berlo, p. 12.

18. Paddock, p. 50.

19. Pasztory, 1997, p. 24.

20. Benson, et. al., p. 15.

21. Wigberto Jimenez-Moreno in Paddock, p. 41.

22. Brinton, 1894, p. 50.

23. Berrin and Pasztory, pp. 60, 101ff.; and Museo Nacional, 1994, pp. 37–38.

24. Redfield, 1953, p. 22.

25. Waters, p. 47.

26. Proskouriakoff and Joyce, p. xx.

27. Wauchope and West, p. 485.

28. Paz, *Labyrinth*, 1985, p. 37.

29. Valades, p. 20; and VanKirk, p. 197.

30. Berrin and Pasztory, p. 143.

31. Ibid., p. 159.

CHAPTER V

1. Léon-Portilla, 1964, p. 124; and Thomas, p. 474.

2. Wolf, p. 107.

3. Nicholson, 1957, pp. 199–200.

4. Terry, p. 304.

5. Léon-Portilla, p. 32; and Rodriguez, p. 63.

6. Carrasco, p. 73; and Kubler, 1990, p. 91.

7. Paz, 1972, p. 89.

8. Evans and Berlo, p. 19; and Moctezuma, 1991, p. 4.

9. Tedlock, ed., p. 366; and Covarrubias, 1954, pp. 78ff.

10. Moctezuma, 1991, p. 3.

11. Kubler, 1990, p. 83.

12. Moctezuma, 1991, p. 24.

13. Lopez Austin, p. 123; and Sahagún, 1997, p. 223.

14. Carrasco, p. 88, citing Alfredo Lopez Austin's important book, *Hombre-Dios*. Lopez Austin is credited with the creation of this evocative term.

15. Campbell, 1973, p. 345; and Campbell, 1981, pp. 167–182.

16. Thomas, p. 649; and Mead and Calas, p. 413. This reference is drawn from James Mooney's essay, *An Indian Messiah*. Mircea Eliade, 1959, p. 95, analyzes the origins of the concept of the "culture-hero."

17. Durán, *Book of the Gods*, 1994, p. 121.

18. Sejourné, pp. 25ff; and Auerbach, p. 97.

19. Covarrubias, 1947, p. 136. Miguel Covarrubias is especially insightful on this philosophy. He was one of the earliest tellers of the fall of Quetzalcóatl in *Mexico South*, 1947.

20. Castaneda, 1985, p. 1. In the many depictions of Quetzalcóatl and Tezcatlipoca together, they are in the same frame, yet clearly in opposition to each other, bearing contrasting costumes and facing in opposite directions.

21. LeClezio, p. 145.

22. Lopez Austin, p. 42; and Bierhorst, ed., 1984, p. 26.

23. Bierhorst, ed., 1984, p. 26.

24. Florescano, 1995, p. 31.

25. Spence, 1918, p. 65.

26. Gillespie, p. 177; and Rodriguez, p. 13.

27. Coe, *Mexico*, 1984, p. 125. Translated from A. M. Garibay, *Historia de la Literatura Nahuatl*.

28. Anaya, pp. 143ff.

29. Campbell, 1973, p. 217; and Auerbach, p. 169. Erich Auerbach's *Mimesis*, discussing Dante's "connection of god's plan with earthly events," could easily be talking about Plumed Serpent's two identities on earth and in heaven.

30. Wauchope and Ekholm and Bernal, *Handbook of Middle American Indians*, Vol. 10, p. 112.

31. Ashton, p. 10; and Villegas, ed., pp. 38ff.

32. Wolf, p. 122.

33. Gillespie, p. 134; and Fiedel, p. 304.

34. Davies, pp. 322ff.

35. Henderson and Oakes, p. 15.

36. Léon-Portilla, 1964, p. 6; and Léon-Portilla, 1992, p. xxx.

CHAPTER VI

1. Also, Wauchope and Ekholm and Bernal, p. 323.
2. Davis, p. 30; also, Vaillant, p. 54.
3. Eliade, 1959, p. 183.
4. Campbell, 1973, p. 356.
5. Bierhorst, ed., 1984, p. 28; and Brotherston and Dorn, p. 149.
6. Campbell, 1959, p. 460.
7. Campbell, 1959, referencing Daniel G. Brinton, *American Hero-Myths*, 1882; also, Henderson and Oakes, p. 41.
8. Coe, *Mexico*, 1984, p. 102; and Von Humboldt, 1869, p. 109.
9. Foster, translating Motolinia, pp. 32, 87.
10. Correa, et. al., p. 17.
11. Wauchope and Ekholm and Bernal, p. 372; and Thomas, p. 99.
12. Fernandez, p. 29.
13. Pina Chan, n.p.
14. Paddock, p. 89, citing Wigberto Jimenez-Moreno; also, Meyer and Sherman, p. 37.
15. Fuentes, p.55; also, Carrasco, p. 130.
16. Panofsky, pp. 43–44.
17. Kubler, 1990, p. 72.

CHAPTER VII

1. Lopez Ramos, p. 15.
2. Covarrubias, 1954, p. 174, citing Fray Francisco de Burgoa.
3. Winter, p. 13.
4. Lopez Ramos, p. 26.
5. Zwollo, p. 69.
6. Paddock, p. 153.
7. Markman and Markman, 1992, pp. 245ff; also, Marcus, p. 123.
8. Winter, p. 50.
9. Markman and Markman, 1992, p. 247.
10. Winter, p. 59.
11. Covarrubias, 1947, p. 180; also, Winter, p. 75.
12. Winter, pp. 11, 89.
13. Gruzinski, p. 92, citing *Papeles de Nueva Espana*, ed.

Francisco del Paso y Troncoso, 2nd series, Madrid, 1905–1906.

14. Brinton, p. 40, "Nagualism" essay, an anecdote derived from the earlier writings of Abbé Brasseur de Bourbourg.
15. Correspondence, NB with the artist; also, García Bustos' monograph, *Meditaciones Acerca del Arte*, 1995.
16. Mayer, pp. 311–312.
17. Alcina Franch, pl. 233, p. 16.
18. Léon-Portilla, 1964, cited in Alcina Franch, p. 63.
19. Stuart, p. 75; also, Lopez Ramos, p. 18.
20. Campbell, I.1, 1988, p. 114.
21. Nuttall, p. 54.
22. Barbro Dahlgren, *La Mixteca*, 1979, cited in Lopez Ramos, pp. 63, 74.
23. Covarrubias, 1947, p. 188.
24. Ibid., 1947, p. 188.
25. The *Mexica* were the last Aztec tribal group to leave the northwestern-most lands of Mesoamerica and arrive at Chapultepec.
26. Markman and Markman, 1992, pp. 134–135.
27. Campbell, 1973, p. 193; and Moctezuma, 1988, p. 7.
28. Brotherston and Dorn, pp. 150, 259; and Waters, p. 143.

CHAPTER VIII

1. Hultkrantz, p. 215.
2. Hanks and Rice, eds., p. 3.
3. Hultkrantz, p. xii, citing Wigberto Jimenez Moreno, in his seminal essay, *Mesoamerica Before the Toltecs*; and Paddock, p. 41.
4. Perry and Perry, p. 14.
5. Schele and Miller, p. 18; and Miller, p. 36.
6. Markman and Markman, 1992, p. 273, citing Schele and Miller; and Schele and Miller, pp. 5, 103.
7. Tedlock, ed., p. 212.
8. Tedlock, ed., p. 14; and Redfield, 1953, pp. 48, 65.
9. Morley and Brainerd, p. 460.
10. Tedlock, ed., pp. 26–27; and Léon-Portilla, 1988, p. 11.
11. Wauchope and Nash, p. 357.
12. Gossen, ed., p. 19.

13. Rothenberg and Quasha, eds., p. 13.

14. Translation of *Gucumatz*: Tedlock, ed., p. 355; "lord of genius," ibid., p. 212; "primordial beginnings," Lopez Austin, p. 39; "empty sky…" Tedlock, p. 33. This *Popol Vuh* excerpt is translated by Daniel G. Brinton in his "Nagualism" essay: Brinton, 1894, pp. 32–33, from the French of Abbé Brasseur de Bourbourg, Paris, 1861 version.

15. Tedlock, ed., pp. 163–166.

16. Tedlock, ed., pp. 62, 213.

17. Bricker, 1981, p. 148, citing Munro Edmonson's version of *Popol Vuh*; and also Gossen, ed., p. 95; and Recinos and Goetz, p. 16. Tedlock, ed., p. 183, is his more recent variant on Edmonson's (1971) Tohil/Quetzalcóatl translation.

18. Nicholson, 1967, pp. 135–136; and Recinos and Goetz, pp. 16–17.

19. Recinos and Goetz, pp. 16–17 and H. B. Nicholson, 1957, p. 196; and Daniel G. Brinton's earlier 1885 translation of the *Annals*, p. 11, from the original text, but again, with the assistance of Abbe Brasseur de Bourbourg's French version.

20. Edmonson, 1982, p. xii.

21. Reyes, 1950, p. 104; and Edmonson, 1986, p. 31.

22. Roys, ed., p. 83.

23. Todorov, p. 66, quoting Ralph Roys' earlier 1933 version of the *Chilam Balam*; and Léon-Portilla, 1988, p. 51; and Edmonson, 1982, p. xi.

24. Edmonson, 1982, p. 24.

25. Nicholson, 1957, pp. 280–288.

26. Roys, ed., p. 133.

27. Edmonson, 1982, p. 106; and LeClezio, p. 163.

CHAPTER IX

1. Léon-Portilla, 1988, p. 118; and Roys, ed., p. 166.

2. Recinos and Goetz., ed., p. 41; Ferguson, p. 137; and the last great work of Tatiana Proskouriakoff, pp. xvi-xx, 185–192.

3. Redfield, 1953, p. 66; and Von Hagen, 1990, pp. 219–221.

4. Brundage, p. 270; and Ferguson, p. 137.

5. Léon-Portilla, 1964, pp. 69–75.

6. Nicholson, 1967, p. 119.

7. Von Hagen, 1990, p. 219.

8. Wauchope and Ekholm and Bernal, Summary, p. 303.

9. Waters, p. 123; and Gallencamp, p. 170.

10. Zapata Alonzo, p. 25.

11. Museo Nacional survey, p. 16.

12. Coe, *Maya*, p. 123.

13. Zapata Alonzo, p. 24.

14. Kubler, 1990, p. 287; and Nicholson, 1957, p. 293.

15. Spinden, pp. 34, 211. Anthropologist and ethnologist Herbert J. Spinden, of the American Museum of Natural History and the Peabody Museum of Harvard, was a pioneer deciphering Maya art in the early years of this century. Also see Stierlin, p. 168.

16. Andrews, p. 387.

17. Morley and Brainerd, pp. 548–555.

18. MacAdams, p. 99.

19. Landa, p. 89; and Luckert, p. 45.

20. Eliade, p. 32. In *The Sacred and the Profane*, he writes of "orientation [being] made possible" when we reach a spiritual place high above the ground.

21. Coggins and Shane, p. 53; and Léon-Portilla, 1988, p. 70.

22. Ferguson, p. 148.

23. Museo Nacional report, p. 17.

24. Museo Nacional report, p. 64.

25. Redfield, 1950, p. 305.

26. Díaz-Bolio, p. 25.

27. Mundkur, p. 145.

28. Paz, *Labyrinth*, p. 303.

29. LaBastille, p. 76.

30. Wauchope and Ekholm and Bernal, HMAI, Vol. 10, pp. 75ff.; and Bushnell, p. 79.

31. Schele and Friedel, p. 394, also Note, p. 506; and Markman and Markman, 1989, p. 75; and Daniel G. Brinton, 1894, pp. 26–27, citing the 1702 ethnohistorical works of the Dominican priest Francisco Nunez de la Vega.

32. Terry, p. 609; and Luckert, pp. 147ff.

33. Ferguson, p. 203.

34. Shook, pp. 89, 94.

35. J. E. S. Thompson, pp. 66, 120.

CHAPTER X

1. Stierlin, p. 60.
2. Brotherston, 1992, p. 18; and Meyer and Sherman, pp. 56, 58.
3. Paz, 1972, p. 110.
4. Ibid., p. 87.
5. Bierhorst, 1990, p. 10; and Palacio de Velazquez, p. 13.
6. Léon-Portilla, 1980, p. 186.
7. Moctezuma, 1988, p. 18.
8. Bierhorst, ed., 1984, pp. 71ff.
9. Ibid., p. 73.
10. Bernal and Pina Chan, 1968, p. 77; and Emmerich, p. 98. The legend is adapted from the Cronica Mexicayotl.
11. Graulich, p. 245.
12. Bierhorst, ed., 1984, p. 83.
13. Durán, *Book of the Gods*, p. 133.
14. Metraux, p. 114; and Scully, p. 21.
15. Thomas, p. 289; and Florescano, 1995, p. 91.
16. Frazer, p. 259.
17. Emmerich, p. 216.
18. Grateful thanks to Robert Pickering, Director of the Department of Anthropology at the Denver Museum of Natural History, for drawing my attention to the recent and as yet unpublished works by Phil C. Weigand on the remote Occidente region of Mexico.
19. Portillo, p. 44; and Brinton, 1882, p. 121.
20. Bierhorst, 1984, p.69; and Wauchope, Ekholm and Bernal, p. 416.
21. Ibid., p. 154: HMAI, Vol.10, an excellent essay by Agustin Villagra Caleti.
22. Kelly, p. 50; and Saenz, p. 45.
23. Kelly, p. 53.
24. Ibid., p. 39.
25. Kubler, 1990, pp. 48, 149
26. Florescano, 1994, pp. 1–20, predominantly citing Angel Maria Garibay, *Teogonia e historia de los mexicanos*, 1965.
27. Ibid., p. 9; and Evans and Berlo, p. 20.
28. Campbell, II.1, 1988, p. 41.
29. Eliade, 1991, p. 100.
30. Soustelle, 1970, pp. 95–119; and Wolf, p. 144.

1. Antonio Penafiel, ed., *Cantares in idioma Mexicano*, folio 14 (1899, 1904) in the *Biblioteca Nacional*, Mexico City, cited in Léon-Portilla, 1964, p. 11.
2. Meyer and Sherman, p. 67.
3. Stuart, p. 36.
4. Ibid, p. 56.
5. Brotherston, 1992, p. 160, citing *Cantares Mexicanos*, folio 27.
6. Sahagún, 1997, p. 121.
7. Ibid., p. 96.
8. Saenz, p. 19; Gutierrez Solana, p. 3; Wauchope and Cline, pp. 11–14; Alcina Franch, pp. 18, 75; and Sejourné, p. 59.
9. Thomas, p. 57, based upon an anecdote in *De Orbe Novo*, by the courtier-scholar Peter Martyr.
10. Marcus, pp. xvii-xviii, 8, 27, 262; and Alcina Franch, pp. 63, 64.
11. Alcina Franch, p. 69, trans. NB; and Gutierrez Solana, p. 4.
12. Bricker, ed., p. 12.
13. Ibid., p. 9; Marcus, pp. 143, 444; and Wauchope and Cline, p. 487.
14. Reyes, 1964, p. 93; and Reyes, 1950, p. 96.
15. Reyes, 1950, p. 98.
16. Edited by Angel Mario Garibay K., from a 16th-Century Nahuatl-Spanish manuscript by Juan Bautista de Pomar, Mexico City: *Universidad Nacional Autonoma de Mexico*, 1964. Translated into English by Miguel Léon-Portilla with Grace Lobanov, 1969, p. 69.
17. Reyes, 1950, p. 110.
18. Nahuatl text from Indian informants of Fray Bernardino de Sahagún. Facsimile of Volume 8, folio 195. Edited by Francisco del Paso y Troncoso, Madrid, 1907. Translated into English by Miguel Léon-Portilla, 1969, pp. 61–62.
19. Early 16th century Nahuatl 85pp. manuscript folio. Incomplete copy by Charles Etienne Brasseur de Bourbourg, 1865, formerly in *Biblioteca Nacional*, Mexico City; now at University of Pennsylvania, University Museum; translated into English by

Daniel G. Brinton, *Ancient Nahuatl Poetry*, Philadelphia, 1887, p. 111.

20. Brinton, 1887, p. vi.
21. Astrov, ed., p. 311; and Sahagún, 1997, p. 129.
22. Gossen, p. 14.
23. *Florentine Codex*, Vol. II, p. 43. Recorded by Fray Bernardino de Sahagún in ca. 1550. Translated from Nahuatl/Spanish by Laurette Sejourné, in *Burning Water: Thought and Religion in Ancient Mexico*, London, 1956, pp. 150–151.
24. Markman and Markman, 1992, p. 204, citing R. H. Barlow.
25. Sahagún, *Primeros Memoriales*, pp. 56–57.
26. Eduard Seler, *Gesammelte Abhandlungen (Complete Works)*, Vol. II, pp. 1059–1061, Berlin, 1904. Translated from the German by Anselm Hollo, in Jerome Rothenberg, ed., *Shaking the Pumpkin*, 1991, pp. 319–320.
27. Rothenberg, ed., 1991, p. 417.

CHAPTER XII

1. Wauchope and Nash. p. 336; Villegas, ed., p. 26; and Neumann, pp. 145, 268.
2. Brundage, pp. 46, 91; Spence, 1913, p. 107; and Muser, p. 135.
3. Muser, p. 135; and Lopez Austin, p. 352.
4. I am indebted to H. B. Nicholson's 1957 dissertation for the clarity of this structure.
5. John Bierhorst, 1984, p. 97, synthesizes these two crucial roles as "the savior doctrine."
6. Mundkur, p. 86.
7. Nicholson, 1957, p. 29; Soustelle, 1970, p. 52; and Nicholson, 1967, p. 80.
8. MacLachlan and Rodriguez, p. 54; and Brinton, 1894, p. 20.
9. Astrov, ed., p. 314, translation by D. G. Brinton.

CHAPTER XIII

1. Cardenal, trans. by Clifton Ross, pp. 17, 57.
2. Bierhorst, ed., 1984, pp. 96–99; Léon-Portilla, 1992, pp. 4–12; and Brinton, 1887, Note, p. 123.

3. Léon-Portilla, 1992, p. 15; Stuart, p. 148; and Durán, *History*, 1994 ed., pp. 483–493.
4. Thomas, pp. 180ff; and Wallace, p. 159.
5. Sahagún, 1997 ed., p. 9.
6. Cardenal, pp. 17, 57; and Reyes, 1964, essay, "The Early Chroniclers," p. 124.
7. Gillespie, p. 155.
8. Redfield, 1953, p. 126; Thomas, p. 406; and Durán, *History*, 1994 ed., p. 319.
9. Léon-Portilla, 1992, pp. 22–23; and Bierhorst, ed., 1984, pp. 99ff.
10. Soustelle, 1970, p. 231; and Sahagún, 1995 ed., pp. 4–5.
11. Sahagún, 1995 edition, p. 5; Bierhorst, ed., 1984, p. 107; and De las Casas, p. 5.
12. Ruiz, p. 30; and Brading, pp. 22–23, 26.
13. Cortés, p. xiii; Villegas, ed., pp. 60ff., "*la conquista espiritual*"; and Brading, p. 212.
14. De las Casas, p. 71.
15. Cortés, p. 24; Díaz del Castillo, pp. 88–92; and Léon-Portilla, 1992, pp. xxvii, 26–28.
16. Léon-Portilla, 1992, pp. 30–31.
17. Léon-Portilla, 1992, p. xxxiii; and Marcus, p. 196.
18. Paz, *Labyrinth*, 1985, p. 84; and Bierhorst, ed., 1984, p. 105.
19. Wauchope and Nash, p. 317; Sejourné, p. 35; and Vaillant, p. 239.
20. Thomas, p. 205, citing *Florentine Codex*, Chapter XII.

CHAPTER XIV

1. Paz, 1972, p.78.
2. Cortés, p. 70.
3. Waters, p. 23; LeClezio, p. 94; and Reyes, 1964, p. 105.
4. Cortés, p. 72; Thomas, p. 251; and Diego Munoz Camargo and Bernardino de Sahagún, cited in Léon-Portilla, 1992, pp. 38, 40.
5. Cortés, p. 190.
6. Thomas, p. 261; and Meyer and Sherman, p. 109.
7. Léon-Portilla, 1992, p. 41.
8. Léon-Portilla, p. xxvii; and Meyer and Sherman, p. 111.
9. Díaz del Castillo, p. 214.
10. Vaillant, p. 225; and Reyes, 1950, pp. 80ff.
11. Cortés, pp. 84–86 and p. 467, note by Anthony Pagden.

12. Díaz del Castillo, p. 35; Reyes, 1964, pp. 105, 124; and Cortés, p. xxix.
13. Díaz del Castillo, p. 11.
14. Díaz del Castillo, p. 221.
15. Díaz del Castillo, pp. 222–223; and MacLachlan and Rodriguez, p. 61.
16. Léon-Portilla, 1964, p. 67.
17. Ibid., p. 68.
18. Bierhorst, ed., 1984, pp. 108–111, translated from the Nahuatl of Sahagún, 1995 edition, *Florentine Codex* Book XII, by John Bierhorst; Léon-Portilla, 1992, pp. 62–64, adapted from the same source by Angel Maria Garibay K.; and Carrasco, p. 204.

CHAPTER XV

1. Cited in Campbell, II.3, 1988, p. 259.
2. Díaz del Castillo, pp. 220–230.
3. Durán, *Book of the Gods*, 1994 ed., p. 70; Durán, *History*, 1994 ed., p. 375; Durán, *Book of the Gods*, 1994 ed., p. 91–92, 107; also Sahagún, cited in LeClezio, pp. 51.
4. Díaz del Castillo, pp. 236ff.
5. Meyer and Sherman, p. 116.
6. Léon-Portilla, 1992, p. 68.
7. Ruiz, p. 50; and Meyer and Sherman, p. 120.
8. Vaillant, p. 249; and Thomas, pp. 388–389.
9. Léon-Portilla, 1992, p. 74; and Thomas, p. 389.
10. Léon-Portilla, p. 77.
11. Díaz del Castillo, p. 293.
12. Vaillant, p.251, citing Sahagún and Durán; and Cortés, Endnotes by Anthony Pagden, pp. 476–478.
13. Léon-Portilla, 1992, p. 85; LeClezio, p. 37; and Durán, History, p. 79.
14. Léon-Portilla, 1992, p. 87; and Díaz del Castillo, p. 289.
15. Cortés, p. 142.
16. Léon-Portilla, p. 93.
17. Thomas, pp. 443–444.
18. Cortés, p. 157.
19. Vaillant, p. 257,.
20. Léon-Portilla, 1992, p. 109; and Léon-Portilla, 1964, p. 151.

21. Léon-Portilla, 1992, p. 109.
22. Ibid., p. 116.
23. Léon-Portilla, 1964, p. 150; and Léon-Portilla, 1992, p. 122.
24. Cortés, Anthony Pagden Notes, pp. 492–493, 518; and Díaz del Castillo, p. 403.

CHAPTER XVI

1. Ruiz, pp. 54–66; and Liss, 1975, p. 48.
2. Benitez, pp. 21, 39.
3. Lévi-Strauss, 1963, p. 106, less charitably regards it as "ephemeral union."
4. Liss, 1975, p. 69; MacLachlan and Rodriguez, p. 77; and Benitez, p. 147.
5. Ruiz, p. 67; Liss, 1975, p. 69; and Meyer and Sherman, p. 188.
6. Benitez, p. 108.
7. Florescano, 1994, p. 79; Ruiz, p. 67; and Spence, 1918, p. 172.
8. Galeano, p. 137.
9. Wauchope and Cline, p. 29.
10. Grafton, 1992, p. 89; Brading, p. 102; and Spence, 1918, pp. 64–65, 172.
11. Davies, p. 203; Nicholson, 1957, p. 8; and Wauchope and Cline, p. 71.
12. Liss, 1975, p. 128.
13. Meyer and Sherman, p. 186; Liss, 1975, p. 72.
14. H. B. Nicholson, p. 79; Lafaye, pp. 140, 176.
15. Nicholson, 1957, p. 23; Lafaye, pp. 139–40.
16. Sahagún, 1997, pp. 3–4.
17. LeClezio, p. 47; Nicholson, 1957, p. 120; and Campbell, 1981, p. 167.
18. H. B. Nicholson, 157, p. 120.
19. Léon-Portilla, 1980, p. 96, excerpting from Sahagún.
20. Rothenberg, ed., 1968, p. 444, translated from Sahagún Book IV; Nicholson, 1957, p. 29; Brundage, p. 131; and Grafton, 1997, p. 62.
21. Charlot, 1963, p. 148; and Grafton, 1997, p. 58.
22. Alfredo Lopez Austin essay in Edmonson, 1974, "The Research Method of Sahagún," p. 148.
23. Miguel Léon-Portilla essay in Edmonson, 1974. "The Problematics of Sahagún," p. 248.

24. Ruiz, p. 38.
25. Lafaye, p. 157.
26. Todorov, pp. 202–203; and Durán, *History*, 1994, Ignacio Bernal essay, p. 575.
27. Durán, *Book of Gods*, 1994, p. 25.
28. Durán, *History*, pp. 7, 243.
29. Spence, 1913, p. 7; and Durán, *Book of Gods*, 1994, p. 25.
30. Fiedel, p. 305.
31. Durán, *Book of Gods*, 1994, p. 129.
32. Landa, pp. iii-xiv.
33. Ibid., pp. 10–14.
34. Ibid., pp. 88–89.
35. Todorov, pp. 205, 211.
36. Ignacio Bernal in Wauchope and Cline, p. 4; and Angel Maria Garibay in Durán, pp. 12, 575.
37. Spence, 1918, p.69.

CHAPTER XVII

1. Cited in Ramón Eduardo Ruiz, *Triumphs and Tragedy*, p. 37.
2. Paz, 1988, p. 12.
3. Durán, *Book of Gods*, 1994, p. 129fn.
4. Galeano, p. 43, translated from Francisco de Solano, *Los mayas del siglo* XVIII.
5. MacLachlan and Rodriguez, pp. 116, 123, 197; and Benitez, pp. 51; pl. 81, p. 214.
6. Benitez, p. 104; and Liss, 1975, pp. 88, 114.
7. Meyer and Sherman, p. 274.
8. Brading, pp. 274, 280; and Paz, 1988, p. 34.
9. Ruiz, p. 101; Lafaye, p. 191; and Paz, 1988, p. 152.
10. Brading, pp. 390, 459; and Paz, 1988, p. 37.
11. Nicholson, 1967, p. 112.
12. Warner, pp. 302–303; and Note, p. 390.
13. Lafaye, pp. 228, 242; and Warner, p. 302.
14. Benitez, p. 278; and Von Humboldt, 1988, pp. 64, 72, 90.
15. Galeano, pp. 100–101; Ruiz, pp. 146–151; Meyer and Sherman, pp. 288–291; and Warner, p. 304.

CHAPTER XVIII

1. Sinkin, p. 162.
2. Read, p. 18.
3. Paz and Beckett, eds, pp. 96–97.
4. Read, pp. 55–56.
5. Paz, Introduction, 1990, p. 504.
6. Ibid., pp. 499ff, catalogue essay by Fausto Ramirez.
7. Ibid., essay by Xavier Moyssen.
8. Ibid., essay by Xavier Moyssen.
9. The late Guillermo Bonfil Batalla, an anthropologist and founder of the INAH Regional Centers in Mexico, in his final, iconoclastic book, *Mexico Profundo*, refers to the "schizophrenic" birth of the "fictitious" independent state of Mexico, pp. 65–66.
10. Meyer and Sherman, p. 461; Wolf, p. 245.
11. Sinkin, p. 22.
12. Hale, esp. Chapter 7, "Liberalism and the Indian," pp. 215–247; and Sinkin, p. 22.
13. Sinkin, pp. 26–33.
14. Galeano, Vol.II, p. 376.
15. Sinkin, pp. 78–81, 164; and Callcott, p. 76, citing Juárez' Mexican biographer, Rafael de Zayas Enriquez.
16. Sinkin, pp. 169–178.
17. Ruiz, pp. 265–267.
18. Paz, *Labyrinth*, p. 129; and Ruiz, p. 271.
19. Callcott, p. 154.
20. Ibid., p. 158.
21. Meyer and Sherman, pp. 485–486.
22. Toor, p. 540; and Reed, p. 15.
23. Paz, ed., 1985, pp. 539–550, with an excellent catalogue essay on Posada by David W. Kiehl.

CHAPTER XIX

1. Paz, ed., 1985, p. 157.
2. Lafaye, p. 311.
3. Hart, p. xiv.
4. Paz, *Labyrinth*, p. 138; and Galeano, II, p. 25.
5. Wolf, p. 247; and Meyer and Sherman, p. 486.
6. Driver, p. 458.
7. Batalla, pp. 110–111.

8. Galeano, II, p. 26.

9. Womack, Prologue; and Galeano, II, p. 25.

10. Paz, 1990, p. 643.

11. Léon-Portilla, 1992, pp. 165–168.

12. Womack, pp. 400–404, is the definitive translation and analysis of Zapata's *Plan* and its implications.

13. Ibid., Womack text, p. 403.

14. Ruiz, p. 364.

15. Womack, p. 330.

16. Weatherford, p. 170; LeClezio, p. 78; and Paz, *Labyrinth*, pp. 142, 335.

CHAPTER XX

1. Fernandez, p. 151.

2. Galeano, II, pp. 58–59.

3. Reyes, 1964, p. 4; and Charlot, 1972, p. 153.

4. Reed, p. 22; Villegas, ed., p. 159; and Fuentes, p. 39.

5. Paz, 1990, p. 559, Dore Ashton's essay citing Siqueiros; and Campbell, I.1, 1988, p. 8.

6. del Condé, p. 18; Lafaye, p. 205; and Charlot, 1963, p. 89.

7. Fuentes, p. 61.

8. Charlot, 1972, p. 216, citing Vasconcelos; and Alma Reed, p. 69, citing Jean Charlot.

9. Reed, p. 22; and Reyes, 1964, p. 118.

10. Kelly, pp. 215; and Mayer, pp. 316ff.

11. Berrin and Pasztory, pp. 67–68; Reed, pp. 76, 186; and Charlot, 1972, p. 3.

12. Charlot, 1972, p. 341; Hoozee, ed., p. 53; and Herrera, pp. 80–81.

13. Herrera, p. 99.

14. Paz, 1990, p. 618.

15. Rochfort, p. 25.

16. Reed, pp. 75–76.

17. Galeano, II, p. 61; and Charlot, 1963, p. 67.

18. Herrera, pp. 99, 103–104; and Hoozee, ed., p. 131.

19. Hoozee, ed., p. 105; Charlot, 1963, p. 124; and Lévi-Strauss, 1979, pp. 44–45.

20. Rochfort, p. 91.

CHAPTER XXI

1. Orozco Murals, Special Collections, Dartmouth College Library.

2. Orozco, p. 155.

3. Ruiz, pp. 370–371; and Reed, p. 42.

4. Paz, 1990, p. 603.

5. May, p. 220.

6. Rochfort, pp. 26–27.

7. Galeano, II, p. 60.

8. May, pp. 212ff.

9. Hurlburt, pp. 58–59.

10. Orozco Papers, Dartmouth, DL 34–2:10, and 2:13.

11. Orozco Papers, Dartmouth, attachment to Reed letter of May 22, 1932.

12. Orozco Papers, Dartmouth, Brooklyn Eagle clipping derived from handwritten MS on Hanover Inn letterhead, text incorporated in college press announcement, DL 34–2:8.

13. Orozco Papers, Dartmouth. MS, The Frescoes, confirmed to be "in Orozco's hand," in Hurlburt, p. 269, fn. 140.

14. Mayer, p. 332.

15. Orozco Papers, Dartmouth, Lewis Mumford article in *The New Republic*, October 10, 1934.

16. Reed, p. 100.

17. Rochfort, p. 29.

18. Micheli, p. 3; Hurlburt, p. 197; and Paz, 1990, p. 640.

19. Charlot, 1972, p. 329.

20. Rochfort, p. 39; and Hoozee, ed., pp. 15–16.

21. Zapata Alonzo, p. 191.

22. del Condé, essays by Alberto Hijar, pp. 114–137.

23. Genauer, pp. 28ff; and Charlot, 1972, p. 355.

24. del Condé, pp. 140–171.

CHAPTER XXII

1. Lawrence, 1962, p. 677.

2. Lawrence, 1972, p. 90, *The New Republic*, December 15, 1920.

3. Lawrence, 1972, p. 104; Lawrence, 1962, p. 740.

4. Parmenter, p. 278.

5. Nehls, p. 219; and Pasztory, pp. 108ff.

6. Tompkins, pp. 211–216.

7. Nehls, p. 219.

8. Lawrence, 1959, Rexroth Intro., p. 19; and Lawrence, 1972, *Mexico* essay, pp. 104–106.

9. Lawrence, 1962, p. 672.

10. Lawrence, 1927, p. 148; and Lawrence, 1972, p. 100.

11. Lawrence, 1962, p. 672.

12. Gregory, p. 70; Lawrence, 1927, p. vff; and Lawrence, 1976, p. 68.

13. According to William York Tindall's literary sleuthing, it appears that much of Lawrence's depiction of the theology of ancient Mexico in *The Plumed Serpent* derived from this book.

14. Moore, pp. 467–68; Lawrence, 1926, p. 227; and Lawrence, 1995, p. 97.

15. Terry, pp. 170ff.

16. Lawrence, 1976, p. 93.

17. Lawrence, 1923, p. 3.

18. Moore, pp. 470–474; and Lawrence, 1976, p. 99.

19. Lawrence, 1995, p. 29.

20. Ibid., p. 241.

21. Lawrence, 1995, p. 69.

22. Ibid., p. 116.

23. Ibid., p. 118.

24. Ibid., p. 215.

25. Ibid., pp. 325–326.

26. Lawrence, 1962, pp. 747–748.

27. Nehls, pp. 264, 285.

28. Ibid., p. 267.

29. Parmenter, p. 273.

30. Moore, p. 503; Nehls, p. 386; and Parmenter, p. 94.

31. Lawrence, 1962, p. 860.

32. Lawrence, 1926, p. 52.

33. Ibid., p. 84.

34. Ibid., pp. 117–119.

35. Ibid., p. 154.

36. Ibid., pp. 214, 220.

37. Ibid., p. 397.

38. Ibid., p. 455.

39. Lawrence, 1959, pp. 122–126.

CHAPTER XXIII

1. Lafaye, pp. 208, 307.

2. Reed, p. 129.

3. Ibid., p. 156.

4. Ibid., p. 141.

5. Bricker, 1981, pp. 140–141.

6. Toor, p. 353.

7. Reyes, 1964, pp. 97–101. Essay, *Vision of Anáhuac*, 1915.

8. Paz, 1972, pp. 74, 77; and Paz, *One Earth*, 1985, pp. 88, 153.

9. Fuentes, pp. 34, 201.

10. I learned of Tatiana Proskouriakoff, Teobert Maler, John Lloyd Stephens, and Alfred P. Maudslay, among others. Also see John Dorfman's profile of Ian Graham in the September/October 1997 issue of *Archaeology Magazine*, p. 60.

11. Lévi-Strauss, 1963, pp. 7, 23–24, 210.

12. I borrow contemporary American anthropologist James Clifford's useful term.

13. Van Maanen, p. 2. The term "professional stranger" is attributed to M. Agar.

14. Tedlock, ed., p. 356; LaBastille, pp. 51ff; and Bowen, pp. 141–149.

Bibliography

Alcina Franch, José. *Codices Mexicanos*. Madrid: Editorial MAPFRE, 1992.

Anaya, Rudolfo A. *Lord of the Dawn: The Legend of Quetzalcóatl*. Albuquerque: University of New Mexico Press, 1987.

Andrews, George F. *Maya Cities: Placemaking and Urbanization*. Norman: University of Oklahoma Press, 1975.

Arnold, Caroline. *City of the Gods: Mexico's Ancient City of Teotihuacán*. New York: Clarion Books, 1994.

Artaud, Antonin. *Oeuvres Complètes, Vol. VIII: Lettres du Mexique*. Paris: Gallimard, 1971.

Artes de Mexico, No. 32. *Serpientes en el Arte Hispanico*, Alberto Ruy Sanchez, ed., 1996.

Ashton, Dore. *Abstract Art Before Columbus*. New York: André Emmerich Gallery, 1957.

Astrov, Margot, ed. *The Winged Serpent: American Indian Prose and Poetry*. Boston: Beacon Press, 1992.

Auerbach, Erich. *Mimesis: The Representation of Reality in Western Literature*. New York: Doubleday, 1957.

Batalla, Guillermo Bonfil. *Mexico Profundo: Reclaiming a Civilization*. Translated by Philip A. Dennis. Austin: University of Texas Press, 1996.

Baudez, Claude, and Sydney Picasso. *Lost Cities of the Maya*. New York: Harry N. Abrams, 1987.

Benitez, Fernando. *The Century After Cortés*. Translated by Joan MacLean. Chicago: University of Chicago Press, 1965.

Benson, Elizabeth, ed. *Mesoamerican Sites and World Views: A Conference at Dumbarton Oaks, October 16–17, 1976*. Washington, DC: Dumbarton Oaks Research Library and Collections, Trustees for Harvard University, 1976.

Benson, Elizabeth, et. al. *The Cult of the Feline: A Conference in Pre-Columbian Iconography*. Washington, DC: Dumbarton Oaks Research Library and Collections, Trustees for Harvard University, 1972.

Bernal, Ignacio, and Roman Pina Chan. *Three Thousand Years of Art and Life in Mexico, as Seen in the National Museum of Anthropology, Mexico City*. New York: Harry N. Abrams, 1968.

_____. *The Olmec World*. Translated from the Spanish by Doris Heyden and Fernando Horcasitas. Berkeley: University of California Press, 1969.

Berrin, Kathleen, and Esther Pasztory. *Teotihuacán: Art from the City of the Gods*. San Francisco: Fine Arts Museums of San Francisco, 1993.

Bierhorst, John. *The Mythology of Mexico and Central America*. New York: William Morrow, 1990.

_____. *The Mythology of South America*. New York: William Morrow, 1988.

_____. *Four Masterworks of American Indian Literature*. Tucson: University of Arizona Press, 1984.

Bierhorst, John, ed. *The Hungry Woman: Myths and Legends of the Aztecs*. New York: William Morrow, 1984.

Bloch, Marc. *The Historian's Craft*. Translated from the French by Peter Putnam. New York: Vintage Books, 1953.

Boas, Franz. *Race, Language, and Culture*. Chicago: University of Chicago Press, 1940.

Bowes, Anne LaBastille. "The Quetzal, Fabulous Bird of Maya Land." *National Geographic* Magazine, 135.1 (January 1969).

Brading, David. *The First America: The Spanish Monarchy, Creole Patriots, and the Liberal State 1492–1867*. New York: Cambridge University Press, 1993.

Brambila, Rosa. *Teotihuacán Hall, The National Museum of Anthropology*. Mexico City: INAH, 1988.

Braudel, Fernand. *A History of Civilizations*. Translated by Richard Mayne. New York: Allen Lane, The Penguin Press, 1994.

Bricker, Victoria Reifler, General Editor. *Supplement to the Handbook of Middle American Indians. Volume*

Three: Literatures. Munro S. Edmonson, Volume Editor, with the assistance of Patricia A. Andrews. Austin: University of Texas Press, 1985.

Bricker, Victoria Reifler. *The Indian Christ, The Indian King: The Historical Substrate of Maya Myth and Ritual.* Austin: University of Texas Press, 1981.

Brinton, Daniel G. *Nagualism: A Study in Native American Folk Lore and History. Proceedings of the American Philosophical Society,* XXXIII.144. Philadelphia: McCall & Company, Printers, 1894.

_____. *Rig Veda Americanus: Sacred Songs of the Ancient Mexicans, with a Gloss in Nahuatl.* Philadelphia, 1890.

_____. *Ancient Nahuatl Poetry, Containing the Nahuatl Text of* XXVII *Ancient Mexican Poems.* Philadelphia, 1887.

_____. *The Annals of the Cakchiquels: The Original Text, with Translation, Notes and Introduction.* New York: AMS Press, 1969, reprint of 1885 edition.

_____. *American Hero-Myths.* Philadelphia: H.C. Watts, 1882.

Brotherston, Gordon, ed. "Voices of the First America: Text and Context in the New World." *New Scholar* Magazine, X.1 and 2 (1985).

_____. *Book of the Fourth World. Reading the Native Americas Through Their Literature.* New York: Cambridge University Press, 1992.

_____. Translations prepared in collaboration with Ed Dorn. *Image of the New World: The American Continent Portrayed in Native Texts.* London: Thames and Hudson, 1979.

Brundage, Burr Cartwright. *The Phoenix of the Western World: Quetzalcóatl and the Sky Religion.* Norman: University of Oklahoma Press, 1982.

Brunhouse, Robert L. *In Search of the Maya: The First Archaeologists.* Albuquerque: University of New Mexico Press, 1973.

Bushnell, G. H. S. *The First Americans: The Precolumbian Civilizations.* New York: McGraw-Hill, 1968.

Callcott, Wilfrid Hardy. *Liberalism in Mexico, 1857–1929.* Hamden, Connecticut: Archon Books, 1965.

Campbell, Joseph. *Historical Atlas of World Mythology.* *Volume I. The Way of the Animal Powers. Part 1. Mythologies of the Primitive Hunters and Gatherers.* New York: Van der Mark Editions, 1988.

_____. *Historical Atlas of World Mythology. Volume* II, *The Way of the Seeded Earth. Part 1, The Sacrifice.* New York: Harper & Row, 1988.

_____. *Historical Atlas of World Mythology. Volume* II, *Mythologies of the Primitive Planters. Part 3, The Middle and Southern Americas.* New York: Van der Mark Editions, 1988.

_____. *The Mythic Image.* Princeton: Princeton University Press, 1981.

_____. *The Hero With a Thousand Faces.* Princeton: Princeton University Press, 1973.

_____. *The Masks of God: Primitive Mythology.* New York, 1959.

Cardenal, Ernesto. *Quetzalcóatl.* Translated by Clifton Ross. Berkeley: New Earth Publications, 1985.

Carrasco, Davíd. *Quetzalcóatl and the Irony of Empire: Myths and Prophecies in the Aztec Tradition.* Chicago: University of Chicago Press, 1982.

Carver, Norman F., Jr. *Silent Cities of Mexico and the Maya.* Kalamazoo, Michigan: Documan Press, 1986.

Castaneda, Carlos. *The Art of Dreaming.* New York: HarperCollins, 1993.

_____. *The Power of Silence.* New York: Simon & Schuster, 1987.

_____. *The Fire From Within.* New York: Simon & Schuster, 1985.

_____. *The Eagle's Gift.* New York: Simon & Schuster, 1981.

_____. *The Second Ring of Power.* New York: Simon & Schuster, 1977.

_____. *Tales of Power.* New York: Simon & Schuster, 1974.

_____. *Journey to Ixtlan.* New York: Simon & Schuster, 1972.

_____. *A Separate Reality.* New York: Simon & Schuster, 1971.

_____. *The Teachings of Don Juan.* New York: Ballantine Books, 1969.

Charlot, Jean. *An Artist on Art: Collected Essays, Vol.* II:

Mexican Art. Honolulu: University Press of Hawaii, 1972.

_____. *The Mexican Mural Renaissance, 1920–1925.* New Haven: Yale University Press, 1963.

Clifford, James. *Routes: Travel and Translation in the Late Twentieth Century.* Cambridge, Massachusetts: Harvard University Press, 1997.

_____. *The Predicament of Culture: Twentieth Century Ethnography, Literature, and Art.* Cambridge: Harvard University Press, 1988.

Coe, Michael, and Richard A. Diehl. *In the Land of the Olmec, Volume I. The Archaeology of San Lorenzo Tenochtitlán.* Austin: University of Texas Press, 1980.

Coe, Michael, et. al. *The Olmec World: Ritual and Rulership.* Princeton: Princeton University Press, 1995.

Coe, Michael. *Breaking the Maya Code.* New York: Thames and Hudson, 1992.

_____. *Mexico.* New York: Thames and Hudson, 1984.

_____. *The Maya.* New York: Thames and Hudson, 1987.

_____. *The Jaguar's Children: Pre-Classic Central Mexico.* New York: Museum of Primitive Art, 1965.

Coggins, Clemency Chase, and Orrin C. Shane, III, eds. *El Cenote de los Sacrificios.* Mexico City: Fondo de Cultura Económica, 1996.

Correa, Gustavo, et. al. *The Native Theatre in Middle America.* New Orleans: University of Louisiana, Middle American Research Institute, 1961.

Cortés, Hernán. *Letters from Mexico.* Translated and edited by Anthony Pagden. New Haven: Yale University Press, 1986.

Cosío Villegas, Daniel, ed. *Historia Mínima de Mexico.* Mexico City: El Colegio de México, 1995.

Covarrubias, Miguel. *The Eagle, the Jaguar, and the Serpent: Indian Art of the Americas.* New York: Alfred A. Knopf, 1954.

_____. *Mexico South: The Isthmus of Tehuantepec.* New York: Alfred A. Knopf, 1947.

Davies, Nigel. *The Toltec Heritage: From the Fall of Tula to the Rise of Tenochtitlán.* Norman: University of Oklahoma Press, 1980.

Davis, Keith F. *Désiré Charnay, Expeditionary Photographer.* Albuquerque: University of New Mexico Press, 1981.

De las Casas, Bartolomé. *A Selection of His Writings.* Translated and edited by George Sanderlin. New York, 1971.

del Condé, Teresa, et. al. *Los Murales del Palacio de Bellas Artes.* Mexico City: INBA /Americo Arte Editores, 1995.

Díaz del Castillo, Bernal. *The Conquest of New Spain.* Translated and with an introduction by J. M. Cohen. New York: Penguin Books, 1963.

Díaz-Bolio, José. *The Geometry of the Maya and their Rattlesnake Art.* Merida: Area Maya, 1987.

Driver, Harold E. *Indians of North America.* Chicago: University of Chicago Press, 1969.

Durán, Fray Diego. *Book of the Gods and Rites and the Ancient Calendar.* Translated by Doris Heyden. Norman: University of Oklahoma Press, 1994.

_____. *The History of the Indians of New Spain.* Translated by Doris Heyden and Fernando Horcasitas. Norman: University of Oklahoma Press, 1994.

Edmonson, Munro S., ed. and trans. *Heaven Born Merida and Its Destiny: The Book of Chilam Balam of Chumayel.* Austin: University of Texas Press, 1986.

Edmonson, Munro S., ed. and trans. *The Ancient Future of the Itza: The Book of Chilam Balam of Tizimin.* Austin: University of Texas Press, 1982.

Edmonson, Munro S., ed. *Sixteenth-Century Mexico: The Work of Sahagún.* Albuquerque: University of New Mexico Press, 1974.

Eliade, Mircea. *The Myth of the Eternal Return, or, Cosmos and History.* Translated from the French by Willard R. Trask. Princeton: Princeton University Press/Bollingen Series, 1991.

_____. *The Sacred and the Profane: The Nature of Religion.* Translated from the French by Willard R. Trask. New York: Harcourt, 1959.

Emmerich, André. *Art Before Columbus.* New York: Simon & Schuster, 1963.

Evans, Susan T., and Janet Catherine Berlo. *Teotihuacán: An Introduction.* Washington, DC: Dumbarton Oaks Research Library and Collections, Trustees for Harvard University, 1993.

Ferguson, William M., and John Q. Royce. *Maya Ruins of Mexico in Color.* Norman: University of Oklahoma Press, 1977.

Fernandez, Justino. *A Guide to Mexican Art from Its Beginnings to the Present.* Translated by Joshua C. Taylor. Chicago: University of Chicago Press, 1969.

Fiedel, Stuart J. *Prehistory of the Americas.* New York: Cambridge University Press, 1992.

Florescano, Enrique. *El mito de Quetzalcóatl.* Mexico City: Fondo de Cultura Económica, 1995.

_____. *Memory, Myth and Time in Mexico, From the Aztecs to Independence.* Translated by Albert G. Bork with the assistance of Kathryn R. Bork. Austin: University of Texas Press, 1994.

Foster, Elizabeth Andros, ed. and trans. *Motolinía's History of the Indians of New Spain.* Berkeley: Cortés Society, 1950.

Fowler, William R., Jr., and Stephen D. Houston, eds. *Ancient Mesoamerica* Magazine, II. 1 (Spring 1991). *Urban Archaeology at Teotihuacán.* New York: Cambridge University Press, 1991.

Franco, Maria Teresa, ed. *Arqueología Mexicana Magazine. Special Olmec edition.* Mexico City (March April 1995).

Frazer, Sir James George. *The New Golden Bough.* Edited, with Notes and Foreword, by Theodore H. Gaster. New York: Criterion Books, 1961.

Fuentes, Carlos. *A New Time for Mexico.* Translated by Marina Gutman Castañeda and the author. New York: Farrar, Straus & Giroux, 1996.

Fukuyama, Francis. *The End of History and the Last Man.* New York: The Free Press, 1992.

Galeano, Eduardo. *Memory of Fire. I: Genesis. Part One of a Trilogy. II: Faces & Masks.* Translated by Cedric Belfrage. New York, 1985.

Gallenkamp, Charles. *Maya: The Riddle and Rediscovery of a Lost Civilization.* New York: Viking Press, 1987.

García Bustos, Arturo. *Meditaciones Acerca del Arte.* Mexico City: Academia de Artes, 1995.

Geertz, Clifford. *The Interpretation of Cultures.* New York: Basic Books, 1973.

Genauer, Emily. *Rufino Tamayo.* New York: Abrams, 1974.

Gillespie, Susan D. *The Aztec Kings: The Construction of Rulership in Mexica History.* Tucson: University of Arizona Press, 1989.

Gossen, Gary H., ed. *Symbol and Meaning Beyond the Closed Community: Essays in Mesoamerican Ideas.* Albany: Institute for Mesoamerican Studies, University at Albany, State University of New York, 1986.

Grafton, Anthony. "The Rest of the West." *The New York Review of Books* (April 10, 1997), pp. 57–64.

_____. *New Worlds, Ancient Texts: The Power of Tradition and the Shock of Discovery.* Cambridge: Belknap Press of Harvard University Press, 1992.

Graulich, Michel. *Myths of Ancient Mexico.* Translated by Bernard R. Ortiz de Montellano and Thelma Ortiz de Montellano. Norman: University of Oklahoma Press, 1997.

Gregory, Horace. *D. H. Lawrence: Pilgrim of the Apocalypse. A Critical Study.* New York: Viking Press, 1957.

Grove, David C. *Chalcatzingo: Excavations on the Olmec Frontier.* New York: Thames and Hudson, 1984.

Cruzinski, Serge. *The Conquest of Mexico: The Incorporation of Indian Societies into the Western World, 16th–18th Centuries.* Translated by Ellen Corrigan. New York: Polity Press, 1993.

Gutierrez Solana, Nelly. *The Painted Books of Prehispanic America. In Masterkey: Anthropology of the Americas, Vol. 61, No. 1.* Los Angeles: Southwest Museum, 1987

Hale, Charles A. *Mexican Liberalism in the Age of Mora, 1821–1853.* New Haven: Yale University Press, 1968.

Hanks, William F., and Don S. Rice, eds. *Word and Image in Maya Culture: Explorations in Language, Writing and Representation.* Salt Lake City: University of Utah Press, 1989.

Hart, John Mason. *Revolutionary Mexico: The Coming and Process of the Mexican Revolution.* Berkeley: University of California Press, 1987.

Hay, Clarence L. *The Maya and Their Neighbors: Essays on Middle American Anthropology and Archaeology.* New York: Dover Press, 1940.

Henderson, Joseph L., and Maud Oakes. *The Wisdom of*

the Serpent: The Myths of Death, Rebirth and Resurrection. Princeton: Princeton University Press, 1990.

Herrera, Hayden. *Frida: A Biography of Frida Kahlo.* New York: Harper & Row, 1983.

Hoozee, Robert, ed. *The Mexican Muralists.* Ghent: Europalia, 1993.

Hultkrantz, Ake. *The Religions of the American Indians.* Translated by Monica Setterwall. Berkeley; University of California Press, 1979.

Hunter, C. Bruce. *A Guide to Ancient Maya Ruins.* Norman: University of Oklahoma Press, 1974.

_____. *A Guide to Ancient Mexican Ruins.* Norman: University of Oklahoma Press, 1977.

Huntington, Samuel. *The Clash of Civilizations and the Remaking of World Order.* New York: Simon & Schuster, 1996.

Hurlburt, Laurance P. *The Mexican Muralists in the United States.* Albuquerque: University of New Mexico Press, 1989.

Jung, C. G., and C. Kerenyi. *Essays on a Science of Mythology: The Myth of the Divine Child and the Mysteries of Eleusis.* Translated by R. F. C. Hull. Princeton: Princeton University Press/Bollingen, 1978.

Jung, C. G. *Four Archetypes: Mother – Rebirth – Spirit – Trickster.* Translated by R. F. C. Hull. Princeton: Princeton University Press, 1992.

Kelly, Joyce. *The Complete Visitor's Guide to Mesoamerican Ruins.* Norman: University of Oklahoma Press, 1982.

Krauze, Enrique. *Mexico: Biography of Power.* New York: HarperCollins, 1997.

Krickeberg, Walter, et. al. *Pre-Columbian American Religions.* London: Werdenfeld and Nicolson, 1968.

Kubler, George, assisted by Eve Merriam. *The Louise and Walter Arensberg Collection of Pre-Columbian Sculpture at the Philadelphia Museum of Art.* Philadelphia: Philadelphia Museum of Art, 1954.

Kubler, George. *The Art and Architecture of Ancient America: The Mexican, Maya and Andean Peoples.* New Haven: Yale University Press, 1990.

LaBastille, Anne. *Birds of the Mayas. Maya Folk Tales.* Westport, NY: West of the Wind Publications, 1993.

Lafaye, Jacques. *Quetzalcóatl and Guadeloupe: The Formation of Mexican National Consciousness.* Translated by Benjamin Keene. Chicago: University of Chicago Press, 1976.

Landa, Friar Diego de. *Yucatán Before and After the Conquest.* Translated with notes by William Gates. New York: Dover Press, 1978.

Lawrence, D. H. *Quetzalcóatl: The Early Version of the Plumed Serpent.* Edited by Louis L. Martz. Redding Ridge, Connecticut: Black Swan Books, 1995.

_____. *Letters to Thomas and Adele Seltzer.* Santa Barbara: Black Sparrow Press, 1976.

_____. *Phoenix: The Posthumous Papers of D. H. Lawrence.* Edited by Edward McDonald. New York: Viking Press, 1972.

_____. *The Plumed Serpent (Quetzalcóatl).* New York: Alfred A. Knopf, 1926, 1969.

_____. *The Collected Letters, Volume II.* Edited by Harry T. Moore. New York: Viking Press, 1962.

_____. *Selected Poems.* With an introduction by Kenneth Rexroth. New York: New Directions, 1959.

_____. *Mornings in Mexico.* With an introduction by Richard Aldington. London: Martin Secker, 1927, 1950.

_____. *Studies in Classic American Literature.* New York: T. Seltzer, 1923.

LeClézio, J. M. G. *The Mexican Dream: Or, the Interrupted Thought of Amerindian Civilizations.* Translated by Teresa Lavender Fagan. Chicago: University of Chicago Press, 1988.

Léon-Portilla, Miguel. *The Broken Spears: The Aztec Account of the Conquest of Mexico.* Translated from Nahuatl into Spanish by Angel Maria Garibay K. English translation by Lysander Kemp. Boston: Beacon Press, 1992.

_____. *Time and Reality in the Thought of the Maya.* Translated by Charles L. Boilès. Tulsa: University of Oklahoma Press, 1988.

_____. *Native American Spirituality.* New York: Paulist Press, 1980.

_____. *Pre-Columbian Literatures of Mexico.* Translated

from the Spanish by Grace Lobanov and the author. Norman: University of Oklahoma Press, 1964.

Lévi-Strauss, Claude. *Myth and Meaning.* New York: Schocken Books, 1979.

_____. *Tristes Tropiques.* Translated from the French by John and Doreen Weightman. New York: Penguin Books, 1977.

_____. *Structural Anthropology.* Translated by Claire Jacobson and Brooke Grundfest Schoepf. New York: Basic Books, 1963.

Liss, Peggy K. *Mexico Under Spain, 1521–1566: Society and the Origins of Nationality.* Chicago: University of Chicago Press, 1975.

Lopez Austin, Alfredo. *The Myths of the Opossum: Pathways of Mesoamerican Mythology.* Translated by Bernard Ortiz de Montellano and Thelma Ortiz de Montellano. Albuquerque: University of New Mexico Press, 1993.

Lopez Portillo, José, et. al. *Quetzalcóatl in Myth, Archaeology and Art.* New York: Continuum Books, 1982.

Lopez Ramos, Juan Arturo. *Esplendor de la antigua Mixteca.* Mexico City: Editorial Trias, 1990.

Lowry, Malcolm. *Under the Volcano.* New York: Reynal & Hitchcock, 1947.

Luckert, Karl W. *Olmec Religion: A Key to Middle America and Beyond.* Norman: University of Oklahoma Press, 1976.

MacAdams, Cynthia, photographs. Text by Hunbatz Men and Charles Bensinger. *Mayan Vision Quest: Mystical Initiation in Mesoamerica.* San Francisco: HarperSanFrancisco, 1991.

MacLachlan, Colin M., and Jaime E. Rodriguez O. *The Forging of the Cosmic Race: A Reinterpretation of Colonial Mexico.* Berkeley: University of California Press, 1980.

Marcus, Joyce. *Mesoamerican Writing Systems: Propaganda, Myth and History in Four Ancient Civilizations.* Princeton: Princeton University Press, 1992.

Markman, Roberta H., and Peter T. Markman. *The Flayed God: The Mesoamerican Mythological Tradition, Sacred Texts and Images from Pre-Columbian Mexico*

and Central America. San Francisco: HarperSanFrancisco, 1992.

_____. *Masks of the Spirit: Image and Metaphor in Mesoamerica.* Berkeley: University of California Press, 1989.

May, Antoinette. *Passionate Pilgrim: The Extraordinary Life of Alma Reed.* New York: Paragon House, 1994.

Mayer, Ralph. *The Artist's Handbook of Materials and Techniques.* New York: Viking Press, 1984.

McDonald, Edward ed., *Phoenix: The Posthumous Papers of D. H. Lawrence.* New York: Viking Press, 1936.

Mead, Margaret, and Nicolas Calas, eds. *Primitive Heritage: An Anthropological Anthology.* New York: Random House, 1953.

Métraux, Alfred. *Twin Heroes in South American Mythology,* in *Journal of American Folklore,* Volume 59. Philadelphia, 1945.

Meyer, Michael, and William L. Sherman. *The Course of Mexican History.* New York: Oxford University Press, 1995.

Michelli, Mario De. *Siqueiros.* New York: Harry N. Abrams, 1968.

Miller, Mary Ellen. "Imaging Maya Art." *Archaeology Magazine* (May/June 1997).

Moctezuma, Eduardo Matos. *Tula.* Mexico City: INAH, 1991.

_____. *The Mask of Death in Prehispanic Mexico.* Mexico City: Garcia Valadés Editores, 1988.

Moore, Harry T. *The Priest of Love: A Life of D. H. Lawrence.* London: Penguin Books, 1976.

Morley, Sylvanus, and George Brainerd. *The Ancient Maya.* Revised by Robert J. Sharer. Stanford: Stanford University Press, 1983.

Mundkur, Balaji. *The Cult of the Serpent: An Interdisciplinary Survey of its Manifestations and Origins.* Albany: State University of New York Press, 1983.

Museo Nacional de Antropología, Mexico City. *La Arqueología Mexicana en el Umbral del Siglo XXI: Proyectos Especiales de Arqueología.* Mexico City: INAH, 1994.

Muser, Curt. *Facts and Artifacts of Ancient Middle America.* New York: Dutton, 1978.

Nehls, Edward. *D. H. Lawrence: A Composite Biography.* Volume II. Madison: University of Wisconsin Press, 1958.

Neumann, Erich. *The Origins and History of Consciousness.* With a Foreword by C. G. Jung. Translated from the German by R. F. C. Hull. Princeton: Princeton University Press/Bollingen, 1970.

Nicholson, H. B. *Topiltzin Quetzalcóatl of Tollan: A Problem in Mesoamerican Ethnohistory.* [Unpublished dissertation, Harvard University, 1957]

Nicholson, Irene. *Mexican and Central American Mythology.* London: Hamlyn, 1967.

Nuttall, Zelia, ed. *The Codex Nuttall, A Picture Manuscript from Ancient Mexico.* New York: Dover Publications, 1975.

Olson, Charles. *Mayan Letters.* Edited by Robert Creeley. Palma de Mallorca: Divers Press, 1953.

Orozco, José Clemente. *Autobiografía.* Mexico City: Ediciones Occidente, 1945.

_____. Special Collections, Dartmouth College Library.

Padden, R. C. *The Hummingbird and the Hawk: Conquest and Sovereignty in the Valley of Mexico, 1503–1541.* Cleveland: Ohio State University Press, 1967.

Paddock, John, ed. *Ancient Oaxaca: Studies in Mexican Archaeology and History.* Stanford: Stanford University Press, 1966.

Palacio de Velazquez. *Arte Precolombino de Mexico.* Milano: Olivetti Electa, 1991.

Panofsky, Erwin. *Studies in Iconology.* New York: Harper & Row, 1939.

Parmenter, Ross. *Lawrence in Oaxaca: A Quest for the Novelist in Mexico.* Salt Lake City: G.M. Smith, Peregrine Smith Books, 1974.

Pasztory, Esther. *Teotihuacán: An Experiment in Living.* Norman: University of Oklahoma Press, 1997.

Paz, Octavio. *Essays on Mexican Art.* Translated by Helen Lane. New York: Harcourt, Brace & Co., 1993.

_____. Introduction. *Mexico: Splendors of Thirty Centuries.* New York: Metropolitan Museum of Art, 1990.

_____. *Sor Juana, Or, The Traps of Faith.* Translated by Margaret Sayers Peden. Cambridge: Belknap Press of Harvard University Press, 1988.

_____, ed. *Mexican Poetry: An Anthology.* Translated by Samuel Beckett. New York: Grove Press, 1985.

_____. *One Earth, Four or Five Worlds.* Translated by Helen Lane. New York: Harcourt Brace Jovanovich, 1985.

_____. *The Labyrinth of Solitude and Other Writings.* Translated from the Spanish by Lysander Kemp, Yara Milos, and Rachel Phillips Belash. New York: Grove Press, 1985.

_____. *The Other Mexico: Critique of the Pyramid.* Translated by Lysander Kemp. New York: Grove Press, 1972.

_____. *Claude Lévi-Strauss: An Introduction.* Translated by J. S. and Maxine Bernstein. Ithaca: Cornell University Press, 1970.

Perry, Richard and Rosalind. *Maya Missions: Exploring the Spanish Colonial Churches of Yucatán.* Santa Barbara: Espadaña Press, 1986.

Pickering, Robert B. "Discovering the Occidente," *Archaeology* Magazine (November/December, 1997).

Pina Chan, Roman. *Quetzalcóatl, Serpiente Emplumada.* Mexico City: Fondo de Cultura Económica, 1990.

Prescott, William Hickling. *History of the Conquest of Mexico.* Boston: Harper and Brothers, 1843.

Proskouriakoff, Tatania. *Maya History.* Edited by Rosemary A. Joyce. Austin: University of Texas Press, 1993.

Read, John Lloyd. *The Mexican Historical Novel, 1826–1910.* New York: Instituto de las Españas en los Estados Unidos, 1939.

Recinos, Adrian, and Delia Goetz, eds. and trans. *The Annals of the Cakchiquels.* Norman: University of Oklahoma Press, 1953.

Redfield, Robert. *The Primitive World and Its Transformations.* Ithaca: Cornell University Press, 1953.

_____. *The Folk Culture of Yucatán.* Ithaca: Cornell University Press, 1950.

Reed, Alma. *The Mexican Muralists.* New York: Crown Publishers, 1960.

Reyes, Alfonso. *Mexico in a Nutshell and Other Essays.* Translated by Charles Ramsdell, with a foreword by Arturo Torres-Rioseco. Berkeley: University of California Press, 1964.

_____. *The Position of America and other Essays.* Selected and translated from the Spanish by Harriet de Onis. New York, 1950.

Ricard, Robert. *The Spiritual Conquest of Mexico.* Translated by Lesley Byrd Simpson. Berkeley: University of California Press, 1966.

Rochfort, Desmond. *Mexican Muralists: Orozco, Rivera, Siqueiros.* New York: Universe Publishing, 1993.

Rodriguez, Antonio. *A History of Mexican Mural Painting.* London: Thames and Hudson, 1969.

Roth, Michael S., with Claire Lyons and Charles Merewether. *Irresistible Decay: Ruins Reclaimed.* Los Angeles: The Getty Institute for the History of Art and the Humanities, 1998.

Rothenberg, Jerome. *Shaking the Pumpkin: Traditional Poetry of the Indian North Americas.* Revised Edition. Albuquerque: University of New Mexico Press, 1991.

Rothenberg, Jerome, and George Quasha. *America a Prophecy: A New Reading of American Poetry From Pre-Columbian Times to the Present.* New York: Vintage Books, 1973.

Rothenberg, Jerome, ed. *Technicians of the Sacred: A Range of Poetries from Africa, America, Asia and Oceania.* New York: Anchor Books, 1969.

Roys, Ralph L., ed. *The Book of Chilam Balam of Chumayel.* Washington, DC: Carnegie Institute of Washington, 1933.

Ruiz, Ramón Eduardo. *Triumphs and Tragedy: A History of the Mexican People.* New York: W. W. Norton, 1992.

Ryan, Judith. *The Jaguar and the Feathered Serpent.* Melbourne: National Gallery of Victoria, 1981.

Saenz, Cesar A. *Quetzalcóatl.* Mexico City: INAH, 1962.

Sahagún, Fray Bernardino de. *Primeros Memoriales.* Paleography of Nahuatl Text and English Translation by Thelma D. Sullivan. Norman: University of Oklahoma Press, 1997.

_____. *Florentine Codex. General History of the Things of New Spain.* Translated from the Aztec into English, with notes and illustrations, by Arthur O. Anderson and Charles E. Dibble. Santa Fe: School of American Research, 1955.

Schele, Linda, and David Friedel. *A Forest of Kings: The Untold Story of the Ancient Maya.* New York: Morrow, 1990.

Schele, Linda, and Mary Ellen Miller. *The Blood of Kings: Dynasty and Ritual in Maya Art.* Fort Worth: Kimbell Art Museum, 1986.

Scully, Vincent. *Architecture: The Natural and the Manmade.* New York: St. Martin's Press, 1991.

Séjourné, Laurette. *Burning Water: Thought and Religion in Ancient Mexico.* London: Thames and Hudson, 1956.

Shook, Edwin M. *The Temple of Kukulkán at Mayapán.* Washington, DC: Carnegie Institution, 1954.

Sinkin, Richard N. *The Mexican Reform, 1855–1876, A Study in Liberal Nation-Building.* New Haven: Yale University Press, 1968.

Sociedad de Antropología y Etnografia de Mexico. *Quetzalcóatl* [journal], Vol. I, No.1. Mexico City, 1929.

Soustelle, Jacques. *Daily Life of the Aztecs on the Eve of the Spanish Conquest.* Translated from the French by Patrick O'Brian. Stanford: Stanford University Press, 1970.

_____. *La Vie Quotidienne des Aztèques.* Paris: Hachette, 1959.

Spence, Lewis. *The Magic and Mysteries of Mexico: The Arcane Secrets and Occult Lore of the Ancient Mexicans and Maya.* Van Nuys, California: Newcastle Publishing, 1994 reprint of 1918 first edition.

_____. *The Myths of Mexico and Peru.* New York: Dover Publications, 1994 reprint of 1913 first edition.

Spinden, Herbert J. *A Study of Maya Art: Its Subject Matter and Historical Development.* New York: Dover Press, 1975 reprint of 1913 edition.

Sten, Maria. *Codices of Mexico.* Mexico City: Panorama Editorial, 1978.

Stephens, John L. *Incidents of Travel in Central America, Chiapas and Yucatán.* Washington, DC: Smithsonian Institution Press, 1993.

Stierlin, Henri. *Art of the Maya, from the Olmecs to the Toltec-Maya.* New York: Rizzoli, 1981.

_____. *Ancient Mexico.* Lausanne: Benedikt Taschen, 1967.

_____. *Mayan Architecture.* Lausanne: Benedikt Taschen, 1963.

Stuart, Gene S. *The Mighty Aztecs*. Washington, DC: National Geographic Society, 1981.

Sweeney, James Johnson, and Alfonso Medellín Zenil. *The Olmec Tradition*. Houston: Museum of Fine Arts, 1963.

Taggart, James M. *Nahuat Myth and Social Structure*. Austin: University of Texas Press, 1983.

Tedlock, Dennis, ed. and trans. *Popol Vuh: The Definitive Edition of the Mayan Book of the Dawn of Life and the Glories of Gods and Kings*. New York: Simon & Schuster, 1985.

Terra, Helmut de. *The Life and Times of Alexander Von Humboldt*. New York: Alfred A. Knopf, 1955.

Terry, T. Philip. *Terry's Guide to Mexico*. Hingham, Massachusetts: Rapid Service Press, 1943.

Thomas, Hugh. *Conquest: Montezuma, Cortés and the Fall of Old Mexico*. New York: Simon & Schuster, 1993.

Thompson, J. Eric S. *The Rise and Fall of Maya Civlization*. Norman; University of Oklahoma Press, 1954.

Todorov, Tzvetan. *The Conquest of America: The Question of the Other*. Translated from the French by Richard Howard. New York: Harper & Row, 1984.

Tompkins, Peter. *Mysteries of the Mexican Pyramids*. New York: Harper & Row, 1976.

Toor, Frances. *A Treasury of Mexican Folkways*. New York: Crown Publishers, 1947.

Townsend, Richard. *The Ancient Americas: Art from Sacred Landscapes*. Chicago: Art Institute of Chicago, 1992.

Vaillant, George C. *Aztecs of Mexico: Origin, Rise and Fall of the Aztec Nation*. Garden City: Doubleday, 1947.

Valades, Adrian García. *Teotihuacán: The City of the Gods*. Mexico City: G.V. Editores, 1995.

Van Maanen, John. *Tales of the Field: On Writing Ethnography*. Chicago: University of Chicago Press, 1988.

VanKirk, Jacques, and Parney Bassett-VanKirk. *Remarkable Remains of the Ancient Peoples of Guatemala*. Norman: University of Oklahoma Press, 1966.

Von Hagen, Victor Wolfgang. *Maya Explorer: John Lloyd Stephens and the Lost Cities of Central America and Yucatán*. San Francisco: Chronicle Books, 1990.

_____. *South America Called Them: Explorations of the Great Naturalists: La Condamine, Humboldt, Darwin, Spruce*. New York: Alfred A. Knopf, 1945.

Von Humboldt, Alexander. *Personal Narrative of a Journey to the Equinoctial Regions of the New Continent, 1799, 1804*. Abridged and translated by Jason Wilson. New York: Penguin Books, 1995.

_____. *Political Essay on the Kingdom of New Spain*. Edited by Mary Maples Dunn. Norman: University of Oklahoma Press, 1988.

_____. *Vues des Cordillères et Monuments des Peuples Indigènes de l'Amérique*. Paris, 1869, illustrated folio based upon text of 1810 edition.

Wallace, Lew. *The Fair God, Or, The Last of the 'Tzins: A Tale of the Conquest of Mexico*. Boston: Houghton Mifflin, 1894.

Warner, Maria. *Alone of All Her Sex: The Myth and the Cult of the Virgin Mary*. New York: Vintage Books, 1976.

Waters, Frank. *Mexico Mystique: The Coming Sixth World of Consciousness*. Chicago: Swallow Press, 1975.

Wauchope, Robert, General Editor. *Handbook of Middle American Indians, Volumes Fourteen and Fifteen*. Howard F. Cline, volume editor. Guide to Ethnohistorical Sources. Austin: University of Texas Press, 1975.

_____. *Volume One*. Robert C. West, volume editor. Natural Environment and Early Cultures. Austin: University of Texas Press, 1971.

_____. *Volume Eleven*. Gordon F. Ekholm and Ignacio Bernal, volume editors. Summary. Austin: University of Texas Press, 1971.

_____. *Volume Ten*. Gordon Ekholm and Ignacio Bernal, volume editors. Archaeology of Northern Mesoamerica. Austin: University of Texas Press, 1971.

_____. *Volume Six*. Manning Nash, volume editor. Social Anthropology. Austin: University of Texas Press, 1967.

Weatherford, Jack. *Indian Givers: How the Indians of the Americas Transformed the World*. New York: Fawcett Columbine, 1988.

Weigand, Phil C. *Éhecatl: Primer Díos Supremo del Occidente*, in IV Mesa de Trabajo, Origenes y

Desarrolo de la Civilización del Occidente, Colegio de Michoacán, 1–3 Agosto, 1990. In press.

Weston, Edward. *The Daybooks, Volume I, Mexico.* Edited by Nancy Newhall. Rochester: George Eastman House, 1961.

Wilford, John Noble. "Human Presence in Americas Is Pushed Back a Millennium." *The New York Times,* February 11, 1997, pp. 1, C4.

Williams, William Carlos. *In the American Grain.* New York: New Directions, 1956.

Wilson, E. O. *Naturalist.* New York: Warner Books, 1995.

Winter, Marcus. *Oaxaca, The Historical Record.* Mexico City: Editorial Minutiae Mexicana, 1995.

Wolf, Eric R. *Sons of the Shaking Earth.* Chicago: University of Chicago Press, 1959.

Womack, John, Jr. *Zapata and the Mexican Revolution.* New York: Knopf, 1968.

Woodward, C. Vann. *The Future of the Past.* New York: Vintage Books, 1989.

Wright, Ronald. *Time Among the Maya: Travels in Belize, Guatemala and Mexico.* New York: Weidenfeld and Nicolson, 1989.

Zapata Alonzo, Gualberto. *Descriptive Guidebook to Chichén Itzá.* Merida: Libros, Rivistas y Folletas de Yucatán, 1984.

Zwollo, Tonny. *The Lost Paradise: Architecture and Ecology in the Oaxaca Valley.* Delft, The Netherlands: Entre Monte Albán y Mitla, 1993.

Index

Illustration Credits

62 Photograph by the author.

62 Photograph by the author.

64 Limestone relief. Stela number 15, Yaxchilan. Maya, 770 A.D. 87.5 X 82.2 cm. The British Museum.

65 Tattooed face of Priest from Upper Temple of the Pyramid of the Magician, Uxmal. Maya-Toltec, 9th century A.D. Collection Museo Nacional de Antropologia, Mexico City. Published by permission of the Coordinacion Nacional de Asuntos Juridicos, Instituto Nacional de Antropologia e Historia (INAH), Mexico City.

66 Collection of the Peabody Museum, Harvard University. Terminal Classic period, A.D. 800–900.

67 Photograph by the author.

68 Engraving by Frederick Catherwood, in John L. Stephens, *Incidents of Travel in Yucatán, Volume I* (New York: Harper & Brothers, 1843). General Research Division, The New York Public Library, Astor, Lenox and Tilden Foundations.

69 Engraving by Frederick Catherwood, in John L. Stephens, *Incidents of Travel in Yucatán, Volume I*.

70 Photograph by the author.

71 Photograph by the author.

72 Alexander Von Humboldt. *Vues des Cordillères et Monuments des Peuples Indigènes de l'Amerique.*

73 Fray Diego Durán, translated by Doris Heyden, *Book of the Gods and Rites and the Ancient Calendar.* (Norman: University of Oklahoma Press, 1994).

74 Plumed Serpent (Quetzalcóatl). Museo Missionario Etnologico, Vatican Museums, Vatican State. Scala/Art Resource, New York.

75 Exhibition Dioses del Mexico Antiguo, College of San Ildefonso, Mexico City. (December 9, 1995– May 5, 1996). Curated by Eduardo Matos Moctezuma. Photograph by the author.

76 Aztec/Mexica. Late Post-Classic (A.D. 1300–1521). Collection Museo Nacional de Antropologia, Mexico City. Published by permission of the Coordinacion Nacional de Asuntos Juridicos, Instituto Nacional de Antropologia e Historia (INAH), Mexico City.

81 *Codex Telleriano-Remensis.* Collection Bibliothèque Nationale, Paris.

86-87 Aztec (Central Mexico). Snake with Human Head in Mouth. Philadelphia Museum of Art: The Louise and Walter Arensberg Collection.

88 Sahagún. *Florentine Codex.*

89 Dumbarton Oaks Collection.

91 Durán. *Book of the Gods and Rites and the Ancient Calendar.*

93 Sahagún. *Florentine Codex.*

96 Durán. *Book of the Gods and Rites and the Ancient Calendar.*

99 Durán. *Book of the Gods and Rites and the Ancient Calendar.*

100-101 Bibliothèque Nationale, Paris.

104 Photograph by the author. Published by permission of the Instituto Nacional de Bellas Artes y Literatura, Direccion de Asuntos Juridicos, Mexico City. © Estate of Diego Rivera. Licensed by VAGA, New York, NY.

105-106 Photograph by the author. Published by permission of the Instituto Nacional de Bellas Artes y Literatura, Direccion de Asuntos Juridicos, Mexico City. © Estate of Diego Rivera. Licensed by VAGA, New York, NY.

108 Transparency number 1731(3). *Florentine Codex –* Lam XVI #52. AMNH Photo Studio. Courtesy Department of Library Services, American Museum of Natural History.

110 Sahagún. *Florentine Codex.*

111 Sahagún. *Florentine Codex.*

113 Grant Smith/Corbis-Bettman.

115 Robert Wauchope, General Editor. Howard F. Cline, Volume Editor. *Handbook of Middle American Indians. Guide to Ethnohistorical Sources, Volume XIV, Part III.* Fig.93. Published by permission of the University of Texas Press, Austin, 1975.

122 Pedro Antonio Fresquis. Our Lady of Guadalupe, ca. 1780–1830. National Museum of American Art, Smithsonian Institution, Washington, DC. Hemphill Collection/Art Resource, New York.

125 Underwood/Corbis-Bettman.

126 Corbis-Bettman.

128 Corbis-Bettman.

130 Museo Nacional de Artes e Industrias Populares, Mexico City. Published by permission of SOMAAP, Mexico City.

132 Museo Nacional de Artes, Mexico City. Published by permission of SOMAAP, Mexico City.

133 Museo Nacional de Artes, Mexico City. Published by permission of SOMAAP, Mexico City.

134 Photograph of painting by Baldwin H. Ward. Collection Corbis-Bettmann, New York.

136 Collection The Metropolitan Museum of Art. All rights reserved.

138 Hirshhorn Museum and Sculpture Garden, Smithsonian Institution. Gift of Joseph H. Hirshhorn, 1966. © Estate of David Alfaro Siqueiros. Licensed by VAGA, New York, NY.

140 Corbis-Bettman.

141 Corbis-Bettman.

144 Gelatin silver print, 7 7/16" x 9 5/16". Collection Museum of Modern Art, New York. Gift of David H. McAlpin. Copy print © The Museum of Modern Art, New York. Copyright © Center for Creative Photography, Arizona Board of Regents.

146 Photograph by the author.

149 Photograph by the author. Published by permission of the Instituto Nacional de Bellas Artes y Literatura, Direccion de Asuntos Juridicos, Mexico City. © Estate of Diego Rivera. Licensed by VAGA, New York, NY.

151 Gelatin silver print, 9 11/16" x 7 7/16". Collection Museum of Modern Art, New York. Purchase. Copy print © 1998. The Museum of Modern Art, New York. Copyright © Center for Creative Photography, Arizona Board of Regents.

154-155 Fresco, 120" x 205". Hood Museum of Art, Dartmouth College, Hanover, New Hampshire. Commissioned by the Trustees of Dartmouth College. © Estate of José Clemente Orozco. Licensed by VAGA, New York, NY.

157 Watercolor and gouache, 45.1 x 45.1 centimeters. Hood Museum of Art, Dartmouth College, Hanover, New Hampshire. Purchased through gifts from Mr. and Mrs. Peter B. Bedford; Jane and Raphael Bernstein; Walter Burke, Class of 1944; Mr. and Mrs. Richard D. Lombard; Nathan Pearson, Class of 1932; David V. Picker, Class of 1953; Rodman C. Rockefeller, Class of 1954; Kenneth Roman, Jr., Class of 1952; and Adolph Weil, Jr., Class of 1935. © Estate of José Clemente Orozco. Licensed by VAGA, New York, NY.

158 Brush and ink on paper, 34 x 25.1 centimeters. The Museum of Modern Art, New York. Purchase. Photograph copyright © The Museum of Modern Art, New York.

159 Pyroxaline on celotex and plywood. This is a reconstructed version of the original, which was moved to the Tecpan Building in Tlatelco, Mexico City, in 1964. (Rochfort, p. 189). Published by permission of the Instituto Nacional de Bellas Artes y Literatura, Direccion de Asuntos Juridicos, Mexico City. © Estate of David Alfaro Siqueiros. Licensed by VAGA, New York, NY.

160 Published by permission of the Fundacion Olga y Rufino Tamayo, Mexico City.

161 Gelatin-silver print, 34.2 x 26 centimeters. The Museum of Modern Art, New York. Gift of Mrs. Nickolas Muray. Copy print copyright © The Museum of Modern Art, New York. Published with the permission of Mimi Muray Levitt.

162 Collection the Harry Ransom Humanities Resarch Center, The University of Texas at Austin.

167 Collection the Harry Ransom Humanities Research Center, The University of Texas at Austin

169 Collection the Harry Ransom Humanities Research Center, The University of Texas at Austin. Photograph by Dorothy Brett.

170 Published by permission of SOMAAP, Mexico City. © Raúl Anguiano Valdez. Licensed by VAGA, New York.

172 Photograph by Bodil Christensen. Frances Toor. A Treasury of Mexican Folkways. © Crown Publishers, New York, 1947.

173 Photograph by C. Volpe/VIREO (Visual Resources for Ornithology), The Academy of Natural Sciences of Philadelphia.

Excerpts

PublicAffairs is a new nonfiction publishing house and a tribute to the standards, values, and flair of three persons who have served as mentors to countless reporters, writers, editors, and book people of all kinds, including me.

I.F. Stone, proprietor of *I. F. Stone's Weekly*, combined a commitment to the First Amendment with entrepreneurial zeal and reporting skill and became one of the great independent journalists in American history. At the age of eighty, Izzy published *The Trial of Socrates*, which was a national bestseller. He wrote the book after he taught himself ancient Greek.

Benjamin C. Bradlee was for nearly thirty years the charismatic editorial leader of *The Washington Post*. It was Ben who gave the *Post* the range and courage to pursue such historic issues as Watergate. He supported his reporters with a tenacity that made them fearless, and it is no accident that so many became authors of influential, best-selling books.

Robert L. Bernstein, the chief executive of Random House for more than a quarter century, guided one of the nation's premier publishing houses. Bob was personally responsible for many books of political dissent and argument that challenged tyranny around the globe. He is also the founder and longtime chair of Human Rights Watch, one of the most respected human rights organizations in the world.

For fifty years, the banner of Public Affairs Press was carried by its owner Morris B. Schnapper, who published Gandhi, Nasser, Toynbee, Truman and about 1,500 other authors. In 1983, Schnapper was described by *The Washington Post* as "a redoubtable gadfly." His legacy will endure in the books to come.

Peter Osnos, *Publisher*